PSYCHOSYNTHESIS

NEW PERSPECTIVES AND

CREATIVE RESEARCH

The Best of The Synthesist Journal

editor: Will Parfitt

PS AVALON
Glastonbury, England

PS Avalon
Box 1865, Glastonbury
Somerset, BA6 8YR, U.K.
www.willparfitt.com

book design: Will Parfitt

ISBN
978-0-9562162-0-5

CONTENTS

5

INTRODUCTION

Psychosynthesis is an approach to self development that includes our spiritual as well as our physical, emotional and mental needs. Psychosynthesis aims to move us away from fragmentation and pain and towards integration and joy through including both the lighter and the darker sides of life.

These days we all know only too well how the act of one person can and does have a profound effect on us all; equally we are all responsible for the effect we have collectively on both the planet as a whole and on each individual. In the early stages of this new century, the two areas of most concern are our individual and collective responsibility. In an article published in the early 1990s, I suggested that Psychosynthesis, being truly integrative and holistic, is the most important psychology for the 21st Century as it gives us a perspective that can bring meaning to both our individual and collective acts. So does this grand claim have any validity?

Psychosynthesis is applied in many different areas of life, and the primary aim is to apply Psychosynthesis to whatever areas of life our deepest inner sense of values leads us. Doctors, social workers, teachers and business people of all types train in Psychosynthesis and it is respected in many different areas of work. It can also be applied in the home, in relationships, in child rearing and all aspects of daily life. It is usefully applied in creative endeavours, including writing and art, both its creation and appreciation.

The articles in this collection clearly demonstrate that the values and practices of Psychosynthesis are increasingly relevant to our modern world, exploring as they do a myriad of different ways of understanding Psychosynthesis and its application. It is central to Psychosynthesis, however, to remember that it is not about applying techniques but learning to live with a vision that comes from deep within.

We have moved into a new world where each individual has their own unique way of perceiving and interacting with the world based not only on the past traumas and so on that were experienced during childhood, as is presented in the Freudian world view. We also have potential, the 'future' within us which, through proper attention, can be brought to life and manifest in ways that bring a deep sense of purpose and meaning to life. In our modern world anything that increases our sense of meaning has to be good. Psychosynthesis does just that, helping us become, as in the title of Piero Ferrucci's classic Psychosynthesis book, *what we may be.*

Psychosynthesis was founded by Roberto Assagioli, an Italian doctor, in the early 20th century when he realised the Freudian approach he had learned not only ignored but actively berated spiritual beliefs. Assagioli did not want to deal with just the 'basement' of the psyche, where all our old traumas are stored, but also with the 'upstairs', as it were, where we connect to our potential. Important as it is to analyse the past so we become more effective in our lives, we also need to look to our potential and find ways to develop and grow.

Psychosynthesis works to uncover the creative and spiritual energy within each of us which can illuminate whatever are our areas of interest. Psychosynthesis is a consciously inspired vision of how the best psychological and esoteric understandings of the human psyche can be applied in a relevant, meaningful way that should work for everyone whatever their beliefs. Over the course of his life Assagioli fine-tuned the system, not to create an eclectic mishmash but a potent synthesis. Thus we find in Psychosynthesis elements of various therapies, from analytical through humanistic to transpersonal, coupled with practices adapted from spiritual and esoteric traditions.

To hold and nurture his vision, he always referred everything back to his basic model, called 'the egg diagram', which is a simplified version of the Kabbalistic Tree of Life, and which will be described in some detail at the end of this introduction. The influence of Kabbalah on Assagioli was considerable and, because of its inclusive vision, enables Psychosynthesis to incorporate many systems and techniques without being diluted or corrupted.

As well as from Kabbalah, Psychosynthesis has influences from Christian mysticism, Raja Yoga, Buddhism, Gnosticism, Theosophy, Rosicrucianism, Hermeticism and Alchemy. Assagioli admired the work of Dante, for instance, which he felt synthesized the masculine and feminine approaches of Christian mysticism. He saw in Dante's *Divine Comedy* an archetypal description of the processes each individual goes through in their developmental journey through life. Whilst writing about Dante, Assagioli also mentions troubadours, particularly concerning the imagery of the rose (also used by Dante.) He aligns Psychosynthesis with Gnosticism through asserting: 'Psychosynthesis appreciates, respects and even recognises the necessity of [faith] but its purpose is to help to attain the direct experience.'

There are many versions of Alchemy but they all generally agree that 'a common substance' is subjected to a series of operations to obtain an end product called the philosopher's stone, the elixir of life, or just simply gold. Whether taken on a purely physical level or seen metaphorically, the alchemical process takes a dead thing, impure, valueless and powerless, and transforms it into a living thing, active, invaluable and transformative. This exactly describes the work of Psychosynthesis and, with a little thought on the metaphor involved, shows how the process of Psychosynthesis can be applied in all human endeavours, perhaps even especially in the creative and business worlds.

Hermeticists believe the two most important powers of the human psyche are will and imagination (both properly tempered by love.) We use imagination to create the world in which we live, and will is the force by which we maintain it. The key to a meaningful life is then aligning personal will with transpersonal Intent (True Will or Purpose.) As Assagioli put it, we then can '*begin to discover the secrets we are looking for, and attain a conscious contact with the Existence of which we are an inseparable part.*'

THE EGG OF BEING

(adapted from Psychosynthesis: The Elements and Beyond)

The main Psychosynthesis map (diagram on next page) is called 'the egg of being' or, more simply, 'the egg diagram', and represents the whole psyche. The three horizontal divisions of the egg stand for our past (1), present (2) and future (3). All three are constantly active within us, although in different ways. This is obvious when we consider the present moment – after all, we are here and now not then and there! Within this present moment, this 'here and now', we carry the past with us in the form of all our memories and experiences whether we remember them or not. It is everything from the past, in one sense, that makes us what we are in the present moment. In another sense, perhaps more 'esoteric' but no less real, we also carry the future within us. It has not happened yet, but all of us have right now the potential to become something else, to have new experiences, to find new ways to express ourselves. Or perhaps someone's potential might be to always remain the same, to experience or express nothing new – but that, too, is something they carry within themselves.

If we look at the egg of being in this way, we can see it is a complete map of the continuum of time. Whilst its primary focus is on the present moment, because that is, after all, the moment in which we want to use the map, like all good maps it will help us tune into where we have been (the past) and where we are going (the future). By reference to the past, we can get a clearer understanding of where we are in the present moment. This then helps us decide where we want to go and how to get there.

The egg of being is chiefly concerned, however, with our inner journey and so its 'divisions' represent the different aspects of ourselves as individual beings, and our connection to other beings too. As your familiarity with the map increases, so does your familiarity with the different aspects of yourself.

(1) [see diagram] represents the lower unconscious, our personal psychological past which includes repressed complexes, long-forgotten memories, instincts and physical functions over which

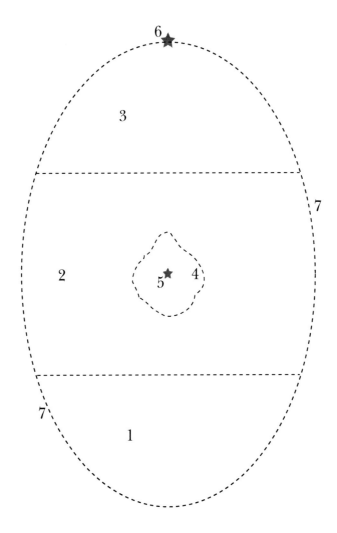

The Psychosynthesis Egg Diagram

we (ordinarily) have no conscious control. All our fundamental drives and 'primitive urges' are part of this realm as are the activities of basic bodily functions. It is primarily the repressed material, often experienced in the form of unconscious controls upon us, phobias, obsessions, compulsive urges and so on, with which we are primarily concerned in Psychosynthesis.

When we explore our lower unconscious it helps our growth because as we learn to integrate more of these 'older' or repressed aspects of ourselves, the more whole we become. When we release previously repressed energies, we feel healthier, have more energy available to us, and feel more freedom in our lives. (2) represents the middle unconscious, the place where all states of mind reside which can easily be brought into our field of awareness (4). For example, in our readily accessible 'middle unconscious', we carry all sorts of information and knowledge that is not always relevant but is readily accessible if we need to connect with it.

The middle unconscious also holds suppressed material. This differs from repressed material that has been 'pushed down' into the lower unconscious. With repressed things we no longer 'remember' or own them as part of us. Suppressed material, on the other hand, we know is there, it is just that we are choosing, for one reason or another, not to bring it out at this moment. There is nothing wrong with suppression, but we have to be careful that things that we suppress in our consciousness do not get completely forgotten, and then become part of the contents of our lower unconscious from where they will start controlling us rather than us controlling them.

The field of awareness (or consciousness) (4) is shaped like an amoeba to emphasize how it is constantly changing as our field of awareness changes. Originally it was simply shown as a circle, but I prefer to shape it like an amoeba to emphasize how it constantly changes. The field of awareness is constantly alive with sensations, images, thoughts, emotions, feelings, desires and impulses all of which we can observe and act upon or not as we see fit.

Our field of awareness is constantly fluid, changing as our feelings or thoughts or sensations send us information about our environment. If we become really cut off from our experiences it can be as if the amoeba of awareness 'encysts', it hardens its semi-permeable skin and stops letting through clear messages, either from inside to outside or vice versa. Part of the work of Psychosynthesis is to bring freedom of movement to our amoeba, and to increase our awareness of its function and abilities.

(3) represents the superconscious, our evolutionary future, the region from where we receive all inspiration and illumination, however we experience it. Indeed, true inspiration can come to us in artistic or scientific, very grand or very simple ways. It is the source of our 'inner genius' and is thus perhaps the major area of exploration for us when we wish to more clearly and successfully move into our future. Perhaps the most obvious way that most people connect with their superconscious is through insights and 'inspirational flashes' that just seem to appear in their consciousness. Usually such insights, and other similar experiences, show that the superconscious has been contacted.

The exploration of these three realms, the lower, middle and higher unconscious, is one of the main tasks of Psychosynthesis. Any distinction between higher (or super) unconscious and lower unconscious is developmental, not moralistic. The lower unconscious is not bad, or in some sense not as good or as important, it is simply earlier in our evolution. It is described as 'lower' simply because it is behind us, and forms the 'foundation' of our present awareness. The superconscious is not merely an abstract possibility but a living reality with an existence of its own. Calling it superconscious (or 'higher' unconscious) does not mean it is above us or better than us in some way, but is merely meant to describe the sense that as we evolve and move towards it is as if we are raising our consciousness into new experiences. Alternatively, when insights come from this realm of the unconscious, we often get a sense of things 'dropping into place'.

(7) represents the collective unconscious that is common to all living beings. We are not isolated pieces of individuality, we are

not islands, so although at times we may feel isolated and alone, in reality we are part of a collective field in which all other beings play a part. There is a constant and active interchange between us and all other sentient beings, whether we are aware of this or not.

Note how in the egg diagram the lines are dotted to show there are no rigid compartments impeding free interplay between all these "levels". If we become too rigid it is as if the egg 'hardens' and our work might be to crack it a little to let more fluidity into our lives. On the other hand, if we are too sloppy, too 'nice' for our own good, if we find it difficult to separate ourselves from other people, then it is as if the spaces in the egg have become too large, letting in (or out) too much. Our work is then to strengthen the eggshell, and create more of an individual identity.

(5) is the personal self, our individual 'I' who experiences all these different states of consciousness. It is the 'I' that experiences itself as having thoughts, emotions and sensations. It is not these changing contents of consciousness (thoughts, emotions, sensations, and so on) but is the inner you that experiences these contents. Generally during life we do not experience this 'I' in a very clearly defined way. The more we work on ourselves through Psychosynthesis, the more we can start contacting the 'I' and making it a living, experienced reality in our consciousness. In one sense we could say on both a psychological but also a physiological level, that the more we get in touch with our 'I' the healthier or more whole we become.

This personal self is a reflection or spark of the spiritual or transpersonal Self (6) that is both universal and individual. The realization of this 'transpersonal' Self is a sign of spiritual success and achievement. Awareness of the personal self is the primary goal of Psychosynthesis, being the place from where we can effectively direct the personality. This leads to a clearer and fuller contact with, and understanding of the Spiritual Self.

TRUE SELF, FALSE SELF
Leaving the Punch and Judy Show

Mike Stillwell

"I am not writing this as an attack on therapy or psychosynthesis. Indeed I am a profound believer in both. But let's use the tools of our profession to look at just what it is we do, and to check whether we are coming from ego or self. Let's see if we can use the map we've developed to see when things are going one way or the other."

INTRODUCTION

I would like to explore how training in counselling and psychotherapy in general, including Psychosynthesis, can either lead us towards identification with a true self or a false self, and the impact that this may have on our clients, supervisees and students. I would also like to show how Psychosynthesis in particular can give us the tools to describe and address this.

In order to do so I would like to establish a simple map with which to define aspects of self and their relationships, based on perceived points of agreement between several different theories of human nature.

I will first begin by drawing attention to the similarities between the act of formulating a theory base to understand human nature, and the therapeutic process which can support healing and evolution within human nature, and the aspects of self which comprise human nature. This is in order to show that the map, the purpose of the map and the subject of the map are all linked. It is said that 'the map is not the territory', but unless it's pretty similar to the territory then it's not much of a map. And if I stop here and there and point at parts of the landscape that are related to these themes but which won't quite fit into such a tight brief – forgive me. The landscape and views are just so interesting I couldn't help stopping to have a look.

THEORIES OF HUMAN NATURE

I believe there is something of the truth in all theory bases that attempt to describe what a person is, and how we operate and develop. If that is the case then formulating a theory base may be an integrative one of construction rather than one of rejection. We look for the similarities and not the differences in order to find a synthesis.

One approach to formulating a theory base may be to take generalisations based on past experience (both our own experience and that of others), compare them with each other for areas of common ground or relationship, and update them according to our own current experience.

THE THERAPEUTIC PROCESS

If each unit of learning is a generalisation about ourselves, others and the world, then rigidly-held generalisations based on past experience, and the strategies based on these generalisations, may be unhelpful to us unless they are questioned, rearranged and updated in the light of new experiences.

With this in mind, the opportunity to update past experience according to new information, with the chance to see how this alters or fits in with existing structures and strategies, may be a very large part of what we offer as therapists – may actually be a large part of the therapeutic process, in other words.

ASPECTS OF SELF

The focus of this piece of writing is one concept of 'self' in all it's aspects; – that we tend to identify our consciousness with one or other of a set of psychological aspects that act as 'sub-selves'; that these aspects are generalisations based on past experience; that it is they and their relationships with each other that can be updated in the light of new experience, and that often the more primitive expressions of these aspects aren't too happy about being updated.

MY SELF

My self-experience and my experience of others leads me to believe that many or all of us switch between identifying with different aspects of ourselves that act like separate personalities within the personality. A few minutes of self-observation, or of listening to a conversation between other people, seems to provide me with experiential proof of this.

Whether we call them sub-personalities or ego-states, one or other of this collection of self-concepts seems to take charge of who we are at any particular time. Each has a set of thoughts, feelings, behaviours, wants, needs, phrases, agendas, a view of the world and the people in it, and so on. When I'm thinking it's generally one of these doing the thinking, or two or more of them talking within me. When I have feelings, I often feel whatever the part of me that I'm identified with always tends to feel, so that 'how I am' depends on 'who I am' at that moment, or which bit of me is 'up' and in charge of my sense of identity.

These aspects can be viewed in terms of our inner experience, such as "I have a 'critic' as a psychic element that drives and criticises me"; or in terms of ourselves in the larger world, in which case I might actually be identified with my critic and act it out; or experience my critic through a person or institution outside of me that I have projected it onto. Whether we look at infra-psychic (within us) or interpersonal (between us) settings, it's our same aspects relating in the same patterns of behaviour.

Because of the confusion between the infra-psychic and the interpersonal spheres, we can often create the sorts of relationships and dramas in the outside world that our sub-personalities get up to inside us.

AN INNER MODEL

It may be that we take in (introject) people, places and events from the world around us as symbols and containers for our own inner forces, taking in information and building up a virtual model of characters, settings and patterns of behaviour. The headings that we file these things under seem common to people in general (are archetypal).

The activity of taking in new information so as to update the inner model (feedback) could be seen as part of the learning process, which affects not only what we know but also who we are. There is, or can be, a constant comparison of old with fresh data as our inner model changes in the light of new input. The activity of referring to the inner model in order to negotiate outer situations (feed forward) can be used to rehearse actions in imagination and to extrapolate possible outcomes or our own and other's behaviour.

Similar to a game of chess, our inner model has places and settings (the board), characters based on our observations of others and ourselves (the pieces), potential actions based on the individual nature of the pieces (the moves) and also complex relationships between all these things over time (the game).

I will later return to the question of who are moving the pieces (of who are the players) when we again focus on the 'true self / false self' aspect of this paper.

ADMIRING THE VIEW

The 'characters' that inhabit this inner model are our sub-personalities and ego-states (that is to say, 'who we are sometimes'), and it is these aspects, and the relationships between them, that can change according to the updating process, like a living filing system.

So if the settings, inhabitants, and patterns of event of this virtual inner model are generalisations based on individual personal observation and experience, filed under archetypal headings, we can draw some conclusions.

Dealing with the past, the perceived present, and the projected future, may often instead be dealing with different functions or 'areas' of this inner construct. If our inner model contains, or is, who we are, then feed-back (new information) may in some circumstances be seen as a threat to a stable identity. Strategies to limit, misinterpret or deny may be developed by the ego and ego-states (more on this later).

A tendency to try to change the outer world to match the inner world (a distortion of 'feed-forward') may be a factor in some circumstances. We, or some part of us, may attempt to update outer reality rather than being updated ourselves.

A therapeutic model or theory base may be an attempt to portray a generalised view of this inner world and it's dynamics, with particular interest in how positive change may be supported when working with others.

If this is the case then we need to be sure if we are seeing clients in the context of a generalised theoretic structure in order to understand their own unique structure – using our theory of inner models to help us in seeing how the entirety of their inner world is affecting who they are and what they are becoming - or whether we are seeing the client as a two-dimensional piece in our own inner world of aspects and relationships.

The difference is between seeing the client's potential and pathology, or seeing them as a bit-part player in terms of our own potential and pathology.

To say that we use the outer world in order to give form to inner energies is perhaps to present a more static picture than is the case. We each have a 'set' of inner energies, but we can invent or borrow new off-the-peg sets of containing forms for those energies in an instant. Dreams seem to be an example of such invention, using things from the prop cupboard of our unconscious to express the state of play within us. Every time we hear a story, whether true or invented, every time we hear a joke, watch a film, play a game or engage with a new set of ideas, we are playing a complex game of 'snap' by instantaneously matching our own inner energies with the system of containers presented to us. It is somewhat like a driver getting into a variety of vehicles, or trying on a variety of gloves.

One may gain some understanding of this from the discipline of seeing every story as portraying the aspects – settings, characters and events – of just one person. These even applies to jokes of just a couple of lines. A situation is described where we are led to believe that a syntropic force of evolution is in operation, only to have our view reversed. The simpler the story, the more obvious the fact that a story is being told of the struggle between a real and a false self. Between ego and soul.

Complex stories, whether Dante's Divine Comedy, or the more recent Lord of the Rings, Harry Potter, and Star Wars, give us a far more comprehensive picture of the our human make-up and the hard-wiring of who we are.

Many people seems to be familiar with the experience of 'one bit of me thinks (this) while another thinks (that)'. Expressions such as 'arguing with myself', 'I told myself' etc. are very common.

I notice that, particularly when working with addictions, people very often describe a devil, imp, monkey or gremlin on one shoulder who is saying, 'Go on, one won't hurt you' or 'Go on, you've been good, you deserve one', while perhaps an angel of conscience stands on the other shoulder, wagging a finger. If the sense of self, or connection with will, of the person in the centre is weak, they can be torn between what can seem a self-destructive rebel and a prim critic.

In this simple example of the basic struggle, you will notice three main characters. Depending upon which belief system we are using we might see a struggle between lower and higher nature – the animal and the divine within us, with the human as us at the centre. Alternatively we might see a Child aspect on one side who has no thought of consequences, with the Parent aspect/s on the other, and with us as the Adult in the centre - the one who can make a choice. Or perhaps we might see id on one side, super-ego on the other, with us as the ego in the centre who can listen to it's advisors and then decide what to do – or perhaps with which to identify.

My point is that since the energies we are looking at are complex then we might profitably hold all of these belief systems in mind, rather than deciding that one is right. Areas of communality between various systems will give us some reasonably firm ground from which to explore our territory.

AN INNER FAMILY

Lets start our exploration with the more primitive aspects of self. Perhaps we can put together the ego-states and 'drama triangle' of Transactional Analysis with the Freudian model of the id, ego, and the 'rules' and 'care' aspects of the super-ego.

PARENT, ADULT, CHILD

You may be familiar with the concept of 'Parent, Adult and Child' from T.A., which at it's very simplest divides Parent into Critical and Nurturing, and Child into Adapted and Free.

The Critical Parent as an inner figure is a container for all that we record from others about rules, and getting it right or wrong. The Nurturing Parent as a figure is an inner container for all that we have recorded from those around us about giving care. The headings of Critical and Nurturing Parent are universal and part of our hard-wiring, though what is recorded there is individual to our own experience.

The Child is a self-recording, and the main aspects or headings are Adapted (how we had to be in order to get our needs met and express our qualities as best we could), and Free, which is a Child aspect free of the rules of the critical Parent and the Care of the Nurturing Parent.

> *CRITICAL PARENT   NURTURING PARENT*
> *ADULT*
> *FREE CHILD   ADAPTED CHILD*

Between the Parent and Child aspects is another figure which is a heading under which is recorded all we have observed or experienced about managing ourselves (including the other ego states) and the world. This is the Adult.

THE DRAMA TRIANGLE

Also from T.A. is the somewhat simpler version of this known as the Drama Triangle. It portrays the dynamics of a personality where the ego is not present or is so weak it can only survive by continually identifying with and projecting out the other ego-states. The more negative aspects of Critical Parent, Nurturing Parent and Child become highlighted, portrayed here as Perpetrator (or Persecutor), Rescuer (or Enabler) and Victim.

PERSECUTOR   RESCUER
VICTIM

The dynamics of the Drama Triangle are called 'games', and these will shortly be described in some detail.

FREUD, EGO, SUPER-EGO, AND ID.

SUPEREGO
EGO
ID

[definitions of Id, Superego and ego from Wikipedia]

THE ID

The Id (Latin, "it" in English, "Es" in the original German) represented primary process thinking — our most primitive need-gratification type thoughts. The Id, Freud stated, constitutes part of one's unconscious mind. It is organized around primitive instinctual urges of sexuality, aggression and the desire for instant gratification or release.

THE SUPEREGO

The Superego ("Über-Ich" in the original German, roughly "over-I" or "super-I" in English) represented our conscience and counteracted the Id with a primitive and unconscious sense of morality. This primitive morality is to be distinguished from an ethical sense, which is an egoic property, since ethics requires an eligibility for deliberation on matters of fairness or justice. The Superego, Freud stated, is the moral agent that links both our conscious and unconscious minds. The Superego stands in opposition to the desires of the Id. The Superego is part of the unconscious mind, and based upon the internalisation of the world view, norms and mores a child absorbs from parents and the surrounding environment at a young age. As the conscience, it is a primitive or child-based knowledge of right and wrong, maintaining taboos specific to a child's internalisation of parental culture.

THE EGO

In Freud's view the Ego stands in between the Id and the Superego to balance our primitive needs and our moral beliefs and taboos. ("Ego" means "I" in Latin; the original German word Freud applied was "Ich".) He stated that the Ego consists of our conscious sense of self and world, a highly structured set of unconscious defences that are central in defining both individual differences in character or personality, the symptoms and inhibitions that define the neuroses, and ultimately serving as the executive branch of the mind which leads to action. Relying on experience, a healthy Ego provides the ability to adapt to reality and interact with the outside world in a way that accommodates both Id and Superego.

ESTABLISHING A BASE LINE

To begin with, then, I'd like to come up with a basic diagrammatic portrayal of these elements of the personality. I'm going to be quite mix-and-match about it, so I'll draw on terms from various of these models. I would suggest keeping in mind the image of a passion flower, which has different arrangements of petals and stamen around a single centre.

The 'Parent, Adult, Child' model shows two main aspects of the recorded 'Parent', then an 'Adult' central aspect, and then shows two main aspects of the self-recording which is the Child. There is the child that had to adapt to get it's need met, and the 'free' child who does not adapt to outer (and now inner) parental restrictions.

Next, the drama triangle portrays the personality at a time when the ego is weak. All three ego-states are powerful yet it is their worst aspects that are highlighted. The child aspect depicted is a self-recording based on the experience of not having needs met. The 'care-giving' aspect is stuck in disabling concern for others, while the 'rules-based' aspect is here simply an abusive perpetrator.

The Freudian model shows the personality with an ego present which develops as a buffer between id and superego, but which does not distinguish between aspects of superego based on 'rules' and 'care', or between aspects of id.

None of the models here distinguish between a healthy ego on the one hand, and the more popular and derogatory understanding of ego as 'self-centredness and an inflated feeling of pride in your superiority to others' on the other.

None of these distinguish between the ego and self, or indeed the Higher Self, and we will be introducing Psychosynthesis and Kabbalah soon in order to do this, but for now we'll stay with the lower personality and it's dynamics in it's most primitive form.

AN INNER FAMILY

To say again, there follows a look at the more primitive expressions of these aspects. We will look at the bigger picture later.

Just for now, and as a temporary measure of convenience, lets put together the concepts of adapted child, victim, and id together to describe a self-recording of early needs – what those needs were, how we had to be in relation to others as a very young child in order to get those needs met, and how we felt when they weren't met. And just for now we're going to call this amalgam of concepts the 'Victim' in order to be clear that we're looking at a very dependant and primitive aspect of the child.

As well as recording it's own early self-experience, the child seems to record the actions and words of others, and particularly it's parents, under the headings of 'getting it right' and 'looking after', so that it can apply the recordings under these headings to itself during the parent's absence. We have all seen young children telling themselves off ("Mustn't do that!") or comforting themselves.

The Inner Parent that's about 'getting it right' has been termed the Superego or the Critical Parent, and, when it's more about 'getting it wrong' or controlling others by putting them in the wrong or indeed just pure abusiveness, as the Critic, and the Perpetrator or Persecutor.

The Inner Parent that is a container for recordings of behaviour to do with 'looking after' and 'care' has been termed the Nurturing Parent, and, when it's a distortion of care used in an attempt to control, as the Rescuer or Enabler.

These Inner Parents contain huge chunks of how we perceived our parents and other important adults, but are not simply based of one parent each. They are not unbiased recordings but are based on a child's interpretation of adult behaviours and so can be extreme caricatures of the people we grew up with. Teenagers in particular seem to confuse the inner and outer parents, which may be helpful in separating.

The three aspects we have looked at are all about control, and we might call them 'hurt' (child), 'hurtful' (critic), and 'helpful' (rescuer), or perhaps we might see them as 'needy, 'nasty' and 'nice'. Or perhaps as carrot, stick, and donkey.

We can see them as a 'done to' bit which is the Victim aspect, and then the two aspects which seek to act on the child in different ways – through criticism, and through concern. But all three are about moving blame, responsibility and bad feeling from one to the other, and not being the one left holding the badness when the music stops, like a horrible game of musical chairs.

It may be they had their origin in the perinatal experience of being a point of awareness and feeling and needs which is acted upon what may seem to be two powers greater than itself; – by a containing an nurturing force, and by another force which squeezes and pushes it into the world. This perhaps is our first experience of the triangle of awareness, love and will.

Because we are purposely looking at the more primitive aspects of the characters of our inner nursery dramas, we will also take a negative view (for now) of the ego.

We'll view the ego as referring to a container for a child's recordings of managing and coping behaviour as witnessed in the adults around them, but we'll see it as weak and having particularly strong and distorted 'Critic', 'Rescuer' and 'Victim' aspects to deal with.

We'll see the ego as ego-centric, ego-inflated and egoic, and in terms of the most negative of the 'self' words – self-important, self-serving, self-absorbed, self-justifying, self-centred, self-referential, and of course, selfish.

The ego as seen from this perspective is like the manager of a firm who wants to look good, and who has no hesitation in making others take the blame when anything goes wrong; – something like the manager in 'The Office'.

It wants to be seen as bigger and better and shinier than anyone else, and is based on self-centred fear. Fear of losing something is has, fear of not getting something it wants.

As well as looking good and avoiding blame it's other priorities include the satisfaction and management of instincts such as those for survival, pleasure, freedom from discomfort, financial and emotional security, sexual and social relationships, the satisfaction of ambitions, attention and self-esteem.

It has essentially evolved to manage the id's pressing instinctive needs, as well as forming like a blister of awareness where the child (id) and parent (superego) aspects rub together, and so has to be skilled at juggling, soothing, holding a perspective that needs will be met but not quite yet, or satisfying needs in fantasy and imagination.

Yet in the example we are looking at we will highlight the idea of the ego in service of the id rather than managing it. We will see the ego as under pressure from the ego-states which should be it's advisors - advisors about riles and direction (Critic), about care and responsibility (Rescuer), and about bottom-of-Maslow's-pyramid needs (Victim) – but which instead have become tormentors.

SOME PRIMITIVE EGO DEFENCE MECHANISMS

If an inner advisor becomes troublesome then identify with it. It takes two to fight and now there's only one - me! I am the Victim (Critic/Rescuer).

If an inner advisor becomes troublesome then put it out there on a person or institution in the world. Once it's projected outwards it's not in here.

Deny the troublesome aspect or problem even exists. In fact deny that any aspects or problems exist. "Having Sub-personalities must be a Multiple Personality Disorder, because normal people don't have all these 'bits'. "All problems are due to faulty wiring on a chemical or cognitive level, and all other psychology is bunkum."

When the ego is struggling to manage it's troublesome inner family of 'advisors' AND to deal with outside problems then obviously things would be a lot simpler if we could get rid of either the inner or outer world, or at least limit the amount of information coming from one or both.

You can make your own list of ways to do this, but one in particular I'd like to highlight is the option of recreating 'past' (or rather inner) relationships in the outer world, so that there is no subjective difference between the inner and outer worlds. We exist in a world of predictable dramas, like a horrible 'Groundhog Day' of bad feeling and of harm to self and others.

Substance misuse can help a lot to creating and maintaining this state of continual and predictable drama, but is optional.

As the ego, find ways to satisfy each of the ego-states in turn; thus, from the ego's point of view, alleviating the pressure. This is linked to the defence above.

(Before continuing I should state that as well as having a downward-pointing triangle of the aspects mentioned, with an ego in the centre and a hurt child below, it would also be profitable to keep on mind a diagram like a 'quincunx'; – like the five-spot of a die – with an additional child aspect which would be 'happy' next to 'hurt'. This is the 'feels-good' child that is so much a part of this pattern, particularly when addiction's involved.. But we'd have too many diagrams! There is an aspect demanding pleasure regardless of cost, like a flip side of the hurt child, and this 'free child' is one of the ego-states which the ego experiences as a pressure).

Let's take the example of self-injury as a coping mechanism. All three (or four) of the aspects are satisfied. The Critic clamours for someone to hurt and punish, the rescuer wants to make someone feel better, the Victim needs to feel hurt and alone, while the Free Child needs to feel pleasure. A person who self-harms can experience all of those things in the space of a few seconds; - hurting themselves, giving themselves relief, feeling pain and seeing blood while alone, and feeling pleasure.

Something like alcohol use offers the same things but with a longer timeframe – the space between pleasurable activity and negative consequences is often more a matter of hours.

Other defence mechanisms could be discussed but the main idea is that of the problem-solving ego trying to control what it can't control and so creating problems. It will be obvious that all of these strategies affect how we are and so come to control and limit us. The weaker the integrity of the ego then the more extreme these behaviours become, to the point where there are no longer ego strategies but simply ego-states relating directly without an ego acting as a buffer. Indeed in the Drama Triangle it's often difficult to see if an ego is present as anything other than a battleground where the ego-states struggle for control of the identity.

On the other hand the ego can be too powerful, using it's own and other's ego-states' interpersonally in order to establish control based on the ego state's approaches. Dealing with someone who is 'borderline psychopathic' in this way can feel like playing chess with an octopus.

A too powerful ego may also see it's advisors simply as threats and seek to eliminate them. An interesting example of this can be found in 'the tragical comedy or comical tragedy of

Mr. Punch'. Mr. Punch, Judy, the baby, the policeman and Joey the clown may be seen as the ego, the rescuer, the victim, the critic and the free child respectively. I recommend a viewing of the show with this in mind. The best joke of all is the Punch and Judy man, who operates the puppets that operate the man.

THE CRITIC

The Critic can be a judge, policeman, ogre, witch, tyrant, bully, dragon, abuser, bad parent, or strict teacher. It may be angry, hurtful, shaming, belittling, blaming, directive, cruel, stern, finding fault, controlling, excluding, arguing, attacking, disapproving, punishing, putting down, opinionated, always right, prejudiced and making others feel small and stupid.

When we are identified with our Critic we often attack people for seeming to us to be exactly as we ourselves are acting. We also often feel ourselves to justified because we see ourselves as a Victim or as Rescuing some poor (and often hypothetical) person from the person we are attacking.

The Critic can attack people for any reason, although often the issue is about looking after – we attack people for not looking after others, ourselves or themselves, and we feel justified in so doing. We speak in absolutes – 'You always...' or 'You never...' When the Critic takes over we see things in a very black and white way. Good and bad are simple, and we're being forthright for another person's own good, or because they deserve being taken down a peg or two, or in another's defence, or our own.

THE RESCUER

The Rescuer can be a guardian angel, fairy godmother, Mr. Fix-it, pillar of strength, superhero, sorter-outer, martyr, mother's-little-helper, knight in shining armour, nurse, hero, or just a 'You're so good to me – what would I do without you?'

It does for others what they should be doing for themselves, and what it should be doing for itself. On the surface it is about giving a yard to get an inch back, but underneath is a 'parentesized child' – a child who looks after needy or chaotic parents in the hope that one day they will look after the carer. It is a hopeless child's recording of what a good mother should be – selfless, untiring, without needs – and because this is impossible it is a shell covering a powerful mechanism to exercise control over others so as to get them to look after it without having to admit this is the case. Unfortunately, because if the time that the recordings took place, these covert needs that it is trying to meet are those of an infant. And there is also a script that goes with these needs that says that this experience of being cared for can never actually happen.

I can sometimes spot my Rescuer is activated in client work. I feel idealised, enjoy the gratitude I receive, am tempted to break boundaries, see my client as a 'poor thing' and feel angry on their behalf, do not challenge them appropriately, become anxious about getting it right and about their possible criticism, and my self worth becomes identified with that which I offer.

THE VICTIM

The Victim controls in order to depend, While the Rescuer may be co-dependant in that it gets self-worth from what it gives, the Victim gets self worth from what it receives. We may seek to have relationships where another person plays Rescuer to our Victim and offers comfort, attention and support to us in the areas of our hurt feelings, how we are eating or sleeping, whether we are happy and if bad people have upset us. We may use the threat of our disappointment, anger or inability to cope/survive as a hidden stick to keep the Rescuer in line, perhaps enforcing this with cautionary of how we punished previous failed Rescuers. We may reward our Rescuer with whatever a 'pretend baby' has to offer, which might include allowing the other to project their own neediness onto us and to give us the support they are unable to offer themselves, or a feeling of power over us or themselves and a feeling of purpose in their lives.

When the Victim is 'up' in us we may use the promise or threat of our own Rescuer or Critic to ensure that we get more support than we give.

The Victim's nature is that of being it's own recorded infantile needs, since it is based on the self-experience of a very young child. In fact it is a recording of those needs being felt but essentially unmet. It may have learnt to find attention and love and to experience feelings of control through, for instance, being weak, being ill, being angry and throwing tantrums, being sexual, or accepting violence, or getting into scrapes from which it is rescued. Yet it has also recorded how it feels for those needs to be unmet, and so the experience of being alone, let down and disappointed, despairing and without support. That which the Victim fears has already happened. It will regularly experience these feelings, and so whatever the person playing Rescuer does or doesn't do the Rescuer will regularly be seen as a bad Rescuer, another name for which can be Critic.

When we are identified with our Victim, based as it is on the perspective of a very young child, we cannot conceive that it is not the job of other adults to look after our feelings and well-being at their own expense or at the expense of others that they care for. We believe that our neediness and demands and way of using people is offering something valuable to our relationships, and we expect that if we attack others for not looking after us then they will apologise and make more efforts to do so in future. The shortfall between these expectations and the reality of adult relationships can torment us.

The Victim aspect is, in short, a professional 'poor thing' that can see others only in terms of their being good or bad parents - as nice or nasty, as helpful or hurtful. Adult behaviour on the part of another may not be recognised as such, just seen as being mean or critical. People are good or bad containers for our feelings, that is all. The Victim will tend to set up one person or institution or substance as both good and bad, which may be an attempt to move towards wholeness by re-experiencing the dichotomy of a good/bad split.

DRAMAS AND GAMES

Games are a way of passing blame and bad feeling around between ego-states projected out from our inner world onto the world of interpersonal relationships.

The sort of dynamics which take place between the aspects within a single person now spills out to infect the pattern of our lives and outer relationships with the same repeating nursery dramas. Our outer world also becomes a Punch and Judy show.

Under the heading of 'Rescuer' I described earlier an example of this aspect activated in me in my client work. Taking this example, let's say that I manage to make my client feel like a dependent Victim, or that my Rescuer was evoked because they were already identified with a Victim aspect. What are the possibilities?

Well, I might lose my boundaries to the extent that I was so accommodating about changing appointment times, excusing missed sessions without being challenging, allowing myself to be caught up in their life such as visiting them in hospital after an OD, going to a meeting with them to support them etc. that there would no longer be a therapeutic space separate from their lives for them to come to. I would have been sucked into the pattern of their lives and thus lost my ability to operate as a therapist.

I would become just one more Rescuer in competition with all the others, wishing I was as helpful as the counsellor they see at a different project and glad the client likes me more than they do their social worker or psychiatric nurse.

Another possibility is that they come each week and talk about this crisis and that crisis, until suddenly it strikes me that the crises are not interruptions to the client's life but their preferred way of living, and that crises and dramas are the building blocks of my relationship with them too. I feel justified in becoming angry and critical and rejecting 'for their own good', or perhaps I just tell them tersely that we will be finishing in three weeks without offering an honest explanation. I have become identified with the Critic, while they exit with a few more things to add to their Victim C.V. and another experience of a bad Rescuer to talk to their next therapist about.

Another possibility is that I try to help my 'poor thing' client, break the boundaries, listen while they rant or wail about this or that person that let them down, always with a certain anxiety they'll punish me if I don't support them, and then suddenly it happens and I am seen as letting them down. The baseball bat that I've always sensed was behind their back encouraging me to be the good Rescuer finally comes out.

Perhaps they attack me verbally or even make a complaint. They move to Critic (though still feeling like an injured Victim) while I am knocked into the Victim position. Everyone has moved round one, like a Mad Hatter's tea party.

With this one example it is possible to begin to see what a game or drama looks like. Two or more people (sometimes many more) become identified with ego-states, one or more of them switch which they are identified with and / or are projecting, and there is bad feeling. Blame is passed around like a hot potato. The wrongness or fault which is passed around is not so much a product of the individual drama as in the fact that the desperately juggling ego, or any single one of these ego-states, or this whole pattern of relating via dramas and games and confusion between the inner and outer worlds simply does not work. It is not possible to effectively run a personality or a life based on these aspects and strategies as portrayed. The ego as portrayed, if present at all, is a creator of confusion.

LEAVING THE PUNCH AND JUDY SHOW

With a sense of relief we will now move from the lower personality into the personality proper, and look at these aspects in a more developed and healthy form.

The 'Critic' we will now call the Inner Father, and as well as it's more negative and critical side is now also seen to be an element of the personality based of giving direction, teaching, guidance, mentoring and support. It may be a recording mainly based on good fathering (from whichever parent or adults this is received). It helps us to get things right rather than only attacking us for getting them wrong. It can be a source of much practical information about living, provides structure, and at heart is about thought, rationality, will and purpose.

It leads by example, being able to support itself as well as others. This is not to say it is the opposite of the Critic, but that it is these other things as well.

The 'Rescuer' we will now call the Inner Mother, and is seen to be about care-giving and responsibility, but without only being disabling through over concern. It may be a recording mainly based on good mothering (from whichever parent or adults this is received). It helps us to grow and develop through facing challenges, and shows us how to care for ourselves enough to engage with and enjoy life without becoming over-extended or exhausted. It is intensely practical, and is also about feeling and heart and love and understanding. It supports by example, being able to care for itself as well as others. This is not to say that it is the opposite of the Rescuer, but that it can be these other things as well.

The Victim we will now call the Inner Child, and as well as dependence is also seen to be about awareness on many levels, and vulnerability, experiment, playfulness, creativity, wonder, and enquiry. It is not adapted to our particular history, nor is it free of the Parent's direction and care. It is the child of our Spirit, and together with our Inner Parents contains our potential to self-actualise. This is not to say it is the opposite of the Victim, but that dependence is one distorted aspect of it's nature, and it is these other things as well.

The ego we will call the Inner Adult, and as well as the side of it's nature based on self-centred fear, it is at it's best also about self-management and interaction with the world based on self-awareness. It can best be described by what it is not – the ego and ego-states of the Punch and Judy show. It's agendas are not only based on defence and attack but includes an understanding of ourselves as part of a larger world. As a practical example it would understand that being a courteous driver helps the whole system to operate. It takes advice from it's advisors – the Inner Parents and Child – in order to not only see how to balance self-interest with the larger good, as part of a society.

The ego is essentially about the past. It references it's own past experience and that of it's advisors in order to negotiate current situations, but has the ability to update it's strategies in the light of new information. It is, under ideal circumstances, teachable.

It has imagination in order to run simulations of possible outcomes, and can also be an observer to it's own inner world and how that world affects and is affected by the outer. It this way it holds part of the potential of the self.

This is not to say that the Inner Adult as now described is the opposite of the negative aspects of the ego, but that it is these other things as well. It is more rounded, like a person who has virtues and vices, strengths and weaknesses.

It is at it's best in it's correct role, which is as a function of the self, which is itself connected with and in service of the Higher Self. The ego can be a good servant but a very poor master indeed.

An ego which admits it is of itself powerless to run things is one foundation for a self.

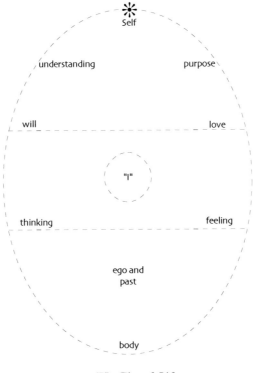

The Tree of Life

A Larger Context

We have looked at the Punch and Judy Show of the lower personality, and now are beginning to look at how those same elements can look in the context of a healthy personality. Now we need to develop a larger map on which to place these elements.

In order to do this we will look at The Egg Diagram of psychosynthesis (see page 11) and the Tree of Life of Kabbalah (see simplified diagram opposite). I will not attempt an explanation of the Egg Diagram here, except to say that among other things it is a diagrammatic representation of the psyche. Similarly I will not attempt an explanation of the Tree of Life here, except to say that among other things it is a diagrammatic representation of the psyche. I'm going to use it here to fill in some of the detail of the Egg Diagram and so develop our map.

As stated at the beginning, it is wisely said that 'The map is not the territory', but unless the map is pretty similar to the territory it's not much use as a map. Let's use this one as it stands for the mean time, just for the purpose of this paper. And I'm going to suggest a correspondence between what we have been looking at and the Tree of Life diagram. I suggest we think of the Inner Parents, Adult and Child as evolving into the lower part of the Tree. That doesn't mean they are the same thing but they correspond. Think of the parts of the Tree as addresses where you can often find these aspects in a purer form, showing their core qualities in a purer form.

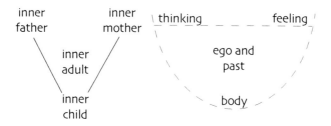

We may have idealised these inner aspects in comparison to their more primitive origins, but at least we know where to find them, and what they are at this level.

What of the more basic, primitive 'Punch and Judy Show' expressions of these aspects? Since we're equating the Inner Child with the 'Body' depicted at the bottom of the Tree, we'll place all of them at the bottom sphere, since they are parents and adults as seen through a child's eyes. They are rightly part of the id.

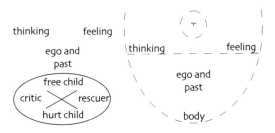

On our diagram of the Tree is an aspect named the 'I' or the self. How does it differ from the ego? Well, in respect to the extremely house-trained version of the ego we termed the Inner Adult, I can imagine some would feel there was little or no difference at all. But the ego and self are built on a different basis. The ego can fully identify with any aspect, or project it out, or ignore it as if it did not exist. The self is dis-identified from all aspects and aware of all aspects.

The ego is based on the past, since it is a recording drawing on other recordings for information. It negotiates the outer world by looking inward into a virtual inner world. Perhaps I could use the example of a robot vehicle, or a missile, referring to an inner map constructed in it's computer brain in order to negotiate the outer terrain. The robot vehicle may use sensory equipment to update it's inner map, but it is looking within for it's reality on order to steer. A real-world obstacle not on the inner map could not be avoided. The ego is the same, but for a variety of reasons already described it has a tendency to try to change the outer world to match it's virtual map.

The self, however, is based in the present, in the now, in the realm of 'what is'.

Earlier on I outlined the idea of both a theory base and also the aspects of the personality as a set of generalisations. The tendency to identify with one theory, or with one aspect of the personality, is essentially limiting and may even be the same thing. Each of the aspects of the personality has an individual recorded belief system and perspective, and it may be that a personal process of comparison and evaluation of theory bases and approaches, updated in the light of new information, reflects an integration of personality elements. In this respect we are looking at far more than the development of an intellectual construct.

In connecting with the bigger picture we start to move away from the control-based perspective of the ego and ego-states, towards one of service to something greater.

THREE LEVELS

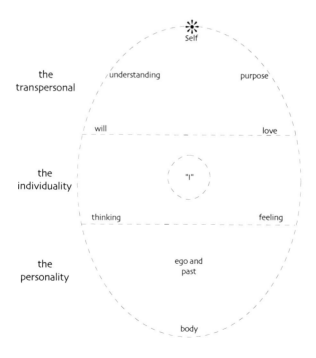

At the bottom of the Egg Diagram/Tree of Life we can see the ego at the centre of a triangle. We're not saying that the id and instincts and the Inner Child are the same as the vehicle of the body, but that there are certain convenient correspondences between them. We are not saying the Inner Father is the same as the realm of thoughts, simply that it has a certain rational base and so is linked to this realm. We are not saying that the Inner Mother is the same as the realm of feelings, but that it has a 'feelings' base and so could be seen as corresponding with this sphere.

Another name for this part of the Egg is the 'lower unconscious', and it may seem strange to place the ego – our sense of identity – in the centre of this area until we recall that the ego lives in the past, and that it's view of the real world is seen through the lens of the past. It is submerged in a realm of complexes, recordings, associations and projections, and is itself a recording. It is a point of consciousness in the unconscious. It continually matches current situations with past ones, to the extent that it cannot differentiate between the two. It's job as manager, and it's primary asset of imagination, are also it's main limitations. It works only for it's own benefit, and it is only the fact that it tends to identify with other elements of the personality that means it works for the good of the whole person at all. In psychosynthesis we have a tendency to believe that we start in the centre and go up and down in our explorations. This should bring things into perspective.

In the centre of the Egg/Tree we see the 'I' or self. In the same way that the ego is the centre of the personality, so the self (with a small 's', and also known as the personal self) is the centre of the individuality. Taking the self as the centre of a hexagram, with upward and downward pointing triangles joined around it, we could look at Thoughts, Feelings, Love and Will as an 'X' shaped cross of functions of the self, and with the function of imagination of the ego (or the sensation of the body) as a lower point, and the function of intuition as a higher point that shows a connection to the three Transpersonal spheres above. Indeed one of the defining truths about the self is that it stands as mediator between the personality below and the Higher Self above – the

Higher Self as the centre of the Transpersonal realm. The self stands with one hand down to help the personality, one hand up for support to the Higher Self.

THE STAR DIAGRAM AND THE HEXAGRAM OF THE SELF

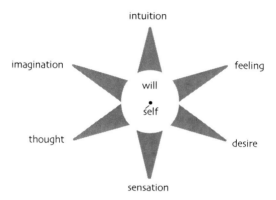

In looking at the role of the ego as a function of the self, we'll just stop and take in the view for a moment as we are looking at hexagrams. It may be that the Star Diagram of psychosynthesis was developed from the planetary hexagram which corresponds to the Tree of Life, but with the function of Will placed in the centre to demonstrate it's importance in PS, which then confuses the other correspondences.

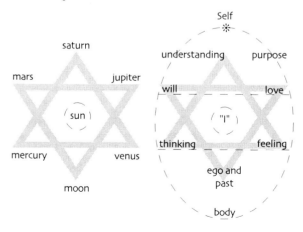

ENOUGH MAP-BUILDING ALREADY

Even with trying to maintain a brisk pace, and hardly pausing to admire the view at all, it has taken a lot longer that intended to get to the point of the paper – the ways in which we can betray our selves and our clients.

It might be said that the history of our lives is the history of the struggle between the ego and the soul, between a false self and a real self. One could write at length about the differences between the two, but in essence the ego sees itself as the centre of the universe, and uses interpersonal games involving ego-states to act out it's struggle.. The self is based on a living trust in the moment to moment reality of a Higher Self.

The ego wants to claim the brilliance of the self as it's own. It is like a hand holding a diamond, with the rays flashing between it's fingers. It says, 'This is mine, this is me'.

In the realm of counselling and psychotherapy, and indeed in any of the helping and supporting professions, we can take one of two broad approaches to client work. One is a problem-solving approach which involves managing and directing others, while the other involves creating a setting for the client to explore and discover and learn. The first requires faith in oneself and one's approach, the second requires faith in the client - or at least faith in a process in which therapist and client participate.

At the beginning of this paper we said that the therapeutic process might, in part, be an opportunity to update past experience according to new information, with the chance to see how this alters or fits in with existing structures and strategies. With the first approach in mind we might listen, decide what the problem is, then offer the solution. This would be very appropriate for a GP or clinical psychologist perhaps, and here we have a medical model of treating a patient. But therapy is/can be very different from this. As a therapist we might be quite brilliant in examining the client's life and relationships, comparing them with past and now inner aspects, and offering interpretations, images and exercises in order to 'crack the nut' and cure the client.

But with the second approach in mind we might work to create a space and a supportive relationship for whatever is waiting in the wings to present itself. We may work hard at building a good structure, which in many respects is an exercise of self-management rather than managing the client. We might confront the client not so much with our opinions as with our reactions, offered as information. In the first approach we are the pilot. In the second approach we are the co-pilot. In the second approach one acknowledges a power greater than oneself as directing the work at all times. In the first approach if there is an acknowledgement of a Higher Self, then It is on the back of a tandem. We steer and it does the peddling when we're going uphill.

In psychosynthesis terms we might see the first approach as will-based and the second as love-based. It is when the therapist claims to be coming from will, or from Father-energy, rather than supporting and mirroring back the client's will, that I begin to feel concern. Is it really will, or is it the control of the ego being exercised?

Psychosynthesis is, unfortunately, seen as a psychology of will. 'Unfortunately' because it is so easy to mistake the self-will of the ego for the will that is a natural function of the self. So easy to impose our will, our ideas, our opinions of 'what needs to happen with this client', our images, indeed our sub-personalities on others instead of creating settings in which the self can begin to emerge and express itself in all it's aspects.

Indeed there is a saying, 'Self is, self is becoming, self is becoming more itself', which I have recently heard changed to, 'Self is, self is becoming, and self needs an ego with which to manifest'. It seems to have become a tenet of belief in PS that the work is about building a strong and healthy ego as a container for the self to emerge, starting with the therapist in training. It seems to make a sort of sense, but some of us must pause to wonder why all the other people connected to spiritual approaches are headed in the opposite direction.

We may be building the ego as a strong container from which the self is to emerge, yet the ego is often in no doubt that the emerging self is the enemy, whether in ourselves or others. So what happens? The ego does as good a job as it can to look as much like the self as possible, but in a distorted way based on control which has to be acted out using others to take on roles in an inner struggle. The ego puts on shawls and dangly earrings and talks about will instead of control. It talks about 'building up a small practice in Docklands' instead of 'using people around me to act out my suppression of the self'. The ego becomes more successful at meeting it's agendas of gaining money, attention, approval and power over others, and also gets a certificate on the bathroom wall.

I am not writing this as an attack on therapy or psychosynthesis. Indeed I am a profound believer in both. But let's use the tools of our profession to look at just what it is we do, and to check whether we are coming from ego or self. Let's see if we can use the map we've developed to see when things are going one way or the other.

Take a look at the Tree again (diagram page 36). We can look at this as a developmental map, as if a seed has fallen from above and is growing upwards. But here the sun that helps it grow has been cut off by clouds.

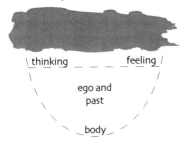

The personality aspects try to survive on their own without being aware of the larger picture. They seek to control each other so as to depend on each other. They are a family cut off from all others, and they battle to try and get from each other and to ape all the things they sense should be there but cannot connect with. The ego poses as the self which 'has' a Higher Self, the Critic rules the thoughts, the Rescuer the feelings, the Child the body and instincts. When the self is glimpsed through the clouds the ego sees it as a fascination and a threat. Oh to have that power and beauty, but how terrible to let go of control! And there is a recorded drama here called, 'This is how I was betrayed, and this is how I now betray myself'. The wound of the emerging self being unacceptable or abused and which originally led to the ascendancy of the ego and ego states as they are is recorded and are still playing.

So we now have an ego that believes it IS the person, and which relieves the pressure from the id by being in service of the id and it's instincts. The ego is continually creating situations which try to relieve the pressures from the parent aspects by finding ways to experience pleasure and harm either together or alternately, AND it needs to try to find a solution to the feared and desired true self, which it does by acting out the original suppression of the self but using others to act the self's role.

Can you imagine being in the ego's place, in the centre of all these pressures? Where would the safest place be?

There's few choices here.

> CRITIC   RESCUER
> EGO
> VICTIM

THERAPY

As a therapist my best choice might be to take the Ego and Rescuer roles, and have my client's act out the Critic and Child ones since the abusive and vulnerable aspects would be top of my list to give to someone out there. I might endlessly explore my client's childhood and their abusive experiences with past figures, while at the same time encouraging them to do the same thing with their current life. I get to manage and direct the work as the ego, and get some kudos as a kindly rescuer who is holding the good parent. If they don't have any past or current dramas involving others we can do some chair work where they can be both Victim and Critic. Then I can convince them that their Free Child is their self. I'll never mirror back the Adult, though.

SUPERVISION

I could be quite fluid and, as the ego, just give the other person whichever ego-state seemed to fit best at any given moment.

Let's say for instance I am running a supervision group, and one of the supervisees brings a client Instead of seeing the client as a whole person I listen for a minute then decide to project one of the ego-states onto them. The client self-harms and so I decide they must be a manipulative Victim. Then I start to act out my Critic and attack the counsellor for being too harsh towards or too care-taking of the client. In other words giving them my Critic or Rescuer while acting it out. In fact it saves a lot of trouble just to attack the counsellor directly for being one of my ego-states without focusing too much on the client. After all the counsellor's a much nearer container than the client.

It is a natural feature of a supervision group that when a client is brought then that client's aspects, which often are echoed by their past and current relationships, start to be unpacked into the group, with group member's taking on roles which chime with their own preferred identifications. As supervisor I will make sure that this process is quickly replaced by my own troublesome aspects being unpacked, and that either my supervisees will walk out carrying them or we will have made sure the client does.

TRAINING

As a trainer I usually have a larger group to work with but a very similar process takes place. Essentially I am not interested in the trainees as people but as sub-personalities. It is in my interest that they become more two-dimensional and stereotyped so that we can create a single makeshift personality out of the group every time it meets. And similar to the supervision group, when dynamics start to emerge I will quickly turn them to the task in hand - making sure that my most personally unacceptable aspects are put out there, and that they stay there. The dynamics of the group will revolve around my stuff, and the same figures will emerge in whichever group I take regardless of the people involved.

The same thing may happen on a much larger scale if I am running a training organisation. I run the organisation as if it were one large personality, with people coming in to finance it as trainees and to run it as staff. Unfortunately the thing I require from my trainees is that they play the part of the emerging self, but are either forced to betray themselves as I was, or leave. I am not interested in them as individual evolving selves but as containers for my projections. I will insist they are projecting things onto me, but never acknowledge it is actually all the other way. And I will try to turn them back from the gate of self-hood. I have to, to tell my story.

I will teach my students they have to reach 'beginner's mind', meaning that I will not value what they have to bring. I will tell them they have to fully identify with sub personalities before they dis-identify, which means not dis-identifying at all. I will teach them everything about the elements of body, feelings, instincts and mind - except that they are responsible for their own. Instead I will teach them that the basis of spirituality is about assertively getting needs met in relationships. I will encourage their self-obsessed Victim and their will-based confronting Critic and their disabling Rescuer in therapy groups, and I will attack adult behaviour as not being engaged. I will encourage the view that dramas are the way to the self.

For students there are also the pressures of studying for the course, paying for it, being in therapy, offering therapy, and having a life. This alone will tend to evoke the earliest survival personalities of my trainees. As therapy and training continually evokes the past and the child, so the evoked child has to try to juggle will well-nigh impossible adult pressures. And in my organisation the students will learn to re-suppress themselves and all the child's fear of not coping that is rolling like thunder under the surface they learn to put on each other, or clients, in a culture of put-downs.

I will stand at the gateway at the safest place of all, on the line, blocking the way to the self and my students will act out all the other aspects of myself that I do not wish to own in myself. I will claim the position of the self, and all the aspects beyond.

So, is all of this a terrible exaggeration? Of course. And is it sometimes like this? Yes. I have intentionally overstated my case for one reason only; – for the person, whether therapist, client, supervisee or trainee, who hasn't understood that sometimes the only thing going on is a power struggle to establish who puts what on whom.

A bleak picture. Ah, but when the clouds clear. What glories!

the 'possibility energy' of the Higher Self breaks through the clouds and transforms the ego and it's three advisors. They open and reveal, in a purer form, the qualities they have carried; a Holy Family that together miraculously become the multi-faceted jewel of the True Self.

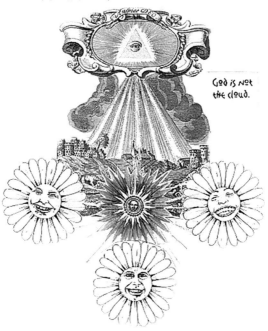

God is not the cloud.

THE BIGGER PICTURE

So, a disturbing vision of what can go wrong; – but psychosynthesis holds a dual focus of not only problems in the personality but the potential of the self emerging though these problems. In a setting where psychoanalysis was still tipped in favour of a medical model focusing on learning through studying the pathology of individuals and conditions where something was wrong, psychosynthesis took the step of looking at individuals and states of being where something had gone very right indeed.

THERAPY

A client visits a therapist. The therapist welcomes them, and offers time, attention and respect. The therapist has a calm and enquiring presence, with love in judgement and a willingness to see all of what the client is and brings. The client speaks, and the therapist waits until they speak again. The therapist holds in mind that 'There is nothing to do, there is nowhere to go'. The therapist works to build a setting and structure and a relationship for the work which is outside the pattern of the client's life and in which that pattern can be looked at and experienced. The therapist does not form opinions about what the client should do, but helps the client to explore all that they are, all that they may be, and all that they can do. The therapist is not so much moving the client from 'A' to 'B' as helping the client to experience 'A' as it really is, and to really 'vision 'B' as it may be and indeed is on some level. The self is 'A', the Higher Self 'B', in some respects.

The therapist brings all that they are to this work, as a self at the centre of their own Egg Diagram / Tree of Life / Star Diagram. They are aware of the different spheres of their experience like a spider with a foot on the web, sensing. They are aware of their own reactions as information, including the stirrings of disabling concern, harsh judgement, and feelings of rejection which indicate early object relations in the work. 'Dramas' are useful in that they provide an opportunity to model a different way of being and invite another to a different kind of relationship.

The client is able to be all that they are, without the fear that yet another person will decide what they should be doing and nag them to do it. Whole worlds of possibility begin to open up. A chance to update according to what is, with the therapeutic relationship as one of the most useful resources since it is that rarest of things - a relationship that can not only be engaged in but also talked about at the same time, without agendas connected with power, or making another person a container for blame or ill-feeling or wrongness, or one's own consciously rejected aspects.

And all the 'issues' and 'stuff', vital though they are, just gives therapist's and client's personalities' something to get on with while their selves connect and get on with the real work.

This is the reality of how it is much of the time. This is the sacred work we do.

SUPERVISION AND TRAINING

A therapeutic training is consistent between what it offers in the counselling room, in supervision, and training; – support to explore material safely in a setting where the therapist, supervisor or trainer is able to register their own reactions and either use them or dis-identify from them, whilst allowing those they support to do the same.

An understanding of the primitive aspects with these games and nursery dramas is vital, partly so as not to act from them and partly to understand that although we cannot afford to get rid of any part of us, we need not take that as an injunction to act those parts out. We need to be aware of these parts whilst at the same time connecting to their expressions on a higher arc. Psychosynthesis teaches us that our potential is already real on some level, and so we can ask for the help and support of higher aspects when seeking to transform the lower.

If this applies in individual therapy, it also applies in other settings. A supervisor, whether individual or group, has an opportunity to support supervisees in exploring the work by giving them space, asking questions, finding creative ways with them to explore the material, holding an awareness of the supervisor's and group's feelings and reactions as being vital material for the work – as long as they are not just acted out unconsciously. There is an attitude of respect for client and counsellor in a spirit of supportive enquiry, and hopefully the therapist bringing the client will leave with a feeling that things have been opened up rather than being boxed up, and will have had a chance to be supported in exploration rather than leaving with others' opinions and suggestions.

If psychosynthesis believes that each person is a group of sub personalities, then group supervision can be incredibly helpful as the supervisor enables the group to use their collective counter transference to experience the client's reality The supervisor does not need the therapist or client to hold personally unacceptable aspects of themselves, and so does not play favourites, does not use the group and clients as containers for their own performance of how their ego and ego-states is suppressing their self. At it's worst a supervisor might use the client as a convenient container as an ego defence against an unacceptable aspect of themselves, of which they are/wish to be unconscious, and possibly encouraging the supervisee to roleplay the client – to identify with them – so as to better use the therapist as an even more convenient container. At it's best a supervisor might hold a structure and awareness which allows not only the therapist, but the client on some level; to experience being seen.

In training, in the main the aim is to support others in their exploration, giving them a safe structure in which to do this. Headings are presented, and a way of exploring these headings, and if there is any truth in what we are teaching then people will discover those truths experientially for themselves. A few simple maps and areas for exploration are given, with much of the teaching being in the presence of the trainers, and there are efforts to avoid great wodges of complex verbiage and brain twisting concepts couched in incomprehensible jargon in favour of practical exercises. Often things are so complex that many mistake understanding for agreement. I'm not sure whether a paper like this would pass my own criteria, unless it was similarly used as a framework for exploration.

And in training, a great many opportunities to rehearse

counselling skills in relation to all the areas of exploration, in small safe settings without fear of judgement by a larger group.

And in the main the various training organisations take each new trainee as a unique individual bringing something that will add to the organisation and the group learning, rather than 'newbies' who should not have an opinion until they have experienced this bit of training or that. Each trainee is seen as a person rather that a sub-personality of the whole. The training will be geared towards most people finishing a manageable-length course, rather than only a fraction reaching the end of six years. The latter way might more reflect a process where only a small number of more successful sub-personalities are needed to run a personality, and the people coming into the training are disposable materials used for a performance which acts out the development of a personality configuration which has suppressed the self.

What is being acted out is the founder's process of development as individuals, rather than seeing the people involved – trainees and trainers – as the point of the whole venture. They are telling a story describing the point where, for them, ego defeated soul. Mainly of course, however, schools are communities of unique evolving individuals.

END WORD

This paper focuses so much on the lower part of the Egg, and on that which is primitive and negative, in writing it I have wondered if I were being simply mean-spirited and critical. My reason for writing it has been my fierce love of psychosynthesis and of what we do, and my own experience of the power of the nursery dramas and of the ego that can try to use the ego-states to manipulate others while trying to claim all that is great and good as it's own.

To simplify what I have been saying, there are many ways at looking at how we are as people, and I tend to think it more useful to hold all of them in mind at different times, without having to manage a precise fit at every level. Putting the Egg diagram and the Tree of life together is particularly useful at glimpsing the bigger picture. It is also interesting to compare Freud's models with the more practical tools of TA; – more practical in that they show these elements active in every human transaction. It is also useful to link those aspects with the Tree, since it puts all of it in the context of our larger potential.

One key idea for me is that we all have a 'set' of headings for parts of self, and that although what we record under these headings is unique, the headings and framework is part of our hardwiring. All these aspects, past, present and potential exist at the same time.

Not only do we each have a set, but every pair of people in relationship tend to divide them up between them. Every group of people, however large or small, tends to do the same. This can lead to people bringing only part of who they are to relationships and groups, and indeed one of a couple (such as a therapist or supervisor) may on certain occasions have an agenda to use this in a way not beneficial to anyone concerned. The same is true of groups and supervisors, facilitators or trainers. Although this is often only an undercurrent or is not present, it stands being discussed.

What I know I haven't adequately portrayed here is the self and the relationship with the Higher Self. I would like to spend at least as many pages doing this – but I will not. I will trust that others will address this and redress the balance. After all, I am not in charge, but I am part of something larger than myself. I trust this.

To end I just want to highlight the Drama triangle as a primitive expression of the more healthy triangle of the developed personality, of the triangle of individuality, and that of the Transpersonal.

In looking at the Tree, follow a line which starts with the hurt Victim and rises up, to the ego, the self-awareness of the self, and beyond. Follow a line from the Rescuer, to the realm of Feeling, and Love, and across to Understanding and beyond. Follow a line from Critic, to the realm of Thoughts, of Will, to Wisdom and Purpose, and beyond, where all meets in Unity.

The Drama Triangle is 'under a cloud', cut off from the sunlight of the Spirit, like a field of daisies on an overcast day trying to get from each other what only the larger world can offer. Such things as Love and Wisdom and Will find abusive and twisted expressions – a testament to the force of life in us all, and even the worst distortions are saying 'This is how I was betrayed, this is how I now betray myself' – are trying to tell a story and so show just exactly where we are stuck. There is an urge to bring in others into the telling of it, which is perhaps the source of mankind's greatest hope and horror.

And how awful to be stuck in endless repeating dramas, like a pass-the-parcel of bad feeling.

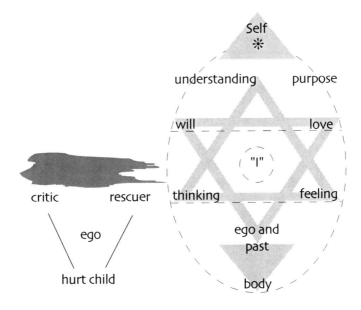

So I guess we have to keep asking ourselves the same questions, over and over. If I look at the two diagrams above, which of them is how I see others? And which of them is how they see me?

We need to keep asking this, so that we can all become All We May Be. And we can develop a self, with the most adult and teachable aspects of the ego integrated and dedicated in service of it, directly from the chaos of the Drama Triangle. The ego becomes convinced that it cannot run the life of the whole person, and that it is not the whole person, – that it is neither the centre of the inner or outer universe – and so in effect serves and becomes one basis, and then a built-in function, of the self which serves the Higher Self. Transpersonal just means 'bigger than me', and is the place of possibility energy. When trying to place one's life on a new basis and a new foundation, one does not build a personality based on satisfying the instincts, and on getting what we want in our relationships, and then hand it over to the self. The experience of self-identification simplifies all the complex agendas, though it is difficult to describe in words. The self is based on the same aspects of child, adult and parents – a holy family – but with right relationship to each other and a connection to something greater-than, and with a knowledge that this something-greater-than is the context of everything. The new basis is the good of all, under the care and direction of something greater - greater in love and greater in power - than oneself. And then acting with every heartbeat as if it's existence is an absolute certainty. Nothing less than this.

The self can operate in the personality and the individuality, rather like Harry Potter growing up in, and spending half the year in, the little world of 4 Privet Drive, Little Whinging, and then moving to Hogwarts to study and to battle the dark forces there. He lives in the 'muggle' world and the 'magical world'. But seriously, you really don't want to build up an ego first. Trust me on this one.

The self is half who we really are, and half who we really want to be. Because I am struck by the difficulty of describing the self, and explaining the difference between the way of the ego and the way of the self, I will finish with a quote. *"The first requirement is that we be convinced that any life run on self-will can hardly be a success. On that basis we are almost always in collision with someone or somebody, even though our motives are good.*

"Most people try to live by self-propulsion. Each person is like an actor who wants to run the whole show; is forever trying to arrange the lights, the ballet; the scenery and the rest of the players in his own way. If only his arrangements would only stay put, if only people would do as he wished, the show would be great. Everybody, including himself, would be pleased. Life would be wonderful…..

"What usually happens? The show doesn't come off very well….Admitting he may be somewhat at fault, he is sure that others

are more to blame... What is his basic trouble? Is he not really a self-seeker even when trying to be kind? Is he not a victim of the delusion that he can wrest satisfaction and happiness out of this world if only he manages well? Is it not evident to all the rest of the players that these are the things he wants? And do not his actions make each of them wish to retaliate, snatching all they can get out of the show? Is he not, even at his best moments, a producer of confusion rather than harmony?....

"Here is the how and why of it. First of all we had to quit playing God. It didn't work. Next we decided that hereinafter in this drama of life, God was going to be our Director. He is the Principal, we are His agents. He is the Father, we are His children.

"Most good ideas are simple, and this concept was the keystone of the new and triumphant arch through which we passed to freedom.

"When we sincerely took such a position, all sorts of remarkable things followed. We had a new Employer."

(Big Book, A.A., 1939, p. 60)

TREE

Roderick Field

The most I,
of all within,
urged tendrils of
tender roots
so down deep,
the black soft earth
reeled but once.
From molten core,
sent strength of ore
and under sky
gave breath, light
and quills of rain.
Through years and time around,
a girth of fathoms
grew, and peeling bark shed,
'til bare and custard white,
sap dizzy in dizzy height,
a tree was born anew.

THE UNIVERSAL SOLVENT

Anonymous

AN ESOTERIC PROLOGUE

In the occult art of Alchemy the term "universal solvent" is used to describe the substance that dissolves all lesser substances and leaves only the purest of metals – gold – at the end of the dissolving process. It is also called the "universal panacea", as it is at the same time the agent of healing for every disease. This substance is referenced to the fourth of seven stages of the alchemical transformation of the soul-metal and is identified with the celestial body of the Sun, the metal gold and in general with the realization of psychic perfection regarding the alchemical task at hand. In the Kabbalah it is referenced to the sixth sephirah – emanation of God – Tiphereth which is identified with Beauty, the Sun, the Sacred Heart, Love.

The correspondence in Hindu religion is the fourth Chakra which is the central of the seven chakras which is all encompassing and reflective of all upper chakras to all lower chakras (and the other way round) as a mirror and as a central unifying point. This chakra is identified with outgoing love. Based on this unifying effect, maybe it is also important to note that the only occult symbol that can encompass all Sephiroth in the Kabbalistic Tree of Life (all ten emanations of God) is the symbol of the feminine (♀). It is identified with Venus, female love, the love of the Great Mother, a love that in its higher form is identified with absolute understanding and in its lower form with unconditional love.

Alfred Adler insisted that the corrective process of the neurotic patient is the transference relationship where the therapist represents the mother-society in a mature reformative way – as opposed to the malfunctioning way the early caregivers (especially the mother) represented society to the infant and caused for malfunctioning or erroneous object formation.

Karen Horney mentions that all psychotherapy patients have the ability to correct their pathological behavior on their own. That the psyche holds the developmental answers but it is hindered in its development by obstacles. All the therapist has to do is remove these obstacles and the self will develop on its own in a healthy way.

Needless to mention the precepts of existential and person-centered therapists all over the world on the importance of principles like unconditional acceptance, reciprocal relations, genuineness and directness. Principles that are essential and indispensable in a relationship that is based on love.

Considering all the above under the prism of psychotherapy we may come to understand deeper the value of the dissolving and transforming effect of love in the therapeutic process. This value we stand to further establish here by virtue of showing the differences with other approaches that are not based on this principle.

SUBJECTIVE VS INTERSUBJECTIVE

One would be tempted to say "objective vs subjective" but most therapists are painfully aware that the term "objective" is as subjective as they come – especially in our trade. Diagnosis only gets more difficult as therapy progresses and therapeutic strategies are very often overturned by the more "objective" reality of the patient. We can therefore safely assume that there is no objective reality to be understood in a therapeutic relation but rather two distinct subjective realities – the therapist's and the patient's – and the space-relation between them. This latter intersubjective frame can only exist if there is a mutual acceptance of the other's point of view as genuinely possessing a potential for objective truth.

Only if there is an acceptance of one's own fallibility and finiteness. This space for the other person in one's heart, not only as an equal but also as a comrade in a common cause, is very much realized in a relationship that involves love because the egotistical selves are dissolved with love and only the true selves remain. One has to empty oneself from one's preconceptions and egotistical defenses to truly open one's heart and mind to a free-flowing alternating intersubjective relationship. One does not give up his wisdom and knowledge in this way but rather frees up space for these to function unhindered by the dams of egoism and its preconceptions.

UNITY VS DUALITY

If we were to promote the idea of intersubjectivity we could very easily come to a new meaning for the therapeutic alliance. When the therapist chooses the intersubjective reality instead of the "objective" reality of his own understanding, a new bond is bound to form between the therapist and the patient. This bond will include a joint front of comrades in arms that view the enemy ahead in a shared way of mind. There is a sense of camaraderie, an idea of common goals. In this frame of mind and soul, both the patient and the therapist can function in truly transforming environment.

The therapeutic aspect of the transference relationship is maximized as the therapeutic team acts in concert as one big therapeutic entity instead of two separate individuals. The sharing of the reformative essence of the therapist is more intense when the relationship is based on love. There is a very intense sharing of souls and the patient's heart is heated up like a piece of iron in the forge and is re-forged in this relationship. Now it is re-forged with the hammer of self-consciousness upon the anvil of the now reassessed perception of outer reality. And it would be unfair to the responsiveness to the therapist to exclude him/her from this process of re-forging.

One cannot but share in this experience and be re-forged to the point where this transforming experience of one's patient reaches one's own soul – whether this is through self-healing or through re-affirmation of one's past transforming moments. Many therapists look back nostalgically to their magic moments with patients. I hold no doubt in my mind that in every single magic moment out there, the feeling of unity between the two is the prevalent one in the relationship. This feeling might not have been born from a loving relationship but such a relationship is surely more apt to lead to such unifying circumstances.

RECIPROCITY VS AUTHORITY

Even though the presupposing of intersubjective realities in therapies leads to the necessary understanding of the patient as an equal in terms of his holding the "objective" truth, there is an even deeper aspect in the experiential aspect of therapy. One has to understand that there is really no way to be an inaccessible authority to the patient. One cannot be objective in being non participating in self-disclosure or in not sharing personal thoughts and feelings with the patient. The idea of a non participating objective therapist is rather a myth and there are at least two reasons for that. First, one cannot consciously hide one's unconscious messages revealed through one's body language and flavoring of speech. Secondly, an absence of energetic participation is very much a participation, as the patient can project upon this blank screen not only his own inner unconscious but also the contents of a very much unilateral transference relationship. By sharing and being forthcoming (of course only under the prism of the client's best interest) the therapist is able to fully explore the present relationship and use it dynamically in a "here and now" analysis that can lead to a resolution of a large range of similar pattern relationships of the patient. An authoritarian approach may provide more insight into the problem but lacks deeply in self-developing for the patient.

If one is to trust Karen Horney and Carl Rogers among others in their saying that the patient holds the keys to the problem of his own development, we must understand the paramount importance that the patient realizes the dynamics of his/her problems on his own so that they can be integrated in his / her developmental schema bring about a profound self-object transformation. It is not without merit that most of our patients rarely remember our most astute comments and interpretations but rather the instances where we provided them with a piece of feedback that was very important to them or a realization they have made on their own in therapy. Sentimental and mental input from the therapist's point of view is nothing but knowledge finite and trivial before the all-devouring jaws of the neurotic defense mechanisms. Whereas the same input approached from a joint point of view addressed specifically to the patient's developmental momentum is infinite and substantial wisdom as it permanently becomes an integral part of the patient's superego ideal. This attuning can best be accomplished in equal empathic relationships, relationships that are best attained through the sincere equality acceptance and oneness that comes from love.

FINITE

When the question of time and space comes into therapy there is either two terrified people approaching a deadly religious problem or a chance to overcome. Usually it is a bit of both, but when true and sincere love is involved in a therapeutic relationship, the question of human finiteness is approached in such a confidence that all involved feel contained by this frame of loving. One often worries about how much love and comfort can one provide as a therapist. How much of oneself can one give in the process, how involved can one become? Will it ever be enough? Will it be worth it, will the returns be appropriate to one's efforts? Will it ever end or will one stay an eternal slave to the patient's needs? Will one have to carry the patient in one's arms forever? How do we ever make sure we handle the endless possibilities of transference the right way to their full potential? Is one's mind and heart ever perfect in treating a patient? Could one live with one's mistakes? Can there be total containment? Can there be total "Holding"? "Mirroring"? Internal Supervision?

One cannot simply refuse these questions. Whether our answer is logical and well thought, there will always be this place in our souls where these questions still burn. And they are supposed to keep burning. Otherwise we would not be truly human-beings that strive upwards.

The answer to these questions is not the same and is certainly different for every therapist. But there is a common denominator in the quality of every such answer. And this is the amount of love the therapist feels for each patient. Only absolute love can produce a unity with the universe that can assuage the metaphysical angst of a soul. And it is the same unity that can contain the similar psychic wound of the patient. The process is dual. It is comprised of the combined efforts of unconditional love-acceptance and understanding-wisdom. One need not give his whole self to patients every time. One can help another to build his/her own fire instead of giving away his/her own burning logs. One can sincerely try his best under the understanding that this means taking into consideration his own self and the other as equals. The line is delicate but very defined if approached under the prism of unconditional love and understanding. The triad of faith hope and love can lead the way to this infinite path. Infinite faith to the unity and harmony of the universe gives birth to the infinite hope for all creatures in this united universe and in itself gives birth to infinite love for the creations on account of the unifying and dynamically evolving nature in all of them. Once such feelings and ideas penetrate in the therapeutic relationship, the wounded soul is magically reheated and the re-forging begins. Love serves as more than fuel in this process. It holds an almost magical ability to dissolve obstacles. Just as the ancient Greeks proclaimed that Love is invincible in all battles, there is no obstacle that can stand in front of unconditional love.

Every unfulfilled wish is fulfilled just by the notion that there is a time and a space for this wish right in front of the patient: in the therapist's soul that mirrors unconditional love. Even the most absurd wishes are fulfilled because the denial of their fulfilling by the therapist is not perceived as rejection since the portrayed love is so unconditional that contains the absurdity and the absurd person as two totally acceptable entities even when the accepting person has a different opinion. There is always space for everything and everyone, even in absolute disagreement. This space is a child of love and not of ethic. If sterile ethics and logical principles were to accept the difference there would not be an acceptance in a sentimental and psychic level but only in a mental level and therefore the person would feel rejected. But love works on all levels and encompasses all. This way the obstacles to the needs are dissolved and the resulting blocked energy is used in a developmental pathway for some long overdue healing.

A Religious Epilogue

'1 *If I speak in the tongues of men and of angels, but have not love, I am only a resounding gong or a clanging cymbal.*

2 *If I have the gift of prophecy and can fathom all mysteries and all knowledge, and if I have a faith that can move mountains, but have not love, I am nothing.*

3 *If I give all I possess to the poor and surrender my body to the flames, but have not love, I gain nothing.*

4 *Love is patient, love is kind. It does not envy, it does not boast, it is not proud.*

5 *It is not rude, it is not self-seeking, it is not easily angered, it keeps no record of wrongs.*

6 *Love does not delight in evil but rejoices with the truth.*

7 *It always protects, always trusts, always hopes, always perseveres.*

8 *Love never fails. But where there are prophecies, they will cease; where there are tongues, they will be stilled; where there is knowledge, it will pass away.*

9 *For we know in part and we prophesy in part,*

10 *but when perfection comes, the imperfect disappears.*

11 *When I was a child, I talked like a child, I thought like a child, I reasoned like a child. When I became a man, I put childish ways behind me.*

12 *Now we see but a poor refl ection as in a mirror; then we shall see face to face. Now I know in part; then I shall know fully, even as I am fully known.*

13 *And now these three remain: faith, hope and love. But the greatest of these is love.'*

1st Corinthians (13)

BIBLIOGRAPHY

Aivanhov O.M. *The Splendor of Tiphareth*, Prosveta 1987
Aivanhov O.M. *The Fruits of the Tree of Life*, Prosveta 1989
Assagioli R. *The Act of Will*, Platts 2000
Frankl V. *Man's Search for Ultimate Meaning*, Perseus 2000
Frankl V. *Recollections, an Autobiography*, Perseus 2000
Jung C.G. *Psychology and Alchemy*, Routledge 1953
 Jung C.G *Symbols of Transformation*, Routledge 1956
Millon T, Davis R. *Personality Disorders in Modern Life*,
                                        John Wiley & Sons 2000
Mitchell J. *The Selected Melanie Klein*, Free Press 1987
Silberer H. *Hidden Symbolism of Alchemy and the Occult Arts*
Storolow R. et al *Psychoanalytic Treatment: An Intersubjective
                              Approach*, Analytic Press 1987
Yalom I. *The Gift of Thereapy* Harper Perennial 2003
Yalom I. *Lying on the Couch*, Harper Perennial 1997
Yalom I. *Momma and the Meaning of Life*, Piatkus 1999

THE ZECHARIAH PROJECT

A Comparison of Models in Psychosynthesis Process
with Old and New Testament Literature

Previn Karian

INTRODUCTION

This essay compares the model of the egg diagram conceived by Assagioli with its application to passages from the Book of Zechariah in the Old Testament, and various related passages in the New Testament, with special reference to John Chapter 10. The processes of inclusivity, integration and synthesis in psychosynthesis are compared with their application in the prophetic vision of this 'minor' prophet, where conflicting transpersonal energies are reconciled and integrated in a remarkable series of metaphors and images.

The original brief to research a relationship between psychosynthesis models and a personal field of interest led me initially to consider comparing Assagioli to Jung and Rogers. The attraction of the latter two was that they represented amplified studies in archetypal and humanist therapeutic approaches, both of which I find myself unconsciously integrating in my own approaches to life and to client work. They were also areas of study in which I wished to deepen and broaden my own understanding and range of interventions. Jung would represent the workings of the higher consciousness, while Rogers the middle and some elements of the lower conscious.

Beginning with summary works by Andrew Samuels ('Jung and the Post-Jungians') and David Brazier ('Beyond Carl Rogers') I found them dry and sterile. I was taken aback at my reaction, because something fundamental was amiss. I could no longer align myself with the easy humanism or the vagaries of archetype that were being presented after the depth of work in Avalon which contained the transpersonal so clearly while moving into both depths and heights of psyche in a seemingly effortless way. Why had they become so hard to read? Why so unsatisfying?

Useful though they were, Jung and Rogers needed to be read directly rather than through their emissaries, while the Book of Zechariah which I stumbled upon during this time stood out with glaring metaphors and imagery of integration, synthesis and reconciliation of transpersonal forces which I knew so well from my past, and from my recent work with PS Avalon. My life circumstance at the time also called me into a re-commitment to living out my belief in the transpersonal, which resulted in my return to Bournemouth where I set up a therapeutic practice.

This direct plunging into and working with transpersonal energy in psychological process in my own life led me to focus on Zechariah and psychosynthesis. In this way, the work stands at a tangent to Assagioli's own interests in both Judaism and Christian spirituality, but imitates his willingness to directly address transpersonal energies with a cognitive intent.

PSYCHOLOGICAL CONTEXTUALISATION OF THE SPIRITUAL

In the opening of Ch.5 in his book Psychosynthesis, Assagioli makes an extremely important admission about those who experience the need to understand the spiritual dimension of their personalities and life. He points out:

'...a personal psychosynthesis for many patients is a much desired and quite satisfactory achievement, making of them harmonious individuals, well adjusted both within themselves and with the community to which they belong and in which they play a useful part. But there have always been a certain number of human beings who were not and could not be satisfied with such a normal achievement, however worthy it may have appeared to others. For such people there must be a different solution, another wider and higher type of psychosynthesis - Spiritual Psychosynthesis.' (Psychosynthesis, Ch5, p.193)

This confession carries with it an implicit elitism which appears to be based on observational fact. The transpersonal understandings and techniques of psychosynthesis can be applied to many individuals who require no more than a sufficient level of self reflective skill to manage the energies which lie above and below the human consciousness. From this, they are able to live adequately harmonious lives and make valuable contributions to individuals and society. Who are those that are excluded from this 'normality'?

I have not been able to discover any writings of Assagioli which discuss pre-incarnational meditation as an exploration of how our spirits/soul may have chosen to incarnate into matter with a specific purpose and intention. But the observable fact is that mankind always carries a minority of people who are too traumatised by either the subconscious or the superconscious to be content with a harmonisation of their everyday lives. Their deep seated agitation emanates from their response to a wounding and the historical and bio-socio-economic contexts in which they exist. Such individuals are preoccupied and engaged with a need to understand spirituality and its expressions, and they find no rest until they do.

For many, rest comes at the end of a journey in art, music, literary, religious or political lives. But with all of these, there is always a sense that the energies that manifested were never fully understood. In the case of the last three in the list, there is also growing dissatisfaction and disillusionment with the crumbling fabric of expressions available to us today in these spheres of activity as they compete in the age of new media, global economies, and the standardisation of culture. Manifestations, protestations, proclamations and experiences of spiritual energy no longer satisfy the hunger of those on spiritual journeys.

It is at that point that Assagioli uniquely offers a psychological context in which spiritual energy can be understood. He notes that individuals can experience spiritual phenomena which then become a fact of their lives. This fact is as real as the troubled repressions of the subconscious, and he uniquely creates the realm of the superconscious as a psychological category that sits above our everyday consciousness in his famous egg diagram. The superconscious is our internal dimension which accesses and holds the spiritual world.

Many great artists, musicians, poets, mystics, psychologists, gurus/teachers and thinkers have become stuck at this point. Lacking the category of the superconscious, they proceeded to become fixated on the contents of the superconscious and its manifold possibilities, shapes and energies. The superconscious has become the only reality for them, and in this fixation and denial of the other aspects of their humanity, they rarely engage with their own shadow and subconscious, while often belittling or dismissing the value of their everyday and current living contexts. Despite the great worth of these spiritual people, there is a lingering sense of something experienced but misunderstood, and therefore potentially dangerous.

The breakthrough in the psychology of the transpersonal (that which lies above and below the conscious ego) comes in Assagioli's major distinction between the Self and the superconscious. Indeed his whole psychology rests on the proposition of an organising Self centre which lies beyond the functioning ego and which is an interface with the Universal or spiritual energies. This higher Self is the incarnated soul, a particle of spirit emanating from the Universal, which journeys through the woundings of life. The rediscovery of this Self through its disidentification with the contents of the psyche is the necessary step and foundation of managing spirituality. Self identification is a prerequisite.

Assagioli then has the two categories to begin contextualising the spiritual. He distinguishes between the superconscious as the realm of existing qualities, essences, archetypes and spiritual energies that shape and call mankind into its future and each individual into his or her destiny. This can be accessed through development and engagement with the will (creative meditation), the imagination (receptive meditation) and cognitive (reflective meditation) faculties (see The Elements of Psychosynthesis, Will Parfitt, pp49-53). But access to the superconscious is not to be confused or enmeshed with the Self.

'It should be pointed out that the reaching up into the realm of the superconscious and its exploration, while approaching the consciousness of the Self, may sometimes even constitute an obstacle to full Self-realisation... One can become so fascinated by the wonders of the superconscious realm, so absorbed in it, so identified with some of its special aspects or manifestations as to lose or paralyze the urge to reach the summit of Self-realization.' (Psychosynthesis, Ch2, pp38-9)

This distinction is made repeatedly by Assagioli. We may be able to experience many forms of spiritual energy, but the experiences and perceptions of the superconscious are NOT to be mistaken with the Self:

'What distinguishes psychosynthesis from many other attempts at psychological understanding is the position that we take as to the existence of a spiritual Self and of a superconscious, which are as basic as the instinctive energies described so well by Freud.' (Psychosynthesis, Ch 5, p193)

While the superconscious can offer a variety of experiences across religions, political and artistic inspirations, and personal callings to serve rather than exploit mankind, these experiences are not permanent phenomena. The Self, however, does remain within each of us as an unchanging interface with both the Universal and our humanity.

'There are people who - either spontaneously or through some strenuous inner exercise of prayer or meditation - can temporarily project their consciousness upwards...getting at times very near to the spiritual Self. But this is a passing condition, it does not last, and they relapse back to their normal level after such intense inner experiences...(This) indirectly explains and emphasizes the difference between becoming aware of the superconscious levels of experience and contents on the one hand, and pure Self-realisation on the other. Self-realisation... means the momentary or more or less temporary identification... with the spiritual Self...In these cases there is a forgetfulness of all contents of consciousness, of all that forms the personality both on normal levels and those of the synthesized personality which include superconscious or spiritual levels of life and experience; there is only the pure intense experience of the Self.' (Psychosynthesis, p 201-202)

The Self here stands permanently outside the superconscious, the daily functioning of the ego ('all contents of consciousness'), and our dysfunctional/functional histories ('all that forms the personality'). The Self, however, is located within us. Somewhere in the make up of the human psyche sits a locus of mysterious, purposeful and intelligent energy which has different behaviours and requirements from mere spiritual experiences.

It is working from this psychological centre which lies outside sub, super and every day consciousness, yet is located within, that leads to the possibility of a place from which and in which synthesis, integration and inclusivity - the healing of mankind - can begin. Rather than neurotic suppression of our past wounding in the subconscious, or escapist projections of our neediness into the superconscious, stepping into a higher Self within enables the psychological health of the spiritual. The Self gives us the possibility of more accurate readings of our super or sub conscious experiences, and enables us to engage the learning we receive into the daily functioning of our ego lives. This is the higher integration of the Self that lies beyond the return to normality which most other psychologies and therapies offer.

'The achievement of integration...can be greatly facilitated by the activation of the superconscious functions, by the realisation of the Self, because those larger and higher interests act as a magnet which draws up the "libido" or psychic energy invested in the "lower" drives. When one of the specific functions of the Self, the will, is recognized and utilised, it too can contribute effectively, by means of its regulating and controlling power, to the harmonious integration, to the bio-psychosynthesis of the whole human being.' (Psychosynthesis, p51)

The integration with higher, lower and everyday energies and levels of consciousness gives Assagioli his unique position in transpersonal psychology. This perspective enables him to warn of the dangers of the absence of the Self in spiritual work, where the energies of the superconscious then flood directly and disruptively into the ego or the personality, causing psychological disturbances:

'(In some cases) the personality is inadequate in one or more respects and therefore unable to rightly assimilate the inflow of light and strength. This happens, for instance, when the intellect is not balanced, or the emotions and the imagination are uncontrolled; when the nervous system is too sensitive; or when the inrush of spiritual energy is overwhelming in its suddenness and intensity...An incapacity of the mind to stand the illumination, or a tendency to egotism or conceit, may cause the experience to be wrongly interpreted, and there results...a "confusion of levels." The distinction between absolute and relative truths, between the Self and the (Ego), is blurred and the inflowing spiritual energies may have the unfortunate effect of feeding and inflating the personal ego.' (Psychosynthesis, Ch 2, p43-44)

Given the working presence of the Self, Assagioli goes on to describe its interaction with the other dimensions of the human psyche. He distinguishes the interplay of Self with superconscious as a 'height' psychology (a term borrowed from Victor Frankl's logotherapy. See Psychosynthesis, ch 5, p197ff) which tries to break into everyday consciousness, while the interplay of Self with sub-conscious belongs to the 'depth' psychology of those such as Jung and Freud who excavate our past histories, dysfunctions and collective archetypal residues which also try to break into everyday consciousness.

In his height psychology, Assagioli speaks of the way in which the superconscious will at times descend into everyday consciousness, while our own efforts can raise our conscious ego into superconscious experiences:

'...at times the conscious (ego) rises or is raised to that higher region where it has specific experiences and states of awareness of various kinds which can be called "spiritual" in the widest sense. At other times it happens that some contents of the superconscious "descend" and penetrate into the area of the normal consciousness of the ego, producing what is called "inspiration." This interplay has great importance and value, both for fostering creativity and for achieving psychosynthesis.' (Psychosynthesis, Ch 2, p38)

His use of the notions of 'ascent' and 'descent' here require clarification. In much spiritual, artistic and psychoanalytic parlance and vocabulary, ascent is a higher climbing into spiritual realms while descent is an exploration of the baser instincts and urges of mankind. However, for Assagioli, contents in either the super or the sub conscious can ascend or descend as he views them as transpersonal, lying above and below the ego. These energies can either break into everyday ego functioning (descent of the superconscious or ascent of the subconscious energies) or the ego can be taken into both realms (ascent into the superconscious or analytic descent into the subconscious. See Transpersonal Development, Roberto Assagioli, Ch2, p24).

As he moves into the dynamics of height psychology, it appears that the superconscious merely contains contents of an invisible nature (qualities, essences, spiritual beings, archetypes) while the Self is engaged with psychological activities, an exercise of the Will which propels the individual and his/her ego towards an enactment of purpose. However, it is the superconscious alone that activates the energy and development of the Self and its Will:

'This raises the all important and not clearly realized difference between "superconscious" experiences and psychological activities and the spiritual Self...The superconscious precedes consciousness of the Self...'
(Psychosynthesis, Ch5, p 198)

We now come to the final piecing together of spiritual contextualsation in transpersonal psychology offered by psychosynthesis. Both super and sub conscious levels hold contents which attempt to express themselves in everyday life and ego consciousness. If either of these contents are denied, they create pathological behaviour or sudden eruptions of their contents into ego consciousness. These differing levels of awareness and perception cannot resolve or integrate themselves through any natural internal processes. They demand that they are regulated or initiated into our lives through conscious choices. The Self and its Will stand outside all of these levels but offer a point from which integration can begin. The Self can connect not only with ego, superconscious and subconscious, but with Universal spirituality in its manifold expressions of myth, symbol, rituals, narratives and interactions with others. In a crucial passage, Assagioli writes:

'What is necessary is to differentiate this superconscious but previously unconscious material from the type of material that may come from the lower levels of the unconscious which have been extensively studied by Freud and his followers. It seems that in some of the extreme cases of irruption from superconscious levels the material that comes arrives – so to speak – almost ready made, and has very little connection with previous experiences. It is not something which arises in the usual way from the lower unconscious as the result of now released but previously repressed experiential contents; it is something new and...sometimes has little relationship to precedent personal experiences of the individual.' (Psychosynthesis, Ch5, p 198)

For the Self to begin integration and synthesis, the first task is to differentiate between contents of the psyche in the superconscious and the subconscious. The subconscious can be accessed through dreams and memories expressed in discourse with the therapist. The superconscious is accessed through imagination, meditative reflection and sensing the directive energies of the Will. This is radically different from the use of the will in NLP which seeks to programme the ego into conventional or personally desired ideals (often a projection of personal need). Hence Assagioli describes superconscious contents in the above quote as 'previously unconscious material...the material that comes arrives...almost ready made, and has very little connection with previous experiences...it is something new, etc'.

This positions the contents of the subconscious with the past and contents of the superconscious with the future. In a radical break even with Jungian notions of the archetypal recently expressed by James Hillman, the superconscious does not emanate from the woundings of individual history or the collective archetypes of our ancestral past. Its contents are not a predetermined image in the seed of an acorn. They are ineffable, indefinable, unknowable and outside the reach of all psychologies which seek to bring the mystery of the universe into the grasp of the therapeutic ego. Only in communion/ connection with a higher Self within do we have a hope of co-operating constructively with these higher forces and contents that allow us glimpses and glimmers of what they might be.

The Self deploys imagination, will and reflective meditation in ways unknowable to the ego, but experienced as hard fact and reality nevertheless. Its primary metaphor is that of a journey, moving between ego conscious, superconscious or subconscious with the purpose of integration, synthesis, inclusivity and healing. It is able to delve into either realms and manage the constructive transition of their energies into everyday living. It appears to emerge in height psychology more than the searchings of the depth psychologists. Most importantly, it enables a profound, rooted and grounded understanding and assimilation of superconscious energies and experiences. The detachment of the Self from all three layers of consciousness (ego, super and sub) remains supreme:

'I would point out here that "superconscious", "unconscious" (subconscious) and "conscious" (ego) are adjectives, that is to say that they are temporary conditions of a psychological fact.' (Transpersonal Development, Ch.2 p.24)

This last point takes us to the application of psychosynthesis contextualising in the Old Testament book of Zechariah and related passages in both Old and New Testament literature. The superconscious contains a number of symbols, narratives and actions which can be grouped together as associated states of awareness. In Transpersonal Development, Assagioli delves into the many nuances of these groupings in Chapters 2, 4, 6 and 13. But all the lists of groups and stages of development are merely transitional markers of the way in which the Self journeys through the superconscious and brings it into everyday consciousness for the use of healing and integration. Zechariah contains some striking examples of symbols and stages of awareness and development which resonate through all Old and New Testament literature, and a reading of the text using the psychological contextualising of Assagioli gives us interesting findings in relation to the relevance of Old Testament texts in spiritual development.

PSYCHOSYNTHESIS MODELS AND PROCESS IN THE BOOK OF ZECHARIAH

The Book of Zechariah, a minor prophet of the Old Testament, contains a strikingly different quality and expression of prophecy, redemption and punishment from the other prophetic texts in

Biblical literature. On reflection, it seems as if the narrative intent is one of healing, integration and bringing times of conflict and violence to an end, while fully acknowledging the presence and impact of violence and punitive dynamics prevalent in spiritual work. If prophetic texts are written primarily to offer people who hear them 'one last chance' of changing their minds and ways (the story of Jonah), then the predictive and fortune telling aspects of any prophetic texts are to be held lightly. An understanding of psychosynthesis contextualising of the spiritual above will enable a first layer of excavation into the many psychological truths that Old Testament literature, read as contents of superconscious revelation, can still hold for us today.

The vibrancy of a call to healing and integration in Zechariah is markedly different from my sense of the other minor prophets, and substantially different from the major prophetic books (Isaiah, Jeremiah, Ezekiel, Daniel). The major prophecies have an apparently dominant orientation to the collapse of Israel's spirituality at political and social levels where prophets battle with rejection from king, society and the religious institutions of the time. Many of the pronouncements of wrath against Israel for her betrayal to God are mixed in a bizarre manner with pronouncements of wrath against her enemies who may go too far in the victories God will allow them. The pronouncements of liberation then appear with a dual political and personal aspect in their proclamation of a Messiah, a redeeming future figure for the restoration of Israel, politically and ethnically linked to King David, who in turn is ethnically linked back to the Patriarchs Jacob, Isaac and Abraham. Zechariah, as text, appears almost to distil the essence of punitive and restoration/liberation process that God will achieve in 3 major groupings of vocabulary.

The first linguistic assumption here is that the text of Zechariah (and indeed all Biblical literature) is a human register and expression of an inspiration attributed to a God who stands outside and within the whole of creation and space-time-matter. This God who remains mysterious, unknowable, ineffable, eternal and infinite is able to manifest aspects of its divinity through appearances, historical and personal events, rituals, language, music and art. The expression of this divinity in the language of sacred texts creates enormous potential for its abuse and misreading in the absence of a psychological understanding of the superconscious, subconscious and conscious ego of the writer and the reader who interact at the moment of reading. However, read from the perspectives of transpersonal psychology, the apparently disparate literature can be seen to hold an internal coherence, consistency and illumination in even the smallest of its details.

In terms of a wide linguistic grouping of imagery, symbolism, metaphors, narratives and pronouncements, it is possible to see the political pronouncements as emanating from the consciousness of the national ego, the punitive pronouncements as a redressing of the unresolved primal subconscious, and the redemption-liberation-integration pronouncements as the offerings of shapes and energy descending from the superconscious. However, outside all of these groupings, there are the remarkable statements of proclamation and declaration which belong to none of these three states of consciousness - they belong to the expression of the Self and its assertions of will in the promise of fulfillment. Unlike the psychosynthesis model where Self is discovered through disidentification with the contents of the psyche, Zechariah shows a Universal Self intervening and profoundly involved in human and personal history, presenting itself within all three states of consciousness in an assertion of deep integration.

NATIONAL EGO

There are a number of punitive verses in Zechariah which are enmeshed with liberation and redemption. Chapter 14 in the book gives a good example of what happens at a psychological level. The first two verses speak of an abhorrent level of violence that will be deliberately invited into Jerusalem, a gathering of 'all the nations to Jerusalem to fight against it'. A plague is then sent to afflict all those who attack the city ('Their flesh will rot while they are still standing on their feet, and their eyes will rot in their sockets, and their tongues will rot in their mouths', vs 12). There is a betrayal of ethnic bonding when even 'Judah too will fight at Jerusalem', implicitly against the other tribes of Israel (vs 14), and the plague spreads to all the animals. The subservience of 'the survivors from all the nations that have attacked Jerusalem' in ritual worship is accompanied by a punishment of no rain for those who don't (vs 17-18), while the book ends with a bizarre exclusion and ethnic extinction ('...on that day there will no longer be a Canaanite in the house of the LORD Almighty' vs. 21).

There are two extreme responses to passages such as these. Those who are consumed with a nationalistic consciousness will take up such texts as a legitimisation of political violence and the enforcement of ethnic divisions and hatred. Nationalistic ego creeps into any ego form which seeks to claim a high moral ground - whether it is Bin Laden's use of Islam to terrorise the US, or the easy moralism of the US to legitimise state violence in bringing down terrorists, or sections of religious institutions which choose to victimize/persecute/ condemn those its moral precepts excludes. At the other extreme are humanists who cite such passages as the reason why they cannot have any associations with recommendations of implicitly legitimised violence towards any aspect of humanity, the animal kingdom or the planet. The former can feed their nationalistic and moral fervour while the latter can fuel their reactive dismissal of outdated and irrelevant spirituality - all from the same text, read purely through the filter of the ego consciousness.

From the transpersonal perspective, what both these readings of the text miss out are the even more bizarre descriptions of redemption that separate the beginning and the ending of Chapter 14, occurring in verses 3-11. These verses bring an entirely different possibility of meaning to precisely what is meant by the LORD who 'will go out against those nations, as he fights in the day of battle' (vs 3). The physical detail in vs 3-11 makes it increasingly difficult to hold a purely political reading of the verses before and after. Yet these are the verses that are repeatedly ignored by those who wish to bang the drums of nationalism-moralism or dismissive humanism. The redemption offered stands beyond the ego, speaking neither to nationalism, moralism or even the potentials and hopes of humanism. It will be looked at in closer detail later.

The difficulty of consistently and coherently holding a political reading of the Zechariah text persists in every passage dealing with judgment against nations. In Chapter 9, Tyre, Ashkelon, Gaza, Ekron, Ashdod and Philistia are not only brought down in power but are also a recruitment place for the future leadership of a restored Judah ('Those who are left will belong to our God and become leaders in Judah' vs7). The oracle in Chapter 12 speaks of a gathering concentration of opposing forces against Jerusalem, where Jerusalem remains as an immovable centre which no longer reflects any political significance, but is protected by a supernatural angelic presence, making the redemption stand outside national or moralistic egotism (vs 7-9). And as if to set the trans-political mode in which the text is to be read, Chapter 2 vs10-13 has a pan-national inclusivity which could only belong to a Universal spirit that celebrates the diversity of peoples it has created.

Understanding spiritual energy or sacred texts in the light of psychosynthesis modelling enables an accurate contextualising of meaning and interpretation from transpersonal perspectives. Psychosynthesis can help to define and limit the role of egotism with its simplistic abuse and misappropriation of the Biblical text which essentially communicates contents of the superconscious. If this is not understood, texts such as those discussed above fall into the grasp of misplaced and distorted nationalistic-moralistic inflation of the ego, producing the common phenomenon of 'white washed tombs', the widespread but unacknowledged religious hypocrisy, moral bigotry and behavioural self-contradiction which forms the congregational nightmare for those involved in pastoral work, or the nightmare of fascist politics which uses spiritual works to inflate a national or personal (so-called 'charismatic') ego. Equally inappropriate, when naïve ego presentations are made of the contents of the superconscious, it can also create a dismissive and reactive arrogance against spiritual texts and contents of the superconscious from the unresearched generalisations of humanists.

Ego without any psychological awareness distorts spiritual energies and the superconscious into an occasion for its own inflation, while inviting equally egotistical reactions to it. Spirituality is used and presented naively, creating a vindictive and false sense of superiority and persecution of those outside the pale, re-enforcing hatred, divisions, prejudice and ignorance in place of informed dialogue.

UNRESOLVED AND PRIMAL SUBCONSCIOUS

It is precisely the protracted egotistic indulgence of their spiritual privileges that led Israel into a distortion, abuse, complacency and defilement of its tradition of superconscious revelation. Where Israel was given the potential of becoming the inspiring beacon of holy living to the nations, it demonstrated a shocking capacity for debauchery and violence, at its worst during the periods recorded in Judges, 1&2 Samuel, and 1&2 Kings – the pre-exilic period.

Chapter 7 of Zechariah continues with this tradition of prophetic warning and exposure. In vs 4-7, the use of ritual as an honouring of the sacred and revealed contents of the superconscious has become (literally) an egotistic feeding of the Israel's national consciousness ('And when you were eating and drinking, were you not just feasting for yourselves?' vs 6). The entire contents of 10 commandments and the first five books of the Old Testament are reduced to the simplicity of two verses of the spirituality that God seeks:

'Administer true justice; show mercy and compassion to one another. Do not oppress the widow or the fatherless, the alien or the poor. In your hearts, do not think evil of each other.' (7:9-10)

But the egotism of Israel is unable to integrate the requests of the superconscious revelation into daily living. The rejection and denial of spiritual life leads to a repression of superconscious energy unable to express its blessings. The result of an absence of spirituality and the superconscious (as modern man without his soul is repeatedly discovering) is desolation. For Israel, this has national repercussions: 'I scattered them with a whirlwind among the nations, where they were strangers. The land was left so desolate behind them that no-one could come or go. This is how they made the pleasant land desolate.' (7:14)

This is far from an arbitrary edict from God. If Israel are the carriers of a specific revelation of the superconscious, then its rejection or denial splits the nation's psyche from its real strengths and its identity. Denial of the superconscious and the appropriation of rituals for the use of the ego leads to a large-scale historic fragmentation of a nation and its people. This is expressed in the internal divisiveness, betrayals, and defilements that multiply with the afflictions of enemies and external political predators. It is not just an inability to manage internal and external that besets Israel here. The absence of the superconscious creates an accumulation of primal subconscious energies gathering with oppressive power on the outside, and creating increasing splitting from within. In short, if the superconscious is rejected, a primal and unresolved subconscious will quickly take its place in the psychic vacuum. This subconscious feeds the ego with a ferocious power dynamic of domination-slavery swings of the pendulum, and manifests as a widescale psychological splitting and fragmentation of either a people or its individuals.

Returning to the punitive passages against the other nations, it is not nationalistic or moral triumph that is being represented here. In Ch 9 where Tyre has 'built herself a stronghold;/she has heaped up silver like dust,/and gold like the dirt of the streets' (vs 3) it is the accumulated belief in possessions and power that will be taken away. In vs 6-7 of the same chapter, it is not just national 'pride' but the reference to primitive beliefs in eating animal and possibly human sacrifices that will be removed ('I will take the blood from their mouths,/ the forbidden food from between their teeth.'). These are the embodiments of the subconscious that replace the superconscious in Israel's national ego.

Chapters 5 and 13:1-6 describe how even the superconscious can be distorted for the needs of an ego increasingly in the grip of a subconscious that requires its own gratification from any source, when the subconscious imitates the vocabulary, tone, images, symbols and rituals of the spiritual (code named 'idolatry' and 'false prophecy' throughout the prophetic texts). The panic and madness of rider and horse in 12:4 when they aggressively surround Jerusalem to bring down the home of the supernatural is in sharp contrast to the riders, horses and chariots of the superconscious in 6:1-8 or 1:7-11. And it is with much pathos that the most significant metaphor of the shepherd brings both superconscious and subconscious side by side in the figures of the worthy and the worthless shepherd of the flock – a symbol of shepherding the soul of a community and the spirits of the individuals – in Chapter 11. For our purposes now, we simply need to note the divisive and unappeasable nature of the collective subconscious, its rejection of the superconscious 'good' shepherd, and the treacherous self gratification of the unworthy shepherd who is content to abandon the sheep after having exploited them for his own appetite and rapacious ends. The power-slavery dynamic of the latter is more attractive to the ego than the worshipful service of the superconscious because the primal subconscious perpetuates a dysfunctional drama that keeps ego neediness, ego drama and ego noise at the forefront of everyday living. Rituals of worship which presence the superconscious are replaced with rituals of appeasement where mankind is enslaved to the spiritual energies emanating from and embodying the subconscious (referred to as idolatry).

It is in this context that we have the imagery of 4 horns 'that scattered Judah, Israel and Jerusalem' (1:19), the idiosyncratic imagery of Chapter 5 with the flying scroll (the self-destruction of all thieves and exploiters as well as those who pervert the cause of justice) and the diaspora (7:14). Our current humanity may believe in its power to manage the primal energies of sex and aggression through a manipulation and development of economic, judicial, legal and political systems. In Zechariah, these activities are presented as an accumulation and acting out of primal subconscious energy, amplified into a full scale spiritual reality in Revelation Chapters 10-13, 15-18 and 20. They do not have the saving power we would like to believe they do, because they do not address the inclusion of the superconscious and its presence.

It is the inclination of the everyday ego to regress into primal and primitive subconscious gratification with its swings from pleasure to pain, violence and a dynamic of oppressive power which feeds the ego with an illusion of control. Even when the energies of the superconscious are offered to or placed alongside the subconscious, the two are not able to integrate or transform the other into a more stable whole. If the energies of the superconscious can inflate the ego with a false nationalism and moral bigotry, the energies of the subconscious reduce the ego to a victimized acting out of power-slavery-survival dynamics in a self-gratification which is amoral, narcissistic, coercive, deceptive and treacherous, satisfying its own hungers and meeting its own survival needs. When the ego is immersed in it, the energies of the subconscious can also imitate the qualities and attributes of the superconscious, though its actions and ends are always primal self-appeasement and self-survival.

INTEGRATION AND
THE CONTENTS OF THE SUPERCONSCIOUS

Assagioli pointed out that the contents of the superconscious can be new, unrelated to any past in the individual, and thus without any immediate cognitive value or explanation. From the perspective of the author of the Zechariah text, this could not be more true. Whilst not quite at a shoulder-to-shoulder level with the prophetic revelations of Daniel, the contents of superconscious revelation in Zechariah may well have qualified him for schizophrenic treatment in the mental health unit of his times.

It is not within the scope of this assignment to research or suggest precise meanings for the contents of superconscious revelation presented here. We merely need to note that there are a total of 8 horses which appear with different functions, 4 craftsmen (suggestive of the role of Hermes) who confront and terrify the 4 horns that unleash the diaspora, the city of Jerusalem, the temple, the stone with 7 eyes, the Branch, the gold lampstand (with 7 lights fed by 7 channels), two olive trees (cf the two witnesses of Revelation 11), the 4 chariots of the spirits that are 'going out from standing in the presence of the LORD of the whole world', the cleansing combined with the crowning of the priest, and the worthy shepherd.

By themselves, these contents of the superconscious revelation given to Zechariah are no more than contents. They do not do anything. They represent powerful energies and forces, but on their own have no direction. When the ego is drawn up into these contents, the result is ego inflation, where the everyday consciousness expands with the energies only as a temporary fact. I may imagine myself to hold or have the energies of the horses or the awareness of the stone with the eyes, but in reality, this would be a delusional ego-inflation. Those energies lie well outside of my everyday living and belong to a different realm, even though I am able to share and participate with them temporarily.

This point is specifically re-enforced in the comparison of the 2 shepherds in Chapter 11. The worthy shepherd has two staffs which he can use – called Union and Favour. But the flock who are diseased and those marked for slaughter react with animosity towards the one representing the benefits of the superconscious and reject him. The powerlessness of the superconscious to transform is contrasted with the power of the primal subconscious to captivate and hold a dysfunctional collective ego. The flock feel more at ease with the unworthy shepherd as their leader. Fragmentation, exploitation and the vengeful energies of the subconscious realms replace Union and Favour.

The superconscious and its contents may be helpful as a guide, encouragement or even an inspiration. But like the law of Moses, it appears to bring with it a heightened sense of condemnation, a knowledge of how dark our being and primal origins can be, and even an energy that is antipathetic to the roots of our humanity in its material ground of indiscriminate sex (procreation-pleasure) and aggression (hunger-survival). The ego collapses into an overwhelming psychosis when faced with the demands or energies of the superconscious after the brevity of inflation. Spiritual heights often make everyday living an impossible task after the intensity of the experiences in the superconscious realm.

With this in mind, the images of integration can now be seen to require something more than the superconscious. The staffs already mentioned are clearly the intention of God in the healing of his sheep/people. Yet the synthesis of 'Union' and its connected blessing 'Favour' do not happen. They require the intervention of a new type of personhood who consolidates three roles: priest, king and shepherd.

Zechariah is first shown the cleansing and restoration of the priest, whose own defilement needs to be dealt with and forgiven in Chapter 3. The priest is described as 'a burning stick snatched from the fire' (3:2), but his restoration is explicitly described as a content and expression of the superconscious:

'Listen, O high priest Joshua and your associates seated before you, WHO ARE MEN SYMBOLIC OF THINGS TO COME: I am going to bring my servant, the Branch. See, the stone I have set in front of Joshua! There are seven eyes on that one stone, and I will engrave an inscription on it...and I will remove the sin of this land in a single day.' (3:9)

The fragile stick on fire is transformed into a branch, the servant not dissimilar to the servant passages in Isaiah chs 40-46. In Zechariah Chapter 6:9-14, this priest is then given the throne in the context of the re-building of the temple: 'Here is the man whose name is the Branch, and he will branch out from his place and build the temple of the LORD...and he will be clothed with majesty and will sit and rule on his throne. And he will be a priest on his throne. And there will be harmony between the two.'

This impulse of integration, synthesis and mission replaces the massive divisions of labour which David had recommended in 1Chronicles 22-29 (in line with the Deutro-Canonical texts), where priests were separated from the singers (prophesy and instrumental worship), with subdivisions of the priests into officials, judges, gatekeepers, guardians and ministers of ceremonies/ rituals, scribes, treasurers and the final division of the army. Priest (spirituality/superconscious representative) and king (authority and power) are combined in a role which involves the rebuilding of the temple of God, a branching out into all peoples to achieve the task revealed by the superconscious.

Furthermore, the city of Jerusalem itself becomes a symbol of energy that stands outside the superconscious. Though a whole field of aggression is constantly pitched against it, even supernatural appearances with the strength of angels are promised to affirm its sanctity and ability to survive all attacks:

'On that day the LORD will shield those who live in Jerusalem, so that the feeblest among them will be like David, and the house of David will be like God, like the Angel of the LORD going before them. On that day I will set out to destroy all the nations that attack Jerusalem.' (12:8-9)

This is a declaration of final resolution that is beyond the capacity of the superconscious to achieve. When the text reads 'I will make Jerusalem an immovable rock for all the nations' (12:3) it is clear that it is not the annihilation of all nations that is meant here. As with the book of Daniel, where the gathering of collective energies accumulate menacingly in the symbols of nations, the gathering of the nations is the final gathering together of the forces of an indiscriminate primal subconscious driven by a reaction to and rejection of the superconscious. The image of Jerusalem as 'an immovable rock for all the nations' is merely image, an offering of the superconscious. What is new here is the opening of the sentence with 'I will'. Here is a will that lies outside both the aggression of the primal subconscious and the unfulfilled offerings and contents of the superconscious.

As Assagioli correctly pointed out as psychological truth, the superconscious in Zechariah proclaims a future that it could not possibly understand or achieve at the time. Much later, the first Christians made enormous use of the superconscious imagery here - Paul turns the body into the temple of God (1Cor 6:19), while Peter sees the imagery of the stone as central to his understanding of the rebuilding of the temple of God as a forgiven people of righteousness (1 Peter 2:4-12). But for Zechariah writing in his time, the result is a detail of imagination beyond the understanding or the will of the ego or the sub or superconscious. The images of resolution were simply beyond the comprehension of Israel in the proposed integration of priest and king, with the additional role of the shepherd. These three form an intrapsychic superconscious representation, alongside the external images of resolution in the city of Jerusalem, the temple and 'all nations'.

Unlike the other images of the superconscious, the images of shepherd-priest-king and the related city of Jerusalem-temple-all-nations form a triad of internal and external symbolic representations. The first triad represents a personhood that can function in everyday living in a very different way to the ego conscious. In the final section entitled 'Pastoral and Therapeutic Implications of Psychosynthesis Modelling', we will see how this comes to represent an alignment or transformation of the ego when it is in connection with a universal Self standing outside ego, sub and superconscious. The defence and formation of the Jerusalem-temple-all-nations triad as an external reality through time is also discussed in the final section as the transformation of the unresolved primal collective subconscious. These two triads of superconscious imagery carry a different quality to the other shapes and imagery listed above. They carry the quality of personhood made up of three interacting subpersonalities rather than the supernatural/archetypal/spiritual contents of the superconscious alone.

The final resolution of a will moving outside all three states of everyday conscious ego, unresolved primal subconscious and the imaginative integration of the superconscious is made explicitly clear in the text of Zechariah. The contents of the superconscious are held in the use of the imagination which reveals the shapes of supernatural energies, presences and movements. This is not a delusional imagination, but one that is receiving an inspired descent of contents from the superconscious reality that was to provide major hermeneutic understanding to the early Christians about the meaning of the life of their founder. It is also through the superconscious that a new personhood is revealed with the hope of an internal and external integration, synthesis and transformation of our primal origins.

INTEGRATION AND THE SELF

The expressions of a Universal Self occur in the text of Zechariah as the will of the LORD. These are not apolitical but anti-political in nature and expressly invert the inflations of any national ego or judgmental moralism and bigotry. The Self is closely allied to the contents of the superconscious in the use of imaginative expression. But the presence of the Self is distinguished by the repeated assertions of its Will.

The whole of the battle gathering around Jerusalem from the perspective of the Universal Self is a transpersonal redemption of the primal subconscious, the deep rooted fears of mankind's psyche regarding existence, the rejection and inability to integrate superconscious with subconscious, and the slavery of the everyday conscious ego to the subconscious. Having just spoken of the downfall of a number of nations who place trust in the achievements of the conscious ego and the gratifications of the subconscious, the text of the shepherd king in Zechariah reads:

'See, your king comes to you, righteous and having salvation, gentle and riding on a donkey, on a colt, a foal of a donkey. I will take away the chariots from Ephraim and the war horses from Jerusalem, and the battle-bow will be broken.

He will proclaim peace to the nations, His rule will extend from sea to sea and from the River to the ends of the earth… I will free your prisoners from the waterless pit. Return to your fortress, O prisoners of hope; even now I announce that I will restore twice as much to you… Grain will make the young men thrive, and new wine the young women.' (9:9-17)

This is not a political battle, and nor is it a psychological one achieved by superconscious revelations alone. In sharp contrast to a vindictive nationalist moralism of the ego-reading of such texts, we have a depth and reach of 'peace' completely out of the grasp of the ego. The subconscious is embraced in a dynamic of forgiveness and put to its use of grounded fertility and harmony in the images of 'grain' and 'new wine'. Texts such as these permeate the redemption and resolution dynamic of the splits between super, sub and everyday consciousness with the presence of a Universal Self, while reflecting the New Testament historiography of the life of Jesus who fulfils these lines. An intervention of the Universal Self is set out as a sacrificial self-immolation which Christians through the centuries have interpreted as the divinity of Jesus on the cross:

'And I will pour out on the house of David and the inhabitants of Jerusalem a spirit of grace and supplication. They will look on me, the one they have pierced, and they will mourn for him as one mourns for an only child, and grieve bitterly for him as one grieves for a firstborn son.' (12:10)

The self sacrifice, in contrast again to either ego or subconscious, is followed by a second diaspora, the scattering and testing of those who turn to and believe in the shepherd-priest-king:

'Strike the shepherd,
and the sheep will be scattered,
and I will turn my hand against the little ones…
I will bring (them) into the fire;
I will refine them like silver and test them like gold.
They will call on my name and I will answer them;
I will say, 'They are my people,'
and they will say, 'The LORD is our God.' (13;7-9)

If this appears to be a bizarre enactment of sado-masochistic pleasure from the perspective of the ego that wishes to gratify the desires of the primal subconscious, it is also a reversal of the diaspora of Israel scattered through punishment at rejecting the superconscious revelations. The answer to the rejected worthy shepherd of Chapter 11 is another shepherd who sacrifices himself for his people. Zechariah's final chapter ends with the most colossal declaration of the presence of the Universal Self in the materiality of this earth. The sufferings and sacrifice of the priest-king-shepherd and his people are not those of the ego or the subconscious, and cannot be achieved by the superconscious being aware of what is to come. A specifically male will, the animus, is restoring its shaping of the world and its relation to that world of its creation. We can now understand the battle as the battle of transformation, integration and synthesis that can only be achieved through the presence of the Self outside and within the super, sub and everyday ego consciousness:

'Then the LORD will go out and fight against those nations, as he fights in the day of battle. On that day his feet will stand on the Mount of Olives, east of Jerusalem, and the Mount of Olives will be split in two from east to west, forming a valley, with half of the mountain moving north and half moving south…Then the LORD my God will come, and all the holy ones with him.

'On that day there will be no light, no cold or frost. It will be a unique day, without daytime or night-time – a day known to the LORD. When evening comes, there will be light.

'On that day living water will flow out from Jerusalem, half to the eastern sea and half to the western sea, in summer and winter. Then the LORD will be king over the whole earth. On that day there will be one LORD, and his name the only name...Jerusalem will be raised up and remain in its place...It will be inhabited; never again will it be destroyed. Jerusalem will be secure.' (14:3-11)

Despite the intertextual links with Revelation chs 21-22, it is the intertextual links with Genesis that give us some hermeneutic possibilities about the transpersonal meanings that could reside here. Prior to the fall, there was no rain. The earth was watered by streams from a single source – a river in the garden of Eden:

'...for the LORD God had not sent rain on the earth...but streams came up from the earth and watered the whole surface of the ground...A river watering the garden flowed from Eden; from there it was separated into four headwaters.' (Gen 2:5-6, 10)

Zechariah's breaking open of the Mount of Olives into four directions and the release of 'living water (that) will flow out from Jerusalem' has a remarkable similarity to the initial configuration of the river in Eden described in Genesis. In Revelation, John speaks of 'the river of the water of life, as clear as crystal, flowing from the throne of God and of the Lamb down the middle of the great street of the city.' (Rev 22: 1). The differences between Eden and Paradise, between past and future, may simply be one of scale, a fulfillment in Paradise of the command to 'Go forth and multiply'. The co-existence/ absence of time past-present-future and the omnipresence of light that Zechariah describes make one shudder at the possibility of universal energy and space where there is no death in time (cuff Rev 21:3-5, 22:5) and where shadow and night are consumed in a final resolution of integrated Self presence.

Only from the perspective of a Self that is outside the superconscious future and the primal subconscious past can any integration be conceived or achieved. The river in Zechariah, which becomes the 'river of the water of life' in John's Revelation, is now a symbol of connection between the human psyche and the eternal/universal source of life. The gateway to the Universal that was so natural to mankind before the Fall opens again with increasing definition as a psychological fact. As the Universal Self reshapes the broken world that rejects and separates itself from the good will of the animus mundi, the waters of life break open in a reconstruction of physical landscape, a metaphor for the change in psychological landscape that occurs when an individual experiences contact and connection with the Universal Will. This sheds much light on John's writings about 'water' in his letters and gospel. More directly, 2 Peter Chapter 2 picks up the Zechariah theme of false prophets-teachers in a dramatic use of the image of water:

'These men are springs without water and mists driven by a storm…they mouth empty, boastful words and, by appealing to the lustful desires of sinful human nature, they entice people… They promise them freedom, while they themselves are slaves of depravity…' (2 Pet 2:17-19)

Rain is further contrasted with springs of water when in the same chapter Peter refers to the flood in Noah's time caused by incessant rain.

The superconscious without the Self is prone to being devoured by the primal needs of the subconscious. But when the impulse behind the redemptive and powerful images of the superconscious is sourced in an act of will from a Universal Self, transformation of the primal subconscious, and integration of the superconscious with the conscious ego take place.

In the tradition of the New Testament that increasingly internalised the Old Testament as metaphors of the emotional and psycho-spiritual redemption achieved in Jesus, it is possible to read the presencing of Universal Self in Zechariah as the transpersonal possibilities of psychological contact and connection with the archetypal animus that shapes the world and its history. In contrast to the egotistical delusions of mankind in its belief that it might control the process and outcomes of world history through nationalistic, political, economic judgments and insular moralism, the Zechariah text speaks of a rigorous transformation process of humility and refinement before the presencing of the Universal Self can even be glimpsed in the superconscious.

The final integration and resolution of the super and sub conscious with the everyday living of the ego conscious can only be achieved from a point outside all three. The Zechariah text speaks of this point as a triumphant Self presencing, the Universal will of God as a locus of energy, movement and integrational ability that none of the other states of consciousness have of themselves. This universal Self and its will is mirrored internally in the human psychological make-up – as the 'new creation' of Paul in Romans 5-8 that replaces the crucified 'old' self on the cross. In Eastern meditation and Jungian psychology, we may speak of the presence of a higher Self or organising Self centre that connects with the transcendental or archetypal.

We carry the mirror of the Universal Self and its Will within us, and this Self (the Christ impulse within) is our gateway to the integrational possibilities of super, sub and ego consciousness which psychosynthesis modelling facilitates and clarifies. The vindictive urges of punishment and bigotry that belong to the ego are replaced with the depth of redemption and integration through forgiveness offered by the Self. The punitive is replaced with the transformational – in John's words, 'There is no fear in love. But perfect love drives out fear, because fear has to do with punishment. The one who fears is not made perfect in love.' (1 John 4:18)

Pastoral and Therapeutic Implications of Psychosynthesis Modelling

The use of psychosynthesis models and categories has been demonstrated in the text of Zechariah to illustrate its usefulness in hermeneutic clarification. The intertextual exegesis that this opens up is outside the scope of this assignment. However, brief comments do need to be made about the practical application of the above.

The misreading of a sacred or spiritual text parallel misinterpretations of the sacred and spiritual life. Many spiritual leaders and those for whom they have responsibility repeatedly fall on the psychological banana skins of inappropriate or abusive applications of spiritual energy. This is just as applicable to those involved in transpersonal therapy. The spiritual disciplines of preparation, reflection and self-assessment both before and after engagements involving the transpersonal need to take these categories of Assagioli into account.

From our reading of the Zechariah text above, we can now see that the categories of superconscious, subconscious and ego conscious are crucial not only to a reading but to the practical application of spiritual energy to everyday life.

The ability of ego to seek inflation through enlargement and inspiration from the energy of the superconscious can be seen as the base for cultic activities, Messianic grandiosities and collective delusions which can occur in the political sphere (Hitler's love of Wagner and misreading of Nietzsche), in the religious sphere (the ritual sexual exposes of TV evangelists in the US or the denial of sexual and alcohol addiction in Islamic states), in art and music (the sensationalist lives of individual artists, the riotous behaviour of crowds at concerts), the therapist's power over the client, and in any form of institutional or hierarchical organization (educational, public sector or commercial). All kinds of spiritual, aesthetic and moral rationales can be drawn as a veil and disguise over the self-inflation of the ego. With an understanding of this psychological dysfunction from the transpersonal categories of the superconscious interacting with the ego, the confusions can be addressed and disentangled. This also throws light on the famous 'vision and thorn' experience of Paul in 2 Corinthians 11 & 12, where his personal suffering of the flesh was given to prevent an egotistical inflation of his superconscious revelations as an apostle – the centre of the Corinthian church divisions.

Where there is ego-gratification, it is likely that spiritual energies are being used to feed the unresolved primal needs of our subconscious past. In the case of Israel, these were noted at the level of a national collective subconscious, but the principle is applicable to the individual. Through visions, dreams, prophecies and other abilities of channeling supernatural energy, imitational possibilities of the subconscious can hold the everyday ego captive in pseudo-representations of the superconscious, described as idolatry, false prophecy and false testimony in Old Testament vocabulary. Distortions of the superconscious occur when the subconscious projects through the ego for gratification of primal needs, able to take the life out of rituals and practices that once belonged to the superconscious, and able to justify the appetites of indiscriminate sex (procreation/ pleasure) and aggression (hunger/ survival). The subtlety here is the use of justifying activities with the imitational vocabulary, symbols, rituals and practices which can feed militaristic brutality, personal vengeance, and sexual licentiousness – or the dysfunctional repression of all of these.

A presentation or clarification of the superconscious alone is likely to provoke reaction, rejection and a regressive movement of the ego towards entrenchment in the subconscious. A calling into a clean, holy, creative, inspired and inspiring future sits as a temporary fact to the everyday ego. The ego can be fixated, crushed by impossible demands or overwhelmed by the contents of the superconscious, but is unable to activate much of the energy into daily living, finding itself propelled in the opposite direction. The introduction and use of the superconscious when attempting to address the grip of the subconscious on the ego again needs to be carefully thought through and introduced when there is sufficient understanding of the needs and the likely behaviour of the reactive subconscious. This again calls for a re-evaluation and much reflection of presentations of inspirational material or techniques to others. The response of the subconscious to the superconscious needs to be acknowledged and worked with as fact.

The superconscious is an imaginal representation of the energies and shapes of the Universal Self. It accesses possibilities on the edge or outside the understanding of the ego, but contains wisdom, truth, insight and relevance to life. It appears to be the favoured realm of Universal expression in all transcendental or metaphysically inclined religions, and also contains the potentials of integration and synthesis of the fragmentation and splitting that afflicts mankind in so many ways. The energy of the superconscious is a powerful reality, but it is often mistaken as permanent, as if it has an automated will of its own. This absence of will and the requirement of the individual to exercise his or her own will is a necessary distinction in all transpersonal work and again needs to be handled with awareness and clarity. The imagination represents, but cannot do all the work itself. Locating the Self within the individual as a locus outside the everyday ego, super and subconscious can now be seen as a crucial part in the achievement of integrating the offerings and revelations of the superconscious with the resistances and transformational requirements of the subconscious. The ego cannot resolve the battle of energies above and below itself. If it is aligned to the Self, the Self can access and interface with the Universal Self, finding movements and resolutions that lie outside the hands of the facilitator and essentially in the hands of the individual being facilitated. Empowering the individual(s) into an understanding of their own transpersonal energies and providing them with sufficient self-reflective strength to integrate and work through their resistances becomes the goal of pastoral and therapeutic work in the light of transpersonal perspectives.

The outcomes of the Self are transformational and inclusive, pan-national and able to confront or embrace the aggression and rejections of the unresolved primal subconscious. This is in contrast to the ego with its punitive, vengeful and vindictive urges being thrown between super and subconscious states. Where the ego inflated by the superconscious would only hate, reject and punish the primal subconscious below it, the Self sacrificially enters into the realms of the subconscious with 'a spirit of grace and supplication'.

The Self stands outside ego noise agitated by contact with either the super or the subconscious. Locating this self as a Christ impulse in prayer and worship before presentation of the superconscious, or through disidentification techniques suggested by Assagioli, become crucial to the application of the will in the integration of the individual. This final section cries out for case study material to show the improvements and variations that can occur in this theme. But as it sits, it provides a framework for managing the often difficult and dangerous dynamics of spiritual energy from above and below the everyday consciousness, offering a pathway of working practice that can access the good will of a Universal animus seeking to restore, bless and be close to its own creation.

We end with a lyrical prayer from Martin Heidegger to sum up the requirement to work from our essence (self) to the essence (Self) of a Universal Being seeking closeness and reconciliation with mankind, rather than the deification of any state of consciousness – a hymn for mankind to be at peace and at home with the essence of the world and its creator:

    '*So long as we do not, through thinking, experience what is, we can never belong to what will be. Will insight into that which is bring itself disclosingly to pass? Will we, as the ones caught sight of, be so brought home into the essential glance of Being that we will no longer elude it? Will we arrive thereby within the essence of the nearness that, in thinging the thing, brings world near? Will we dwell as those at home in nearness, so that we will belong primally within the fourfold of sky and earth, mortals and divinities?... May the world in its worlding be the nearest of all nearing that nears, as it brings the truth of Being near to man's essence, and so gives man to belong to the disclosing bringing-to-pass that is a bringing into its own.*'

(Heidegger, The Question Concerning Technology, p. 49)

BIBLIOGRAPHY

Assagioli, Roberto, *Psychosynthesis*, Aquarian, London (1993)
Assagioli, Roberto, *Transpersonal Development*, Thorsons, (1993)
Bible, *The New International Version*, (1992)
Brazier, David et al., *Beyond Carl Rogers*, Constable, (1993)
Heidegger, Martin, *The Question Concerning Technology*, trans. William Lovitt, Harper & Row, New York (1977)
Parfitt, Will, *Psychosynthesis: The Elements and Beyond*, PS Avalon (2006)
Samuels, Andrew, *Jung and the Post-Jungians*, Routledge & Kegan Paul, London (1994)

SHADOWS OF THE PAST

Ricky N. Lock

Oh life's dance you play me so well, you made me
Fear my own existence, with your games of childhood fears.
You laughed at my insecurities and also gave me hope
To find my own abode – a place to listen to my past rumbles
That honoured the sweet innocent child's dreams.
So clever in your life's dance, so neatly observed
From afar.

Golden thoughts hover, searching for the place
To put all my confusion to rest. To lay my
Young head on my adult shoulders and
Wipe away the salty tears from a neglected childhood.
To hear my unheard thoughts for my child
That calls out to be rescued from
The family of mistrusted deception.

I can see we are all searching to be heard, hoping for
A descending God to help us get through the pain.
And to believe this journey we undertook was
Already in the matrix of his higher plans.
From His safe hands my child's head could
Be cradled from his past shadowy fears.
And then my child's sweet head can be rested again,
Within the dark silence, and taken back before the broken waters
Poured out to life's shadowy past.

Authenticity and Relationship: Conflict or Synthesis?

Alan Robinson

We exist only in the sense that other people acknowledge our existence. And if no one acknowledges our right to be who we are, then we invent ourselves and continue to invent ourselves ad nauseum, until we forget who we were.

The Function of Relationship

"Relationship is inevitably painful, which is shown in our everyday existence. If in relationship there is no tension, it ceases to be relationship and merely becomes a comfortable sleep-state, an opiate – which most people want and prefer. Conflict is between this craving for comfort and the factual, between illusion and actuality. If you recognise the illusion then you can, by putting it aside, give your attention to the understanding of relationship. But if you seek security in relationship you are hindering its function, which brings its own peculiar actions and misfortunes.

"Surely, the function of relationship is to reveal the state of one's whole being. Relationship is a process of self revelation, of self knowledge. This revelation is painful, demanding constant adjustment, pliability of thought-emotion. It is a painful struggle, with periods of enlightened peace.

"But most of us avoid or put aside the tension in relationship, preferring the ease and comfort of satisfying dependency, an unchallenged security, a safe anchorage. Then family and other relationships become a refuge, the refuge of the thoughtless.

"When insecurity creeps into dependency, as it inevitably does, then that particular relationship is cast aside and a new one taken on in the hope of finding lasting security, but there is no security in relationship and dependency only breeds fear. Without understanding the process of security and fear, relationship becomes a binding hindrance, a way of ignorance. Then all existence is struggle and pain, and there is no way out of it save in right thinking, which comes through self-knowledge."

(*Krishnamurti, 1995*)

INTRODUCTION

This paper explores the possible conflict between two fundamental states of being. On the one hand, our need for relationship[1] and on the other, our drive[2] for authenticity.[3] In particular: How is our personal drive for authenticity hindered and/or supported by our need for relationship?

I will also look at the implications for the therapist in the therapeutic relationship. In response, I intend to show that the authentic self can only be realised in relationship; that is, synthesis rather than conflict. And that clients in search of their own authenticity, are best served by a therapist who is prepared to bring her own authenticity into the therapeutic relationship.

OUTLINE

The first section 'What Was Your Face Before Your Parents Gave You Theirs?' considers the question of how, when and why we lose touch with our authentic self in the first place. Starting from the model of human woundedness set out in *The Primal Wound* (Firman & Gila, 1997), but reframing it in an existential context, I put forward the view that fundamentally it is the very real threat of 'non-being', particularly within the family system (the so-called family trance) that causes the 'powerless' child, to betray her true self. Thus, through dependency, the need for relationship takes primacy over her drive to be authentic. Round 1 to our need for relationship.

In the following short section, 'The Authentic Self – A Manifesto', I define the authentic self as a state of being and consider the relationship between truth and authenticity. The 'Manifesto' is very much a personal statement, of what 'being authentic' means to me.

Having looked at how we lose contact with our authentic self and how we might recognise its call, I consider how we can re-connect with our authentic self. Starting from the premise that the authentic self is not something we create, but rather is something we once were, I develop the theme that the first stage in our return to authenticity is essentially away from relationship. More, that the return to authenticity, means that we must chose to re-live and re-experience the existential pain we tried to avoid – to embrace and explore our primal woundedness. Round 2 to our drive for authenticity.

Whilst, the first stage towards authenticity is away from relationship the 'Crucible of Relationship' considers our need for relationship as the context in which we define who we are. The authentic self is now able to embrace relationship, not as an end in itself, through dependency or guilt, but as the only state of being that provides meaning in an existential context. This is the synthesis of drive and need in which the authentic self can begin to realise its purpose. Round 3 – no contest. Relationship is the context. Authenticity is the goal.

As a precursor to considering the implications of the foregoing for the therapeutic relationship, 'The Road to Authenticity' looks at the consequences for choosing to honour the truth of who we are. In particular, that we may have to leave and/or 're-negotiate' existing relationships. At the same time, our fidelity to our own truth, enables us to remain open to the possibility of new and different relationships – including the therapeutic relationship.

The consideration of the implications for the therapeutic relationship starts with the client's perspective. In 'Authenticity and the Client/Therapist Relationship', I have drawn on my personal experience to describe what I believe is the basis of an authentic therapeutic relationship from the client's point of view. 'The Good Enough Therapist', draws attention to the on-going need for the therapist to explore and develop her own authenticity.

What Was Your Face Before Your Parents Gave You Theirs?[4]
or: how we lose touch with our authentic self in the first place.

INTRODUCTION

In my opinion, *The Primal Wound* (Firman & Gila 1997), is a ground-breaking book. It fully honours and builds on Assagioli's pioneering work, updating it, and placing Psychosynthesis at the forefront of the current enquiry into the nature of consciousness and the experience of being. Firman and Gila, have marshalled an impressive range of evidence, and constructed a pervasive and (currently) all-encompassing model of human development that offers an invaluable framework for humanity in general and the Psychosynthesis model in particular.

At the heart of their carefully and scholarly constructed thesis, is a fundamental premise; that the basis of meaning for human beings is found in relationship.

"At the deepest level, human being is relational." (p 32).

That is, relationship with our environment (the external reality), with other human beings, and with our selves (our inner reality, including the relationships with and between the Lower, Middle and Higher Unconscious, the I, the Self, the Higher Self etc.).

AN EXISTENTIAL APPROACH TO THE PRIMAL WOUND

I am not a scientist, and whilst I found the discussion of 'unifying centres', 'authentic personality', 'I-Self relationships', 'splitting', 'survival personalities' etc., important for an intellectual understanding of what are after all fundamentally constructs to support a model of human being, my own proclivities (no doubt born from my own survival personality!) impel me to reframe their constructs (their model) within a philosophical context (another model !)[5]

An existentialist interpretation of Firman & Gila's book is that, if everyone ignored me – that is did not acknowledge me and therefore did not validate my existence – then I could draw one of two terrifying conclusions: (a) I did not exist, or (b) I was alone. Further, I will do anything necessary to avoid the unimaginable terror of non-existence/cosmic aloneness, including denying my authentic self – what Firman & Gila refer to as 'authentic personality' (1997, p 164) and Winnicott (ibid.) refers to as 'the true self'.

In a hostile or non-supportive environment/milieu, this would even include seemingly insane acts designed to provoke hostile reactions from the environment and the people in the environment, because, even a hostile reaction is validation that I exist. Even though the fruits of my provocative acts are likely to be painful for me (physically and psychically), in my battle for existence, pain caused by the actions and re-actions of others, is relationship of a kind, which at least provides me with some acknowledgement that I exist. This 'secondary' pain is in any case, preferable to the primal pain of non-existence/cosmic aloneness, i.e. it is the lesser of two evils. I am in pain, therefore I exist, versus, I do not exist/I am alone.[6]

To put it another way: "We exist only in the sense that other people acknowledge our existence. And if no one acknowledges our right to be who we are, then we invent ourselves and continue to invent ourselves ad nauseam, until we forget who we were." (Robinson, Journal).

Placing this in the context of earliest individual development, we can picture a situation wherein the newly born being views herself as the centre of the universe. "I am." But this is a flawed position since (unknowingly) the newly born baby is totally dependent on the environment and the people in the environment for physical and psychical survival. Therefore – "I am to the extent that my needs: my relationship to food, warmth, etc., are met."

This challenge to our view of our relationship of ourselves to the external reality (the universe) is the origin of the primal wound. Each successive experience of not having our primary needs met, (i.e. non-validation of our existence) is a threat to our concept of ourselves as the centre of the universe (our self-belief). As our self-belief diminishes so the terror of non-existence approaches.

As babies, none of us are ever likely to receive sufficient validation for our existence. We all have, to some degree or another, to adapt to the external environment even though this is at odds with the given inner reality of I as the centre of the universe. As consciousness develops, so do we begin to develop coping strategies, behaviours and beliefs which through trial and error, help to make 'painful' reality more bearable[7]. Note that as previously suggested, coping strategies can be designed to provoke hostile reactions, that is increase the level of secondary pain, to stave off the primal pain of non-being.

At this development stage, and for a long time to come, the individual has little if any power to change things in the external world. Therefore the individual has little choice other than to adopt what ever behaviour is the most effective in minimising the pain of non-being. (Adapt or die.) As these behaviours are perfected and the level of primary pain decreases, this basically 'negative feed-back loop', serves to validate the developed behaviour and beliefs, leading the individual to accept that this is how she must be. The learned behaviour – conditioned reflex actions to environmental stimuli – become the standard way for the individual to relate, and thus cope with, otherwise, painful reality – at the cost of relationship with her authentic self.

Often, these coping strategies are simply palliatives, that is addictions such as alcohol, sex, work, drugs, therapy, esotericism, religion, food, etc., which help to divert the conscious attention away from the source of pain.

In essence, but to varying degrees, the developing individual is never truly her authentic self. Our sense of self (who we are) is a product of our response to and flight from the threat of non-being. As a result, for many of us, our sense of self-worth and therefore self-belief, is built on sand (survival personality, false self etc.,.) Every time we happen upon a situation or experience which cannot be dealt with by any of our previously learned coping behaviours or beliefs, we are lost – even if only dimly felt/experienced – in danger of having to face the terror of non-being which our coping strategies were designed to mask. Thus new coping strategies and beliefs are fostered, with or without the help of friends, acquaintances, professional helpers etc.; new or amended coping strategies designed to bring us back into 'right' relationship with our perception of external and internal reality. The first casualty of these re-adjustment is often our inner reality, our relationship with our authentic self.

THE FAMILY TRANCE

In Firman and Gila's terms, the family is a holding environment and, for the newly born and growing child, the major source of validation (emphatic mirroring). If the family is dysfunctional, that is, if its behaviour is at odds with the growing child's relationship needs, then it is the child, powerless to change the experienced external reality, who has to change and in the process deny/split off from their relationship with their authentic self. Successive adaptations to the family environment, serve to further alienate the individual from their authentic self. Questioning the status quo, the experienced reality, is too painful since it puts the child back in touch with the pain of non-being as well as bringing retribution down on its head from the current external reality — the family trance is thus born and sustained through terror.

John Bradshaw (1997) makes the point that babies/children are innately curious and needy. Yet, they are also entirely dependent on the environment in general, and their 'carers' (a.k.a. parents) to provide for their needs. Thus, if the parents had to repress their natural curiosity as children – because it got them into trouble – then there is a tendency for them to inhibit the child's curiosity too.

In my view this inhibition is experienced by the child as a prohibition against acting in a certain way. As a result, in order not to feel the pain – either physical, because the message was delivered with actual bodily harm or psychological (potential abandonment, non-being etc.), the child 'learns' to modify her behaviour in order to avoid the painful feelings and to get other needs met. Crucially, at this stage in her development, if her needs are not met, she draws the conclusion that there is something wrong with her or the way she behaves.

In general terms, behaviour which gets her needs met or lessens the pain of not having her needs met is preferable to the pain (both physical and psychological) of not having her needs met.2

But the true cost to the child is enormous: she denies her authentic self and the 'survival personality' (Firman & Gila et al) is born.

After many acts of self-betrayal, the need to avoid the additional pain engendered by the shame and the guilt of self-betrayal, serves to further reinforce the 'survival personality'. Thus shame and guilt are added to non-being as experiences to be avoided at all costs. Eventually the shame and guilt of self-betrayal becomes more painful than the original threat of non-being – she has after all abandoned her authentic self. In order to avoid this shame and guilt, she chooses (via suppression) to forget who she is and becomes what the environment wants her to be. This is the primal wound – the shame and guilt she would feel if she acknowledged that she had actually abandoned her authentic self.

I have written elsewhere (Robinson, October 1998) how the Family Trance by its very nature, inevitably impedes rather than assists progress along the road to the authentic self:

"I personally believe that the family environment, (and our parents in particular), has a significant impact on our progress along the road to self-realisation. Where the family environment is generally nurturing and supportive, we are more likely to grow up with an authentic sense of who we are and our possibilities. Where the family environment is hostile and non-supportive, then our chances are limited. As a consequence we may never be able to take any steps along the road to self-realisation, but remain trapped forever within the dysfunctional patterns of our family. Instead of expressing who we are we hide our true natures and become what the environment wants us to be. Thus instead of developing our 'authentic' personality (who we were born to be), we are forced to develop a 'survival' personality."

"Survival personality is an attempt to form some sense of selfhood in the face of the potential pit of non-existence" (The Primal Wound p164)

AUTHENTICITY VERSUS RELATIONSHIP – ROUND 1

It seems to me that from our earliest experiences a conflict exists between our drive towards authenticity and our relationship with the environment, in particular other people in that environment. Chief amongst those relationships being our relationship with our 'primary carers' – our parents in most cases. In particular, our dependency on them to meet our needs for food, warmth and, relationship itself – against the threat of non-being, affords us little choice but to compromise and in my terms, to betray our true self; to turn our backs on who we are.

Round 1 to our need for relationship.

THE AUTHENTIC SELF – A MANIFESTO
OR, HOW WOULD I RECOGNISE THE 'AUTHENTIC SELF'?

The authentic self is a state of being. A state where the expression of one's being 'in the world' is entirely congruent with how one is at any given point in time or space.

Congruency is the key.
• I am what I believe in.
• I am true to what I believe in.
• I act and speak from what I believe in as I understand it.
• It is first and foremost my truth.
• The truth of who I am without compromise.
"Truth is a pathless land." (Krishnamurti.)
Truth is relative and never absolute.
• No one 'knows' the truth.

- I can never know everything.
- What I believe in can only be what I currently know and think based on my life experiences to date.
- What I believe in has changed and will change as my life proceeds.
- I will never stop seeking, questioning and searching for the truth.

This is part of who I am.

- Essentially, I believe in me and my right to be myself.
- Sometimes this brings me into conflict with other people.
- I always strive to honour the needs of others but sometimes this is impossible unless I deny who I am.
- I will not deny who I am for anyone.

Oft times I will get it wrong.

"It doesn't interest me if the story you are telling me is true. I want to know if you can disappoint another to be true to yourself; if you can bear the accusation of betrayal and not betray your own soul; if you can be faithless and therefore trustworthy." (Oriah Mountain Dreamer)

But this too is part of who I am.

My self-imposed task is to bear witness to my own truth and to yours.

This is who I am.

AUTHENTICITY AND SELF-ACTUALISATION

I wish here to draw a distinction between authenticity and self-actualisation as defined by Maslow. It should be clear from the foregoing that for me the need to be authentic is mostly about the need to be 'true to my self, rather than for instance what Maslow's termed 'self-actualisation' which he defined as:

"… ongoing actualisation of potentials, capacities, talents, as fulfillment of a mission (or call, fate, destiny, or vocation), as a fuller knowledge of, and acceptance of, the person's own intrinsic nature, as an increasing trend towards unity, integration, or synergy within the person." (quoted in The Encyclopedia of Reality).

Firstly, note that I do not disagree with Maslow's definition of self-actualisation, merely, that I am not claiming that what I define as authenticity is anything as grand as that.[7] I also accept that the drive towards authenticity may have something to do with fulfilling my potential etc. It certainly has a lot to do with acquiring a "fuller knowledge of, and acceptance of, the person's own intrinsic nature…" It is not that I deny the rest – what may be loosely described as the transpersonal elements – it is just that on the basis of my own experience I have no evidence yet that this transpersonal dimension is real.[8]

"Hello darkness my old friend, I've come to talk with you again…"[9] Or re-connecting with the authentic self. The authentic self is not something we create – it is something we once were.

As I have tried to illustrate above, it is a state of being from which, for reasons of survival, we chose to lose contact with. Regaining what we lost – what, in a sense, we gave away – is not easy. Not only do we have to re-visit and experience again the pain of non-being and alienation, we also have to come face to face with the fact that we abandoned our self. We have to experience the primal wound – the shame and guilt we feel when we acknowledge that we actually abandoned our authentic self.

In particular, we have to re-examine our need for relationship.

AWARENESS AND CHOICE

For me being authentic is essentially about awareness and choice. Being true to one's self is not about acting on every impulse and whim or re-acting to external simulation in a pre-conceived and pre-conditioned way.

Assagioli (1994) approached authenticity from a different starting point than I am proposing. Rather than see it as a state to regain he saw it like Maslow as a state to move into. He does however highlight the importance of choice:

"… I am not recommending that one never be aggressive or that one never fight; I mean that one has the freedom of choice about whether, and to what extent, to give direct expression to the impulse or motive, even if it be one of deeply felt anger or hurt… The point is that choices and decisions are possible. The act of will and intention then involves a decision to accept or not accept an impulse. *Authenticity does not consist in giving in to a bad motive simply because it exists.* (Assagioli, 1994. Authors italics.)

But choice follows awareness. And whence awareness?

I think we have to recognise that the struggle for authenticity is not something the majority of mankind are actively engaged in, nor are ever likely to be. However it is generally acknowledged that throughout history some people have chosen to explore this painful area. Some actively engage, others become drawn in. In the past perhaps, it was the path of the mystic and the ascetic. Since the start of the 20th century, analysis and therapy has provided many a 'route-map for the soul' ; not least of which is Psychosynthesis, " a psychology with a soul"[10]. Often, to paraphrase Jung, it seems to be the task of the second half of life.

I want to pick up the discussion of awareness by referring to Wilber's *Spectrum of Consciousness* (1979). In particular the transition phase between the 'ego' state and the 'transpersonal' which he calls the centaur stage[11]. According to Wilbur:

"… this is the stage where we start to take responsibility for our own development, rather than allowing ourselves to be moved on as if up an escalator… There is a conscious emergence of the real self, and a consequent increase in *spontaneity and autonomy*" (quoted in Rowan, 1993 – my italics)

So the individual begins to take personal responsibility for her own development. Note that implicit in this decision to take responsibility is the recognition (shock?) that hitherto they have not been the masters of their own destiny – as they perhaps fondly believed themselves to be. From this point on 'life' can never be the same. The doors of perception have been opened, albeit only a crack but the individual will never be the same again. Even if she then chooses to ignore 'the call' a degree of background pain will occasionally surface to play a certain havoc with her state of being.

For those who choose to explore the new world they have glimpsed; who seek to reconnect with that part of themselves they long ago lost contact with; who chose authenticity: the path is essentially one of separation from dependence on others, that is ostensibly away from relationship.

There then begins a gradual descent as more and more of what the individual thought of as part of themselves is exposed as something they took on at a stage in their life when essentially they had to chose between survival and annihilation. Like the end product of the gradual stripping away of the layers of an onion, the individual is reduced to nothing. To a primordial state of existential non-being where meaning comes not from our need to survive physically but from embracing the essential terror that fundamentally 'life' is meaningless; that survival beyond the present state is not guaranteed but is a cross on which the false self is crucified.

Note that a particular characteristic of this descent is that basically the individual has to do it alone.[12] "At each stage of our journey so far, society had been on our side, and had said in effect, 'Yes, go on, you are doing well.' But now there is no such boost from society if we want to carry on. We have to do it from own intention and our own will. Society will in most cases put up obstacles instead of helping." (Rowan, 1993)

AUTHENTICITY VERSUS RELATIONSHIP – ROUND 2

Thus the experiences we hoped to avoid as newly born are presented to us again. No longer in a state of total dependency on other people, we now have the opportunity(!) to choose in favour of alienation, pain, anger, outrage, shame, guilt, and existential terror. The price of authenticity! Is it worth it?

Round 2 to our drive for authenticity.

THE CRUCIBLE OF RELATIONSHIP

On the face of it, this return to authenticity, towards being true to my self, is a move away from relationship, e.g.

"I am what I believe in. I am true to what I believe in. I act and speak from what I believe in as I understand it. It is first and foremost my truth. The truth of who I am without compromise."

If only it were that simple!

The truth (as I see it) is that with the responsibility for being true to one's self also comes the responsibility for honouring others.

"My self-imposed task is to bear witness to my own truth and to yours."

It is not about turning one's back on society or other people. As Krishnamurti puts it:

"Relationship is a mirror in which I see myself as I am... Without relationship, there is no existence; to be is to be related..." (Krishnamurti, 1995.)

In his book *The Ethics of Authenticity*, Charles Taylor (1991) writes that the concept of authenticity is relatively new to modern culture, tracing it back to the eighteenth century. The contemporary definition of authenticity is based on the idea that "each of has an original way of being human" (p 28).

"Being true to myself means being true to my own originality, and that is something only I can articulate and discover. In articulating it, I am also defining myself. I am realising a potentiality that is properly my own. This is the background understanding to the modern ideal of authenticity, and to the goals of self-fulfillment or self-realisation in which it is usually couched." (p29)

One of his major themes is the connection between authenticity and – what he terms one of malaises of modernity – individualism. He wants to know whether the trend towards individualism is congruent with being authentic.

He freely acknowledges that many people consider individualism to be one of the major achievements of modern civilisation. We live he says:

"...in a world where people have a right to choose for

themselves their own pattern of life, to decide in conscience what convictions to espouse, to determine the shape of their lives in a whole host of ways that their ancestors couldn't control.

In principle, people are no longer sacrificed to the demands of supposedly sacred orders that transcend them." (p 2) [13]

But he also bemoans the loss of these sacred orders. He writes that people used to see themselves as part of a larger cosmic order, such as the "great chain of Being." This gave meaning to their lives and significance to their activities. Individualism on the other hand:

"...is a centering on the self, which both flattens and narrows our lives, makes them poorer in meaning, and less concerned with others or society." (p 4)

He refers here to a loss of meaning and, I believe, to a loss of relationship.

He is concerned that on the personal level, the contemporary notion of authenticity:

"... fosters a view of relationships in which these ought to subserve personal fulfillment. The relationship is secondary to the self-realisation of the partners." (p 43)

And again:

"Authenticity seems once more to be defined here in a way that centres on the self, which distances us from our relations to others." (p 44)

It seems therefore, if being authentic is defined as 'doing my own thing', 'following my bliss', 'being true to myself', it can be interpreted as a move away from relationship.

Taylor however, is not prepared to give up and accept this version of authenticity. He says that the general feature of human life is its fundamentally dialogical[14] character:

"We become full human agents, capable of understanding ourselves, and hence of defining an identity, through our rich human languages of expression." (p 33).

Here he means language in its broadest sense, to include not only speech but also art, gestures, love etc.

"We are expected to develop our own opinions, outlook, stances to things, to a considerable degree through solitary reflection. But this is not how things work with important issues, such as the definition of our identity. We define this always in dialogue with, sometimes in struggle against, the identities our significant others want to recognise in us. And even when we outgrow some of the latter – our parents, for instance – and they disappear from our lives, the conversation with them continues within us as long as we live." (p 33)

Thus, echoing Firman and Gila (1997), we define ourselves in relationship with other people.

Yet there is more. There exists in us a subtle yet pervasive need to be received, to be seen, to have our unique humanness acknowledged by others. (Taylor uses the term 'recognition'.)

When our identity was largely determined by a social order which itself was taken for granted, 'recognition' was not an issue. However, in an age where most of the old certainties have been swept aside we can no longer take acknowledgement for granted. This creates an anxiety and a tension that did not exist before.

"... in the earlier age recognition never arose as a problem. Social recognition was built in to the socially derived identity from the very fact that it was based on social categories everyone took for granted. The thing about inwardly derived, personal, original identity is that it doesn't enjoy this recognition a priori. It has to win it through exchange, and it can fail. What has come about with the modern age is not the need for recognition but the conditions in which this can fail." (p 48)

So the crucible of relationship serves two purposes. Firstly it is the arena in which we forge our identity. Secondly it is the field in which, through 'external' validation (by the other) we experience our identity as acceptable – or unacceptable.

"On the intimate level, we can see how much an original identity needs and is vulnerable to the recognition given or withheld by significant others. It is not surprising that in the culture of authenticity, relationships are seen as the key loci of self-discovery and self-confirmation." (p49)

This is the theme echoed by Krishnamurti (1995):

"Relationship is a process of self-revelation, of self-knowledge..."

AUTHENTICITY VERSUS RELATIONSHIP – ROUND 3

No contest. Conflict has been replaced by synthesis.

ON THE ROAD TO AUTHENTICITY

It   takes a super-human effort of will and courage for an individual to remain a steadfast witness to her own truth. Potentially, the price to be paid is social and cultural ostracism[15]; loss of relationship with family, friends, work colleagues, employers, landlords, church, creed, race, religion and etc. That is the price she can pay. However, with awareness comes choice! No longer are her compromises motivated by her dependence on the 'other'; on wanting to please them; on not wanting to upset them and etc.

Increasingly she is able to negotiate with her authentic self, on behalf of her authentic self; to mediate between her unfolding personal truth and her need for relationship, community, belonging.

Initially, this will, as often as not, entail a painful separation from relationships which no longer meet these needs. The moving away from these relationships will seem to those she is leaving behind, like a betrayal (and she will have to deal with the guilt of that) but in reality it is the final stage of the beginning of her journey into becoming authentic.

Relationships which no longer nurture or honour her authentic self have to go, or at the very least, have to be recognised as such and 'contained' accordingly. For instance it isn't actually necessary for her to walk away from a long-term friend because she now realise that he has been 'dumping' on her emotionally these last ten years. It may be, that beneath his behaviour she can see a hurt and terrified child who is desperately seeking someone to take care of him and hoping it will be her. She can choose to remain in that relationship and continue to provide support but with awareness and, crucially, on her own terms. Or she can choose to leave.

Although in prospect and in reality this move away

from what are now experienced as ill-fitting and constraining relationships, is terrifying, it is also liberating. Freedom rarely comes without some degree of terror. Now however, for the first time, she is able to choose relationships, jobs, communities, beliefs etc., that reflect who she is in her authentic self. She begins to embody, be and live her truth. Its not a question of fitting in anymore, of selling her self short, to feel loved, wanted and valued. Now the source of validation comes from within, from the honoured authentic self and the truly lived life she has embarked upon.

I don't think it is necessarily a lonely existence. The terror looms large it is true. Krishnamurti said that "Truth is a pathless land". There are no maps, and rightly so, for another's map is not her truth. However as she sets out to find her personal truth she will come into contact with other souls on a similar quest for authenticity. Each of them in some way will have a contribution to make to the ongoing discovery of her own truth.

One of these 'fellow-travelers' may well be a counsellor or therapist.

AUTHENTICITY AND THE CLIENT/THERAPIST RELATIONSHIP

I hope I have shown that the path to the authentic self is within relationship, rather than away from it.

I believe that, whether it is explicit or not to the client or her therapist, she, the client, enters into the relationship with the therapist, believing that the experience will be beneficial. That is, that she will, over time, learn more about her authentic self through the relationship with the therapist.

EXPERIENCING AUTHENTICITY IN THE THERAPEUTIC RELATIONSHIP

"The issue is whether we as therapists can accept the reality of the psyche, the reality of the client's experience. Whether or not a particular incident has objective truth is utterly beside the point. The client, in disclosing this information is telling us something about *the woundedness of the psyche.*" (Gael Rowan, 1999. My italics.)

The major turning point in my own therapy was the moment when for the first time I felt that another human being (my therapist) really understood what it was like to be me.

This experience was later unexpectedly repeated in a group-process context, when, faced with my pain in the form of my unmitigated anger expressed towards members of the group, one person responded in a manner that validated my experience of what it has been like to be me. A form of validation that did not infer any judgment or expectation of me, on the part of the other. In this particular context, a total acceptance of me and my rage which confirmed unequivocally that I had a right to be rageful.

What I have always wanted is simply to be accepted as I am without preconditions or expectations – I know that I am not perfect but I am still worthy of love all the same.

What I have always needed (ached for) has been a simple unequivocal acknowledgement of my inviolable right to be who I am – or bearing in mind the pernicious influence of the family trance, at least who I think I am. More, to experience that acknowledgement in a way that does not diminish either me or the other.[16] Hence insincerity or platitudes have no value at all.

To experience is the key. A mere intellectual understanding of "being seen or received or validated" is not enough. What counts is some act, which may or may not include a verbal response, which shows me that the other understands unequivocally.

Ironically, in my case, it was at the end of a long 'rant' about how I didn't believe I was given due credit for my contributions in the therapy training, when my therapist unexpectedly agreed with me unequivocally. I was stunned and for the first time ever in my whole life, I felt that another human being totally accepted me for who I was – not what I could be or what they wanted me to be.

In hindsight I don't think it mattered whether I was right or wrong. What mattered was that I was not told I was wrong.

To put it more positively; against an expectation of being told I was wrong, I was actually confounded by being told I was right. At a deeper level, my outrage – the 'rant' within me – was totally accepted by the other and therefore validated. It was seen as the product of what had been done to me not who I was.

Not surprisingly, I believe that this is also what the counsellor/therapist must do; put aside all judgements[17] and acknowledge/recognise (to use Taylor's term) the client's right to be who they are.

That is to start with total acceptance of the client.[18] Then as the therapy proceeds, to seek to validate the client's experience of themselves – not the therapist's experience of the client. To see the world through the client's eyes. To share their subjective experience of reality. To seek to understand what it is like to be the client, in the client's world, both in the moment and in the past. In this regard the client's life history – what has happened to the client as the client understands it – is understood as the reason why the client has become who they are. This is not a pathological judgment but a recognition of how things are for the client. The need then is to understand how the client's life experiences have contributed to the client's current experience of themselves; that is their subjective reality and the pain this has caused them, and is currently causing them. Only when the therapist, through immersion in the client's world, has some inkling of what in the past has contributed to their present experience, can the therapist adequately support the client's efforts to heal themselves.

THE GOOD ENOUGH THERAPIST

"The good enough therapist, as Winnicott's good enough mother, will allow the other person in the relationship to experience this: "When I look I am seen, so I exist." (Firman & Gila, 1997 p 231)

Carl Rogers saw three key prerequisites for an authentic therapeutic relationship, as follows:

"(a) The therapist is *congruent*, that is, authentic or 'real' in her/his relationships with clients. In other words, the therapist is not just an anonymous 'expert', but is present as a person.

(b) The therapist experiences and communicates *unconditional positive regard* for the client. Put another way, the therapist has a warm, caring and non-judgmental attitude.

(c) The therapist experiences an *empathic understanding* of the client's inner world, and manages to communicate this understanding to the client."

(Merry, 1990, p 9 – italicized text in the original.)

Points (b) and (c) have been considered in the preceding section.

Point (a) bears further amplification. Merry (1990, p 10), further defines congruence as:

"… that state of being in which we are *most freely and authentically ourselves*, without the need to present a façade, to hide ourselves behind the mask or role of 'expert', for example. It is where our inner feelings are accurately reflected by our behaviour, when we can be received and seen for who we really are." (My italics).

Note that the therapist brings to the encounter the exact same wish as the client – to be received and seen for who they really are. This does not mean that the therapist treats the therapeutic relationship as an opportunity for the gratification of her own needs. What it does mean is that the therapist strives to maintain an awareness of her own feelings and thoughts in her relationship with the client as it unfolds and develops.

Diana Whitmore (1995, p 24) expressed it thus:

"A psychosynthesis counsellor is encouraged to develop a full presence and to approach each client with a universal orientation and an enlarged perspective. What does this actually mean? It means that, given the importance of authenticity and the quality of the human relationship, the counsellor meets the client as a whole person; in other words having her own bodily, emotional and mental processes available."

The authentic therapist strives to be authentic in the therapeutic relationship.

That is to be true to her self and not to deny any of the thoughts and feelings which arise as a result of being present with the client. This includes apparently 'negative' feelings such as anger, irritation, boredom, fear etc.

At times these 'negative' feelings may be supportive of the client[19]. For example, a client is describing a scene from her childhood where she is being unjustly punished. Whilst the client describes this in a 'matter of fact' way, the therapist, may experience anger against the perpetrators. In such instances, the therapist may deem it appropriate to draw attention to this apparent incongruity. "I'm feeling some anger here. Yet I notice that you don't appear to feel any anger. Do you have any thoughts on why not....?" Thus facilitating an exploration of the client's apparent lack of emotion. In this example, it is clear that the anger the therapist feels is on behalf of her client.

But what of those occasions when these less acceptable feelings stem from the therapist's own wounding – the counter-transference[20]?

Here, by definition, the problem belongs to the therapist; and yet if not properly acknowledged as such, will have a negative affect on the therapeutic relationship. The authentic therapist needs to recognise and own these issues which are manifestations of her own shadow. To be authentic therefore the therapist must be aware of her shadow and how it manifests itself in projections, and particularly with the client/therapeutic relationship in mind, the counter-transference.

"Thus the major job for therapists here – far more important than any technique, theory, or intervention – is to recognise and deal with the aspects of themselves that are revealed in the counter-transference." (Firman & Gila, 1997, p246)

"Unless there is such an ongoing cultivation of authentic personality, the therapist will ever remain an ineffective mirror... One cannot form an empathic connection to the many levels of another unless one has established an empathic connection to those levels in oneself." (Firman & Gila, 1997, p 247)

Such awareness can only arise if the therapist herself has explored, and continues to explore her own authenticity, in all probability, as a client in therapy herself.

To return finally to Firman & Gila (1997) and their unifying centres: "Only this development of authentic personality can provide the therapist with the empathic wherewithal necessary to function as a good enough unifying centre within psychosynthesis therapist. This development allows the therapist to connect empathically with the client no matter where the client needs to go, mirroring and facilitating the I-Self relationship over the widest possible range of experience. Where such an external unifying centre is provided, the client can develop an internal unifying centre that, though growing and changing over the years, can support the I-Self connection indefinitely. (p 229)"

CONCLUSION

At the beginning of this paper, I posed the following question:

How is our personal drive for authenticity hindered and / or supported by our need for relationship?

In response, it seems that far from removing us from the need for relationship, our drive for authenticity is only meaningful in relationship.

Secondly, the major implication for the therapist in the therapeutic relationship, is that unless the therapist is in touch with her own authenticity, she will not be able to truly meet the other in the therapeutic relationship.

FOOTNOTES

1 "At the deepest level, human being is relational." (Firman & Gila, 1997 p32)

2 I have purposely used the word 'drive' in this context based on Assagioli (1994): "In considering motivations, then, one is helped by distinguishing between two classes which we may designate respectively as drives and urges, and reasons. Drives and urges can be conscious or unconscious and can be generically regarded as spontaneous tendencies which "move" us or tend to do so...." (p 144)

3 In this paper I use the terms 'authenticity' and the 'authentic

self' in the same sense as Firman & Gila (1997, p227) use the phrase 'authentic personality' to mean "the expression of one's, true I-manes through time."

4 Zen quotation.

5 That is not to say that I any way reject their 'scientific' formulation. As I hope to demonstrate, I am in total sympathy with their ideas. However, for me to be able to make sense of their concepts (that is assimilate and absorb them; make them mine), and look at their implications for my and others ongoing relationship to the environment, each other and our inner selves, I need to integrate them into my own inner model of the human condition.

6 It should be noted that this secondary pain, in all its manifestations, serves to cover/deaden the primary pain/terror of non-being. In time, any or all of the multifarious aspects of this secondary level of pain can become unbearable in themselves and lead the individual to seek further strategies for avoiding the secondary pain. And so on ad-infinitum – ad nauseum.

7 Although I suspect in fact, that being authentic (true to one's self) is a pre-requisite of self-realisation – see also my discussion of Wilber's centaur below.

8 I would not in my terms be authentic if I claimed otherwise!

9 Paul Simon – "Sound of Silence" (1964)

10 Jean Hardy, 1996

11 Sounds like 'centre'-stage – where the I/Self split begins to be healed.

12 Not withstanding the support provided by a therapist or a member of the clergy and etc.

13 A Canadian, Charles Taylor is Professor of Philosophy and Political Science at McGill University. Laying judgment to one side, he like many people, cannot escape his culture, and his upbringing (conditioning.) Therefore when he uses phrases such as "where people have a right to choose for themselves" and "people are no longer sacrificed" and etc., he is of course referring to a very privileged group of people – mostly white, mostly western, mostly educated, mostly financially secure. This does not invalidate his point of view in general terms only in the more specific applications to which he sometimes refers.

14 A view that supports the value of counselling and therapy with its emphasis on the dialogical relationship between the participants.

15 At worst persecution and death!

16 "My self-imposed task is to bear witness to my own truth and to yours."

17 Transference/projection under another name.

18 Surely the true basis for empathy?

19 Projective-identification.

20 "...defined as the conscious and unconscious responses of the therapist to the patient." (Firman & Gila, 1997, p 240)

"Feelings that the psychoanalyst unconsciously directs to the analyzed, stemming from his or her own emotional vulnerabilities and unresolved conflicts." (Davison & Neale, 1998)

ENDNOTES

Page 7

"…coping strategies, behaviours and beliefs.." – often embodied or actualised as sub-personalities. "Subpersonalities..... are learned responses to our legitimate needs: survival needs, needs for love and acceptance, needs for self-actualisation and transcendence." (Molly Young Brown, p94)

"Subpersonalities… develop as a means of meeting some basic need." (Whitmore, 1995, p79)

The particularly 'unacceptable' subpersonalities, that represent, for instance, the need to rage or to destroy and etc., are pushed into the 'shadow'. I disagree with Firman & Gila here. They see the splitting into subpersonalities as preceding the split between authentic personality and survival personality. Since the primal split is created by a wound in the I-Self relationship, it constitutes a split at the most fundamental level of personality organisation. Here one's deepest sense of self-in relationship – one's sense of being is fragmented. We have looked at this fragmentation as a split between the higher and lower unconscious, but there are two other significant splittings to consider. The first of these is the splitting into subpersonalities, the second is the split between authentic personality and survival personality." (Firman & Gila, 1997, p151) In my opinion, the 'needs' which the subpersonalities embody are 'fragments' of the authentic self. Therefore the authentic self is 'a priori'; preceding the development of the subpersonalities, which in turn constellate the survival personality. Surely it could not be any other way since the authentic self is who we were before we began to: "… hide our true natures and became what the environment need(ed) us to be…" (Firman & Gila, 1997. P164.

Page 9

Yet, some children refuse to adapt in such a 'compliant' way. I would suggest that 'difficult' children for instance, are children who have in some part of themselves at least refused to give up on getting their needs met.

Page 13

Of course after independence can come a recognition of our 'interdependence' and our active choice for relationship. However, this seems to me to take us into the realms of the transpersonal, and outside the scope of this paper.

References & Bibliography

Assagioli, Roberto, *The Act of Will*, The Aquarian Press, 1994
Bradshaw, John, *Homecoming*, Bantam Books. 1997.
Davison, C.D. & Neale, J. M. (1998), *Abnormal Psychology Seventh Edition*, John Wiley & Sons, Inc., New York.
Firman, John, & Gila, Ann, *The Primal Wound*, State University of New York Press, 1997.
Hardy, Jean, *A Psychology with a soul* , RKP, 1987.
Krishnamurti, J, *The Book of Life – Daily Meditations with Krishnamurti*, HarperSanFrancisco, 1995.
Merry, Tony, A *Guide to the Person-Centred Approach*, Association for Humanistic Psychology in Britain, 1990.
Matson, Katrinka, *The Encyclopaedia of Reality – A Guide to the New Age,* Paladin Books, Granada Publishing. 1979.
Oriah Mountain Dreamer, *The Invitation – A Guidebook for Living with Integrity, Commitment and Passion*, Thorsons, 1999.
Robinson, Alan, *On Life In General : On Hope In Particular*, Work in Progress
Robinson, Alan, *Paper on The Family Trance*, October 1998.
Rowan, John, *The Transpersonal – Psychotherapy and Counselling*, Routledge, 1993.
Taylor, Charles, *The Ethics Of Authenticity*, Harvard University Press, 1991.
Whitmore, Diana, *Psychosynthesis Counselling in Action*, Sage Publications, 1995.

Wilber, Ken, *No Boundary – Eastern and Western Approaches to Personal Growth*, Shambhala, 1979.

Winn, Denise, *The Whole Mind Book – An A-Z of Theories, Therapies and Facts*, Fontana Paperbacks 1980.

Young Brown, Molly, *The Unfolding Self*, Psychosynthesis Press, Los Angeles, California, 1983

Voyage Through
the Liminal Realms

Rachael Clyne

Change is often prompted by a crisis of some kind; a relationship breakdown, illness, or loss. Rarely do we choose to enter the process of change and transformation. Outer events and our psyche conspire to tug the rug from underfoot, forcing us to question our old perceptions, identity and our circumstances. What begins as apparent misfortune or destruction can eventually bring forth much needed evolution and improvement.

Equally, we may feel stuck in our lives and our relationships. We are dogged by negative thoughts and feelings and we may seek help through counselling and psychotherapy in order to feel better. We agree to enter into a therapeutic journey, little realising what it can entail. We imagine we can keep our lives intact and safe, but there are no guarantees. In order to evolve we must be willing to give up control over what needs to go, and trust that what is really important will be returned to us. Inevitably there are losses along the way. We have to make a voyage into unknown waters, armed only with the slender faith that our psyche knows what it needs. We have to learn to trust the process, to trust that we will survive and emerge to create for ourselves a life more authentic to who we are and ultimately more satisfying.

The therapist acts as a guide, one who is familiar with some of the stages we may encounter on route. Part of her task is to hold the light of faith in the process even when we believe all is at sea or lost.

This series of poems is inspired by the voices of many different people, and attempts to map experiences on an epic journey that is common to us all. The hero, or heroine's journey to the underworld and the odyssey, are myths that express this process of change. The Liminal Realms are an unknown, twilit world, where old identities melt and we must die to be reborn. Familiar reference points no longer apply and nothing is clear-cut here, yet this world has its own laws and language, which we must learn to understand if we are to cross the sea and reach our destination.

PRELUDE

The years of trying
I lost count how many
I know!
I'll go on a course
change jobs
hairdos
stop and wait for a sign
end the relationship
start a new one
give up relationships
go on a detox
what the hell!
I'll drink and smoke
and fuck the consequences!
Stop trying
start trying again
stop drinking and smoking
meditate at dawn
turn vegan
find a therapist
find another one

learn to forgive my parents
· myself
do voluntary work
stop thinking of myself
exercise
love myself everyday.

But everywhere I look
the same life stares back
a mind filled with
grey boxes
the same brick wall
at every turn
walking the same block
day in day out
I'm tired
of searching for
the turning
that will get me
out of this labyrinth.

No gaps
each hopeful chink
leads only
back to the same old
dreary place
each effort merely
serves to strengthen
the wall of failure and frustration
shaking a fist at God
"You said you'd carry me
when I could no longer walk!"
chipping away at hope
reducing it to
a small brown puddle
still declaiming,
in a shrinking voice
"There must be another way!"

1 SPLITTING APART

Then comes the moment
that can no longer
be smoothed over
complied with
arrows of light
burst
the tight brown
pupa case of
my existence.

Eyes shut tight
against the dazzle
scrabbling
to pull edges
together again
this laser blade of truth
no longer affords
the chance to slumber
my life away.

The shock of knowing
things can't go back
the way they were
part of me knows this
and quietly prepares
step by step
for leaving.

Part of me doubts –
am I simply playing
a childish game
of packing socks
and jam sandwiches
into my pyjama case
but never really going?

At the same time
yearning for
the rescuer in waiting
who'll whisk me away
to happy-ever-after-land.

As my wings unfurl
damply
I shrink
from the prospect of flying
not knowing
what kind of imago
I'll turn out to be
butterfly
or beetle?

2 NOWHERE PLACE

In the waiting room
between
who we used to be
and who we need to become
how do we navigate
from where we no longer fit
to where we want to be?

All we can do
is gaze at the view
dead flies on the window-sill
wondering if the view
is a clue.

How long
before the bus comes
to take us to our unknown destination?
Will we know when we get there?
Will it be as we expect
or quite the reverse?

Having
stripped the walls
of old patterns
cleared the furniture
of our dead and departed self
swinging between
trust and frustration
faith and despair
we wonder
where the heck's the door
and where's the fucking key?

3 BORDERLANDS

In the liminal realms
everything
is turned on its head
what was the problem
becomes the solution
the abandoned child
is now the key to love
loneliness that once devoured
a shopping mall of need
becomes the salvation
of standing alone.

In these borderlands
dogged determination
becomes the foe
persistence is terminal
surrender is our only hope
cessation of trying
fruitlessly
to control
what we get to keep
and what we must relinquish.

At the shoreline
of the great sea
it's all up for grabs!
unstinting sacrifice to the sea gods
is the price of passage
trusting their mercy
will return that which truly belongs
the rest washed away on the tides
no matter how
glitter bright it seemed.

4 ASHES

Gazing back
at the shrinking shoreline
my chest heaves
with the sobbing swell
not knowing when
if ever
I'll return.

My old life
a tiny distant line –
all those
broken dreams
lost hope
effort
of waiting
of fitting in
smothering
this seething
rage
now spilling
from my throat
onto the deck
over the stern.

Swept
by wind and wake
and circling gulls
ashes of hate
burn and fade
in the foam
fire and water
salt and flame
is all I am
Who I was
is gone
who I am
is given up
to alchemy.

5 CROSSING

In the bottom of the ship
cars roll against their chains
the hull's metallic creaks
rebound with a snap
filling the underwater gloom
with strange and threatening sounds
against a steady thrum
and stink of engine oil.

It's an act of faith
when there's no visible light
in the middle of a big black
bumpy sea
all we can do is embrace the depth
and if angels
are egging us on
from behind clouds
we haven't a clue.
All that remains
is plodding on

will day ever break?
Will it be a sudden burst
of light?
Or a slow slither
into a grey and dreary morn?

The hull rolls down –
O God we may never come up!
This blackness may be it
only four hours to go
they said
even though we paid our dues
to the ferryman
will we ever reach land?
Incubator or coffin –
we don't want to know
yet this
bare reality
of rise and fall
of life and death
holds something true
memory echoes
lap against awareness
a lengthy labour
a forceps birth:
only four hours to go
till feeding time!

6 SOLSTICE

Lighter now
no longer needing to know
having ceased trying
ancestors whisper in my ear
someone's steering the ship after all
and land will come.

Formless
weightless
no longer angry with my life
weight becomes waiting
waiting becomes peace
and knowledge more certain
that answers will come
the same routine
that weeks ago
filled me with frustration
is just what needs to be done
no longer striving to change
I can wait.

I will light a candle
and celebrate
this standing alone in the dark
kindling the birth of hope
from the place of no choice
the possibility
suddenly arises
of unlimited choices
gazing at the flame
a column of sparks –
my unfulfilled dreams
float up before me
not knowing which will evaporate
into blackness
and which will be the one
to ignite my new life.

Considering each
in the light
of this new faith
I decide
what goes up
will be God's
and what comes down
is mine.

7 STILLPOINT

Suddenly none of it matters
no longer obsessed
by old pre-occupations
of limitation and shortcoming
failure and obstacles
observing instead
myself from afar.

An exquisite moment
of clarity
like watching
a single
raindrop
falling
into
a pool
of silent
water
ah!
the unspeakable beauty
melting
gladly into
eternity
a luminous ocean
Shanti Shanti Om Shanti!

8 SEACHANGE

Something's gone
that I used to drag around
I get the feeling
I'd closed the door on myself
cut off something vital
now I'm open
no more pains in my head
no longer haunted

by fear of being swamped
by that great black
oily wave
carrying its deadly cargo of
flotsam and jetsam.

I'm still bobbing about
on the ocean
but it's a nice ocean
with soft curling waves
everything's less black and white
and I've pink and orange
clothes to match
my new outlook
no more struggle
and all this space inside.

9 COMPLACENCE

How pleasant
to drift
floating free
how easily
given the chance
we become
complacent again –
deluding ourselves
we'll get to keep
the old comfy props
reluctant to undergo
the full tremendum
of transformation
relinquish
our last vestiges
doubting our capacity
for survival –
we cling to the old cliff-edge
with familiar fingers.

Moving through a stage
we tell ourselves
phew that's it!
But it isn't
it's merely respite
from the rigours
of the journey
a bit of r & r
before the next bit

Should we find
we're resting on our laurels
we know that's not really it
for life will come again
and shake the tree
"Move along!
Get on with it!"

We must tip
our last secret hoard
overboard
cast fate
to the winds
and determine anew
to finish the journey.

10 DILEMMA

Now to the heart of it
the final dark secret
on one side
an infant
powerless
forever in a void
being good
in the hope
without hope

waiting
for someone to appear
pick her up
cradle her
feed her
and never let her go.

On the other –
a hermit
resigned
refusing to be here
his cynical scythe
smartly severing
any shoot of hope
with deep dark anger
that must be
preserved
whatever the cost.

For even now
if someone came
and offered
to appease those lifelong cravings:
love, food, security…
nothing
no-one
can Ever – EVER
make up for
what was lost!

Survival lies in forgetting
the pact we made in despair
sincerely believing
nothing would change
refusing to take part
in life
then we wonder
why our life doesn't work

our efforts are as dust
and milk sours on our tongue
failing to recognise
the potency of a vow
what began as
righteous protest
became purgatory
a black hole
swallowing everything into itself.

Be right or be free?
In our commitment to misery
there's a surprising hook
the payoff –
of righteousness of safety
when life gets too close
we flip out
hover in our
sealed bubble
but the cost?
Aaah the cost!

The colours of freedom
banner-bright
beckon like a windmill
twirling in the sand
if I give up this pact
will I betray
her suffering –
lose my safety net?

11 RELEASE

So this is what they meant!
Warmth ripples
in my belly
champagne fizzes

through my veins
as I embrace wholeheartedly
yes!

Cold abandoner
needy devourer
stubborn protestor
every scrap
together in this moment
finally the plot
falls into place
in this last frame.

Filled only with gratitude
and an urge to dive
from the bows
to swim singing
in a joyous sea.

12 WOBBLE MOMENT

Tossing these last remnants
over the side
the deck shudders
doubt bubbles nauseously
as land approaches.

What if I got it wrong
after all?
Will I find myself
flat on my arse
in spiritual pratfall
derided and blamed
by friends and family
as a deluded fool
who sacrificed them all
for some stupid fantasy.

Whatever the outcome
doubtless some will view me thus
envious or bereft
nothing will sway them
I am powerless
as hot salt
sears my cheeks
only faint hope remains
that others may be waiting
on the quay
glad for my sake
I trusted my vision.

13 ARRIVAL

First the sound –
a thunderous clank
as gears change
the signal of land approaching
shudder of metal
slowing down.

Here in the hold
restless limbs are stretched
in mounting anticipation
as is the way of ships
berthing is slow
and laboured
forcing us to wait
even though we know
we've arrived
shouts of those we cannot see
with words we can't quite recognise
secure the vessel
chains and ropes slap
against the side.

At last; the command:
"proceed to upper decks"
sleepily we stumble
up narrow stairs
emerge blinking
into a day
full of hazy sights
as yet undefined
only our feet
endeavour to recall
walking
along the bouncing gangplank
until
we reach
the almost forgotten
sensation of
solid ground.

Attention held
utterly in the moment
careful heed
paid
to each detail
accustoming ourselves
to our new domain
the voyage fades
as we advance
uncertain
yet hopeful
along the quay.

A Patent on God

Influences on Roberto Assagioli

Ellis Linders

My subject for this essay is Gnosticism, Christian Mysticism and the Cathars. Roberto Assagioli recognized man as an inherently spiritual being and sought to return health and balance to the human psyche by promoting spiritual values and insight without involving or adhering to religious creed. This made him somewhat of a maverick in the world of psychology of his, and to this, day. This secular spirituality, I learnt, has its roots in a wealth of esoteric influences. Assagioli's emphasis on soul-making qualities such as Love, Will, Purpose and Imagination came from these rich sources, continuing an ancient and sacred tradition of reconnecting man with her Divine Source.

Assagioli recognized this connection as a profound need within all beings; a yearning that grows stronger the closer we come into our heart, and discover this, her true desire. And so he arrived at the great traditions that helped people walk this path. He, I imagine, must have been intrigued and inspired by the commitment and fervor of these seekers, despite often relentless and cruel persecution. What drove these people was a need for truth that went far beyond the personal; infinitely more powerful than the sum of its parts. I am attracted to these traditions, as was Assagioli, because I believe orthodox religion has left me and many others in spiritual poverty, and I recognize a primal drive within myself that seeks to find my fuller spiritual identity to nourish my being.

So where to start? What questions to ask? Firstly, I needed some knowledge; information and definition. What is Gnosticism? Who were the Cathars? What is the difference between Gnostic, Mystical and Orthodox? Why the threat? Just what was this experience of God that we weren't allowed to know about. Most books I initially came across on the subject were informative on the theological, ideological and political arguments that were used to decide what was in and what was out of the canon. For this reason I understand the New Testament to be largely a political and therefore spiritually limited and limiting document. But I still needed to gain a deeper understanding of the experience of mystical consciousness, this being what inspired Assagioli in his work.

After the history, the mystery... For this I sought to read Gnostic texts and the writings of genuine Mystics. One such source is the 'Pistis Sophia'; a Coptic Gnostic text. It provides an idea of the cosmology that was central to Gnostics thought; of the risen Christ as teacher, the evolution of mankind, commitment to its co-creation and the multifaceted and divine nature of man. These ideas resonate with more contemporary sources such as Theosophy and the Anthroposophical teachings of Rudolf Steiner. Assagioli's Egg-diagram can also be recognized in this as a simplified depiction of a limitless concept.

Original Greek translation of terms, words that took on a meaning of their own over the ages.:
Catholic - Universal
Orthodox - straight thinking
Gospel - Good news
Canon - plumb-line (carpenters term).
Bishop - supervisor
Apostolos - representative
Gnostic - knower
Christ - anointed one
Jesus - Redemption (Hebrew)
Nazarene - Truth (Aramaic)
Heresy - act of choice
Epinoia - creative consciousness
Pleroma - fulfilment
Cathar - derivative of "Purity"

THE MYSTICAL MIND

The words myth, mysticism and mystery are all derived from the same Greek word "musteion", meaning; to close the eyes or the mouth, in other words; darkness and silence.

"The mystical experience of God has certain characteristics that are common in all faiths. It is a subjective experience that involves an interior journey, not a perception of an objective fact outside the self; it is undertaken through the image making part of the mind, often called the imagination, rather than through the more cerebral logical faculty. Imagination is so a God-given faculty. The God of the mystics is not an objective reality but by nature profoundly subjective. Finally it is something that the mystic creates in him or herself deliberately. Certain mental and physical exercises yield the final vision. It demanded great skill, a certain disposition and training, which helps the adept to find his way through the labyrinth path of the psyche. Considerable skill and mental balance is required to handle and interpret the symbols that emerge through the course of concentrated meditation and inner reflection." (Karen Armstrong *A History Of God*)

So this describes the concept of skilful, disciplined, good (purified) Will combined with imagination to arrive at an intimate, fully involved experience of the Divine. Unlike dogmatic religion, which often lends itself to sectarian disputes, Mysticism often claims that there are as many roads to God as there are people. The essential nature of the work is the process of "inner purification to find God at any price". Implicit in this is the perennial philosophy that all the sages of the ancient world had essentially preached a single doctrine: All truth came from God and should be sought wherever it could be found.

"The introspective, imaginative mysticism was a search for the ground of being in the depths of the self. It deprived the mystic of the certainties that characterize the more dogmatic forms of religion. Since every man and woman had a unique experience of God, it followed that no one religion could express the whole of the Divine mystery. Our understanding of our personal lord is colored by the religious tradition into which we were born but it must never be confused with the reality itself…God was discovered to be mysteriously identified with the inmost self. The systematic destruction of ego led to an absorption in a larger,

ineffable reality....a return to man's primordial state of the creation".
(Karen Armstrong)

This then made the "God of the Mystics" an immediate experience that overrides the intermediary of the church, welcoming all varieties of experience, making this level of spirituality a tolerant, inclusive and unifying force. To the mystics the bible had to be read metaphorically, like poetry, if it was to yield the mystery of the sacred. The recurring tragedy of our history into our present is how religion has removed itself from its spirituality through literalism, exclusion, emphasis on doctrinal differences and power-politics – in effect, taking the heart out of the teachings, through rigid interpretation and exclusivity. In the West, since Augustine, the idea of God had become increasingly externalized and had contributed to a very negative conception of human nature, with its emphasis on sin, guilt and struggle.

Central to Gnostic teaching was the rectification of "the Fall of Consciousness"; The "Divine Exile" of Lucifer and of Pistis Sophia (Faith Wisdom), is what the risen Christ came to bring about and what man is co-creative to, as this fall of consciousness happened simultaneously within man, as within the cosmos (as above so below). The purpose of the mystical path was: *"A return to the source of our being; re-unification with Self...by drawing together his dissipated self the mystic would experience the divine presence in personal integration"*. A pretty good description of the methods and aim of Psychosynthesis!

I am aware I am using the terms Mystic and Gnostic as if they were the same. The Gnostics were by nature Mystics. They saw the purpose of their teaching as the realization of Gnosis and to bring their initiates to spiritual maturity where they would experience completely freedom from external authority and become "Christed" themselves – an utterly blasphemous notion to the literalist Orthodox. The Orthodox Church too had Mystics, but this was by no means encouraged, and visionary insight had to stay strictly within the parameters of the doctrine.

One of the central points of contention between Gnostic and Orthodox thinking was that Orthodox creed determined that this fall was somehow "outside" the God-head and isolated this as "evil". Whereas the Gnostics were open to the idea that this too was somehow part of a greater Divine Plan – it had to be, as nothing was beyond the ultimate ineffable God-head. Spirit is in part in a consenting state of exile and limitation in order to achieve Self-Consciousness. Evil in this context is defined as something that has become separated or has entered into a relationship to which it is unsuited; a "forgetting" of true nature: Fallen Angels which have strayed too far from the central source and have become contaminated by the shadow of matter. The Gnostic had to always be aware of the good and evil in his/her own heart and see it as a reflection in microcosm of the war between good and evil in the Universe. This Dualist principle of the two forces good and evil existing alongside each other and within the consciousness of man also, is a basic principle of Gnosticism.

This is why the Kabbalistic Tree of Life is depicted as interrelated pillars that hold each other in balance. When one Sephiroth becomes overly dominant; if for instance we worship one above the other within ourselves, the harmony is disturbed and "evil" enters. However, its origin is still Divine perfection. There is a level on which there is no separation and consciousness is complete. It is this part within ourselves that the mystics are seeking... nothing is separate from the other and man is in intimate co-creation with the Divine Source to fulfill this "knowing". In a way, Spirit is on some level "dependent" upon the world and human beings for its fulfillment, hence the utmost importance of the mystical inner search.

This echoes Rudolf Steiner's teaching on the meaning of Lucifer: Luciferic energy gave ego-consciousness to mankind to explore the Tree of Knowledge (not to be confused with the Tree of Life!). In this process, symbolized as "the Fall", man "forgot" his Divine Origin and became imprisoned in the consciousness of matter. Lucifer is Light without Love. We have, in a way, become addicted to the power Lucifer gave us but, due to our forgetfulness, without the balancing wisdom to use it for what it was intended. Although the Luciferic "enlightenment" has been an important stage in our development and served to set us free from dogmatic fundamentalism during the age of enlightenment, as Lynn Pickford discusses in "The History of Lucifer", the redeeming sacrifice of Christ was intended to bring man back to the Tree of Life. The second coming is not the re-incarnation of Jesus the man, but the awakening of the Christ consciousness in us all, as part of our intended evolution. It is through the love-light of Christ that we can ascend and return to our Divine source. Andrew Harvey echoes this in his book "Son of Man":

" *The second coming will not be the return of an avatar or of a "person" - but will be - if it is to be at all the birth of the authentic "full-grown" Christ-Consciousness in millions of beings who have realized, as the historical Jesus did, the journey into unconditional love for all humanity, the journey of the Christ. It is up to each one of us to take up the terrifying and glorious challenge of Jesus to "Christ" ourselves, so as to be part of this great birth; it is the responsibility of each one of us to imagine, risk, and give everything to participate as fully and fecundly as we can in the evolutionary leap that this birth makes possible."*

Another contemporary Mystic; Teilhard de Chardin describes his understanding of the struggle of evolution as *"a divine force which propelled the Universe from matter to Spirit to personality and, finally beyond personality to God, who is imminent and incarnate in the world, which had become a sacrament to his presence.. Christ in his view was the omega point; the climax of the evolutionary process when God becomes all in all".* (Karen Armstrong).

Rather than science being the enemy of faith, he marries his belief in God with science and follows in the footsteps of those mystics who throughout the ages have used mathematics and science as a means of contemplation. He argues that science shows that the natural world progresses to ever greater complexity AND to greater unity in this variety and is another way of regarding the love that animates the whole of creation.

Due to their constant searching, it seems science and mysticism make easier bed-fellows than science and the established church, or indeed Mysticism and the established church!

In the early years, the followers of Jesus the Christ grew into many different sects, each developing their own interpretations and experience of his message. There existed no defining text on the teachings of Christ. What existed were the accounts of those who "walked with Christ" and who subsequently set forth into the world to teach his message. These were many more than just the 12 apostles we are familiar with in the New Testament. These accounts, together with those received by revelation such as the revelations of Paul, whose essentially Gnostic message was later "appropriated" to be used against the Gnostics, were handed down the generations and eventually put to paper. No apostle is thought or known to have physically written his or her own account. Indeed, among the many theories, it is also believed that the historical Jesus the man never actually existed (Freke and Gandy: "Jesus and the Goddess"), but that the gospel was a Jewish (probably by the Therapeutae and Essenes) reworking of ancient Pagan myths of a dying and resurrecting God. This goes beyond what I am writing about here, but it is very much worth keeping in mind as yet another argument against literalism and to emphasize the Gnostics relationship to myth as profound allegories encoding mystical teachings. The stories and teachings of their spiritual tradition were like signposts pointing beyond words to the mystical experience of the ineffable mystery.

To the Gnostics, the scriptures were to be absorbed at different levels of consciousness at two stages of initiation: The Psychic or Soul level; the "outer circle" where the teaching is focused on the reaching out to others with compassion, and secondly, the "Pneumatic" Spirit level; the "inner circle", where the word teaches the initiate to reach inside and commune with our shared essence of oneness. Lynn Picknett, in her book, "The Templar Revelation", argues among other things, that the apostles of the New Testament never got beyond the Psychic level. That they were not part of Jesus' "inner" circle, with the exception of Thomas and Mary Magdalene....

'*Yeshua said to his students, compare me to something and tell me what I am like. Simon Kefa (Simon Peter) said to him, you are like a just messenger. Matthew said to him, you are like a wise philosopher. Thomas said to him, Rabbi, my mouth is utterly unable to say what you are like. Yeshua said, I am not your rabbi. Because you have drunk, you are intoxicated from the bubbling spring I tended. And he took him and withdrew, and spoke three sayings to him. When Thomas came back to*

*his friends they asked him, what did Yeshua say to you? Thomas said
to them,ilf I tell you one of the sayings he spoke to me, you will pick up
rocks and stone me, and fire will come from the rocks and consume you.'*
"The Gospel of St Thomas" (13)

He wasn't wrong. This esoteric Jesus Christ goes on to
warn Mary: *".....As for you then, be on guard against the world. Arm
yourselves with great strength, or the robbers will find a way to reach
you, for the trouble you expect will come. Let among you understand.
When the crop ripened, the reaper came quickly with sickle in hand and
harvested it. Whoever has ears to hear should hear".*(21)

Jesus understood the danger of limited understanding. He fully
expected, and experienced in his lifetime (whether this was Jesus
Christ as a historical figure or the mystical minds that put pen to
papyrus), the persecution from those who stood to lose earthly
power by his teachings.
*"Yeshua said, the Pharisees and the scholars have taken the keys of
knowledge and have hidden them. They have not entered nor have they
allowed those who want to enter to go inside. You should be as shrewd
as snakes and innocent as doves. (39)"*

He warned to keep these teachings secret and sacred
for those who had "the ears to hear and eyes to see"; i.e. the
Pneumatic initiates of the Inner Circle; the adepts. Not out of
superficial elitism, but to protect of the purity of his symbolic
word. "(62) Jesus said, I disclose my mysteries to those who are
worthy of my mysteries. Do not let your left hand know what
your right hand is doing."

The Jesus "story" is part of the Outer Mysteries of
Christianity, designed for Psychic initiates. The secret teachings
of the resurrected Christ, are designed to be taught to Pneumatic
initiates of the Inner Mysteries, and are found in other Gnostic
Gospels such as "The Book of the Savior", "The Book of the
great Logos according to the Mystery", "The Book of Ieou", and
Pistis Sophia, which accounts for teachings given by the risen
Christ:...."*And it occurred after Jesus had risen from the dead that he
spent eleven years in discourse with his disciples*" (first line of Pistis
Sophia)

THE MYTH OF PISTIS SOPHIA

"The Pistis Sophia is a definitive and unique narration given in the form of Divine dialogue of instruction, revealed by means of questions and answers between Jesus and his closest and most trusted male and female disciples....Sophia guides us through the bondage and liberation of humankind. Liberation comes through Faith (Pistis) and the mysteries of the Christ and the Eternal Father-Mother, manifesting through an inner awakening of the lesser Sophia..... Her fall into the lower worlds initiates a catastrophe that cascades into a rapid sequence of events, bringing about for all of humanity an increasing alienation from our divine origin and a separation from the Infinite Light.....The final restoration is to be revealed by Jesus Christ through purification of the thoughts of Self-Willed, the revelation of the mystery of the forgiveness of sins and the infinite compassion poured forth from the first mystery.." (Hurtak: *Gnostism Mystery of Mysteries*)

The Gnostics had a much more expansive notion of Creation and the Universe than the "God on his throne, looking down on his children beneath". They teach that the God of the Old Testament (Jehovah) we commonly worship, is actually a lesser Creator-God; the Demiurge, maker of all animal bodies and material substances; a deficient image of God, who is under the illusion that he alone is the all powerful "I am a jealous God, there is none other besides me" (Genesis), in the same way that the ego thinks itself an autonomous agent. This explains why the Gnostics considered the World of matter and in extension the physical body, as "evil" i.e.; a not belonging and incompatible energy.

Gnostic cosmology describes a Divine Source, which is ineffable and cannot be known or described, only perceived by its reflection. With an innate creative purpose to "Know Itself", this Source gives birth to itself in pairs of "Emanations", which we understand as Male and Female. At its pinnacle is "the Height"; a pure divine realm containing a complicated and staggering array of Powers, Invisibles, Helpers and Treasuries. Then there is a secondary complex "Aeonic" system containing 13 divisions and 24 Invisibles and 2 Triple powers. In the myth these are all symbolically brought to life as Archetypes. Two of these Aeons of creation are Pistis (Faith) and Sophia (Wisdom). The two upper primal realms are known as the "Pleroma" and are in direct descendence with pure creative force.

Programmed within the Divine Creative Process is the energy of Free Will. It is through this that an aspect of Sophia (her Highest Aspect is indivisible and stays within the Pleroma) is "seduced" by Self-Will to enter lower realms and she becomes trapped by her desire. She finds herself in the darkness of chaos and her light-power taken from her. Using her captured light and grief the lower worlds are created by the Demiurge. Sophia quickly realizes her predicament and calls out to Christ for her redemption. In this she goes through a series of "repentances" for Christ to hear her. She recounts everything that happened to her and realizes her lack of discernment, like a confession, as she recognizes she must take on an entirely new consciousness: "In believing that the light was yours (Divine Source) …. I am bereft of my light…for the light has hearkened to the matter, and will not leave a substance without its purification.." She actively calls for assistance and deliverance by affirming her Faith (Pistis). The message shows that true repentance is the ability to bring about a change on all levels of spiritual attunement so that the old thought forms are no longer present, and bringing new thought forms in alignment with the living light.

The story of Christ here is the bringing of renewed Divine Vibration to the worlds that lie between the High Heaven and Earth. These realms are governed by lesser gods who have become separated from direct Divine Rule after the Fall. Holding Adamic Man, as well as many other worlds, in a limited state of evolution by constricting our consciousness. Christ, due to his purity of High Vibration is uniquely qualified to unlock the gates or "seals" that maintain this limited vibratory level within the nature of Soul-Spirit. He does this by knowing their "names", which act like codes of entry. Christ is in knowledge (Gnosis) of their Divine Origin, which they themselves have forgotten.

Christ is therefore a unifying consciousness of all the worlds of the Cosmos, and in being so, prepares to make possible the ascension of man in accordance to Divine Plan or Purpose – starting with the redemption of Sophia, through the Logos;

the Living Creative Word; one of the highest emanations of the God-force. It is this what the Gnostics understand as the Second Coming, and it is believed by many that these ancient texts have been discovered at this time, nearly 2000 years after they were conceived, because human consciousness has reached sufficient prepared critical mass to receive this information and enter a "New Age" of awakening. On the human level, the purification of the individual leading to self-unity and the final Gnosis is often spoken of in terms of the adept gathering together the soul-stuff scattered throughout his body... Psychosynthesis!

It is worth noting that in this text, it is Mary Magdalene who asks the most questions to Jesus. She, whom Jesus "loved beyond all others". The Feminine, or, the power of Eve, has been regarded as the lesser power by the male-dominated priesthood, but now Jesus will reveal that he has come to re-instate the creative power with the light. Mary Magdalene, like Sophia, once a "fallen woman", who had seven demons cast out of her, exemplifies the purification of the Light; of the Sophia that is being cleansed and raised up to the motherhood of a new creation on all seven levels of conscious reality. Jesus' work with the Divine Shekinah is to restore and elevate the lesser Sophia, and the three Mary figures connected with his ministry in this world exemplifies this emergence. This is why Jesus was manifested through the Virgin Mary; to bring Divine Spirit into the Earthly Mother. And this shows how important it was for Jesus to have female disciples. The redemption of Sophia by the Christ is often described as a marriage; a union, predestined and necessary for the execution of Divine Purpose. Sophia is described by the mystics as "the beloved bride". The marriage of Jesus and Mary Magdalene, whether actual or symbolic, was no secret to the Gnostics.

Misogynism was deeply engrained in Orthodox Jewish Culture; Eve was "made" from Adam's rib to be his "helper", "she" was therefore subservient to "he", as well as blaming Eve, and therefore all women, for the expulsion from the Garden of Eden as punishment for eating the fruit of the Tree of Knowledge of Good and Evil. "To the woman he (Jehovah) said: I will greatly increase your pains in childbearing; with pain you will give birth to children. Your desire will be for your husband, and he will rule over you." (Genesis)

Jesus' tolerance and active inclusion of female disciples was deeply offensive to many, including one of his own most well known disciples, Simon Peter. His aggression is remarked upon by Jesus and fellow disciples in the scriptures. Nevertheless, and not surprisingly, he was later appointed Father of the Christian Church and Catholic keeper of the Key of Heaven.

THE THREAT OF THE FEMININE

"The Secret Book of John" gives us an altogether different interpretation of the "wickedness" of Eve that the Orthodox Church has used to justify its systematic and brutal suppression of the feminine voice throughout our patriarchal history. Rather than Eve being born from Adam's rib, and therefore subordinate, the Secret Book explains that, out of compassion for Adam (Adamic man), the Mother-Father sent him:
"a helper – Luminous Epinoia (creative or inventive consciousness) which comes out of him, who is called life (Eve); and she "helps" the whole creation, by working with him, and by restoring him to his full being, and by teaching him about the descent of his kind, and by showing him the way to ascend"....
"Thus Eve symbolises the gift of spiritual understanding.... The secret book explains that, although God is essentially incomprehensible, the powers that reveal God to humankind include "pronoia" (anticipatory awareness) "ennoia" (internal reflection) and "prognosis" (foreknowledge or intuition), all personified as Feminine presences, presumably because of the gender of the Greek words. But according to the Secret Book it is, above all, the "Luminous Epinoia" that conveys genuine insight." (Elaine Pagels, *The Gnostic Gospels*)
This explains why the Feminine was so respected and revered by the Gnostics. Women were absolute equals and preached and performed baptisms alongside their male counterparts. Something the Orthodox Church was deeply horrified by. For what the Feminine symbolized was nothing less than a path to Spiritual Freedom, threatening the very foundation of the hierarchal church.

A PATENT ON GOD

"The height of arrogance is the height of control of those who create God into their own image" Rhamta, channelled by J.Z. Knight. From *What the (bleep) do we know.*

Perhaps the greatest tragedy and crime against humanity has been that the (exoteric) teachings of Jesus the Christ have been systematically distorted beyond all recognition, and used to smother everything his message stood for, supposedly in his name. The "hidden", esoteric meaning of the teachings of Christ were lost to the many, but bravely kept alive by the few. Many sects of followers increasingly had to go underground for centuries to come, hiding from the tyranny of those who sought to build a hierarchical church, claiming superiority through tailored scriptures to suit their own political needs, which were certainly not open to interpretation.

The early church father Iraneus (130 -202), bishop of Lyons and very much a literalist, nurtured the hope that all Christians everywhere should unite in one church, following the teachings of an authoritative canon, which was to be the guideline for any writing or preaching. Seeking to stem the increasing fragmentation of Christians around the world he wrote his own "definitive" work entitled "Against all Heresies". In this he aggressively condemns the many different testimonies, such as the gospel of Thomas, the book of James and the gospel of Mary, and those who followed them, as "apocryphal and illegitimate, evil interpretations". To Iraneus, Satan was inspiring these so-called spiritual teachers, causing a dangerous threat to the unity of the church and he declared them heretics, frauds and liars. He further claimed that only the gospels of Mark, Luke, Matthew and most importantly John, were "authentic" eyewitness accounts of the life and teachings of Christ.

In the fourth century, under the rule of the newly converted roman emperor Constantine, the construction of a Christian empire began. A coalition of Bishops from churches throughout the empire were instructed to convene at Nicaea to work out a standard formulation of Christian faith and bring about the unity that Iraneus had called for a few centuries earlier. From that historic meeting emerged what is now known as the Nicean Creed, which would effectively clarify "the canon of truth"; the list of 27 writings which would become the New Testament. Henceforth, and to this day, all "revelations" endorsed by Christian leaders would have to agree with this gospel. Aside from deciding on a definitive canon, Athanasius, the then bishop of Alexandria, called for the church to be cleansed from every "defilement" and "apocryphal books". Some courageous Egyptian monks, near the town of Nag Hammadi, defied this order and hid more than fifty books in jars in the desert, where they were discovered in 1947. We owe it to them that we even know about the diversity of early Christian experience, from what became known as the "Gnostic Gospels".

Elaine Pagels in her books 'The Gnostic Gospels' and 'Beyond Belief' investigates the history and nature of the argument against these "other" gospels; why they were deemed so very dangerous to the established church as to prompt such aggressive condemnation and a barbaric inquisition. She focuses her attention on the Gospel of St Thomas and concludes that the gospel of John; pillar of the orthodox canon, was written in the heat of controversy to defend one version of Jesus over that of others:

"What John opposed includes what the gospel of Thomas teaches - that God's light shines not only in Jesus, but potentially in everyone. Thomas's Gospel encourages the hearer not so much to believe in Jesus, as John requires, as to seek to know God through one's own divinely given capacity.... Thomas's gospel draws the different conclusion that the divine light Jesus embodied is shared by humanity, since we are all made in the image of God... Thus Thomas expresses what would later become a central theme in Jewish - and later Christian - Mysticism a thousand years later: That the "image of God" is in everyone, although most people remain unaware of his presence."

John's gospel vehemently denies this; Jesus is unique and different from you and me, man has no innate ability to know God, only through believing in his one and only son Jesus can we find Divine Truth. He also sets out to further damage Thomas's credibility by describing him as a faithless disciple; a "doubting Thomas", because he seeks to verify truth from his own experience. With the re-discovery of these suppressed texts at Nag Hammadi, history shows that early Christians held a very different understanding of the gospel and many of Thomas's contempories revered him as an extraordinary apostle, entrusted with Jesus' "secret words".

THE CATHARS

That Gnosticism is not a homogenous movement is illustrated in the fact that it was the Gospel of John that the Cathars used as their main scripture. The Dualist Catharism was the dominant "religion" of southern France and Northern Italy in the 12th and 13th century. The male Parfaits and female Parfaites entered their priesthood later in life after having served a useful life in the community and gained experience in the sufferings and joys of earthly living. These "perfects" were elders in the true sense of the word. It was their level of consciousness; their inner purity, that determined their election as priests.

Catharism was, like original Christianity, a religion of emanation. Christ was understood to be distinguished above all others by his highly developed psychic capacities such as clairvoyance and the healing of hands. These gifts were not peculiar to just himself but he could ignite others by his own emanation or transmission: The attuning, purifying and strengthening of another's energy body through the potency of one's own. The Parfaits were evolved human beings who developed these gifts within themselves through meditation, fasting, celibacy, initiation and total dedication to the emanation of Goodness (hence their title of bonhommes – "good men"). They understood this earthly world as hell because in it we only achieved our lowest level of sensitivity. Evil is the absence of good and made by Satan. Evil therefore pre-existed the formation of this planet – metaphorically speaking; the Fall occurred in Heaven, not in Eden. God however, is pure love and it was this purity of goodness they connected to when healing and preaching. To the Cathars, the soul was a perpetual active channel of communication between the ego and the spirit and the plane on which the battle of good and evil was fought. The immortal psyche/soul could become purified by living a "good" life throughout its many cycles of incarnation. This needed no intermediary and so was a major obstacle to the Catholic Church which sought to gain control over Cathar lands.

As man purified him- or her- self through leading a blameless life, the Cathars had no belief or need for the doctrine of Grace; something dispensed by the Catholic priesthood in the form of absolutions and privileges; a highly profitable source of ecclesiastical revenue.

In fact, all sacraments held sacred by the Orthodox Church were rejected by the parfaits and their croyants (believers). The Eucharist; the bread and wine turning into the body of Christ, was deemed a pagan derivative of older myth and, as Catharism insisted that the Son of God was not incarnate in the flesh, the whole notion of transubstantiation was to them utterly meaningless. They also did not think much of the sacrament of marriage. Although strongly in favor of its institution, they did not believe that a bona fide union between lovers depended on grace bestowed upon them. They did not consider sexual contact as sinful or taboo and then somehow sanctified at the moment of wedlock. The only sacrament practiced by the Cathars was the Consolamentum, in which the recipient abjures the flesh and dedicates him/herself to the life of spirit. This was administered to the croyants at the point of imminent death, but also used as a primary initiation for the Parfaits.

In this the Parfait had to have achieved such a level of transcendence to be able to leave the physical body and move his/her entire consciousness into the etheric body at will. As Christ on the cross, they had to resist all forms of torture applied to them.

"Do not have pity on the flesh born of corruption, but have pity on the spirit put in prison"…This would explain accounts of Parfaits burning alive on the pyres without appearing to suffer.

This pivotal initiation indicated that the Parfait was capable of further training. The aim was to increase in a controlled fashion (as happened in the many mystery schools throughout history) the psychic power of the individual, to facilitate the ability to heal and to travel astrally to the bedside of those who needed attendance, and, most adeptly, to develop the capacity to emanate to others something of his/her inner pure self. Meditation was only practiced by the Parfaits, as it was recognized that, for those not ready and mature enough for the experience, there was the danger of invasion by lower entities. In fact, mental illness was understood as "initiation gone wrong" in this or a previous lifetime.

They will therefore have understood the force of utter evil that came to root them out; an exoteric church where the level of consciousness of its priests held no importance and doctrine overrode goodness. The pope granted those taking part in the "crusade" full absolution of all sins committed before and in the future. This no doubt contributed to the level of sadistic barbarism that followed. The inquisition, presided over by the Dominican order, was specifically set up in 1233 to erase Catharism. This blood-soaked continuation of self-righteous suppression of dissent set out to abort man's attempt to connect to the true Christ. They systematically dispossessed, starved, tortured and killed, men, women and children with indiscriminate hatred. Justifying and absolving themselves with their own empty sacraments and man-made scriptures. The rooting out of this enlightened culture took seventy years – the inquisition lasted for seven hundred… its former head, now the present pope. The Cathars had removed from people the fear of hell, the very fear on which the Catholic Church had built its empire. As the physical world was created by the lower entity of Satan, life on this planet was hell. The papal inquisition did everything to prove this point.

THEN AND NOW

In order to reclaim our rich and rightful spiritual heritage, we need to understand what we lost and why it is worth our utmost spiritual endeavor to recover that which constitutes our true power.

Somehow Gnostic ideas subsequently survived underground within secret societies such as the Rosicrucians, re-emerging in modern times in the work of influential transpersonal thinkers such as Carl Jung and Roberto Assagioli. Gnosticism itself is therefore evolving. Maybe it would be more useful to speak of a spirit of Gnosticism; an attitude of enquiry building on respect, but not blind acceptance, of the esoteric Wisdom acquired throughout the ages. Certainly issues such as the Gnostic rejection of Matter need to be critically re-evaluated by the modern mind struggling to come into right relationship with our planet.

For the purpose of this enquiry, a picture thus emerges:

Orthodox:	Mystical/Gnostic:
Exoteric	Esoteric
Literalism	Symbolism/ Allegory
Outward Manifestation	Inner essence
Creation	Co-creation
Knowledge	Wisdom
Subjugation	Initiation
The written Word/ scripture	Inner Experience
The Crucified Christ	The Risen Christ
Believing	Knowing
Doctrine	Revelation
Hierarchy	Equality
Male	Male and Female
Original sin	Dualism

"For the Christian Gnostics, the crucifixion of Jesus was not the final crucifixion; the true crucifixion took place in Rome when the ecclesiastical councils insisted upon confining the representation of Jesus to his incarnation under the Virgin Mary – neglecting his existence as the Cosmic Christ and reducing the Holy Spirit to a formula. Not only was the Sophia Bride of the Coptic teachings lost, but also the Chokmah of the ancient teachings de-emphasized. In consolidating Christianity, the early church limited the workings of the Holy Spirit."
(Freke & Gandy)

Enacted time and time again, is the great conspiracy to claim a "patent on God"; to claim to be "chosen" and so to be beyond all human law. In the eyes of the Gnostics this is the delusion of the Self-will. We are our own Demiurge, believing ourselves "holier than thou". In our world today it is the literalists; the fundamentalists, who are not just persecuting the "Gnostics", but are fighting each other for supremacy, as they have done for millennia.

Recently the chief rabbi Andrew Sachs remarked in an interview on BBC radio 4 that: *"To be a spiritual leader is to be guardian of the word, the scriptures. Leaving the scriptures without interpretation is like leaving nuclear fuel without insulation"*.
He was speaking in the context of Islamic and Jewish fundamentalism and was quite rightly emphasizing the responsibility of church leaders to guide their followers mindfully in light of recent conflict. However, history tells us that to claim a "just" interpretation per say, is treading contentious and dangerous ground.

Where there is definition there is limitation. The written word can only ever be an approximation of something indescribable which can only be received through inner experience. As the prophets, the visionaries, the mystics and the Gnostics were all wise to. "The letter kills, but the spirit gives life."(Paul). They teach us we need to be seekers, not believers, and be actively involved in our spiritual growth, knowing we are all One. This is a more demanding God than the one who just tells us what to do. This is a God that calls to re-unite us with our inner magnificent source. Jesus the Christ, we now discover, taught us Truth is found within us; in the purified, compassionate heart; That the Living Word or "Logos" is the guide on the path that leads to Sophia and her Gnosis. It is to be perceived in silence and designed to be an inner expansive force.

The Gnostics were by no means a marginal few. There were many schools and sects across Asia Minor. Best known are the Simonians who followed the teachings of Simon Magus and, by extension, John the Baptist, and the Paulists, inspired by the "unadulterated" revelations of Paul. Two influential Paulist teachers Marcion and Valentinus became in turn founding fathers of a variety of Gnostic sects all over the world, which includes the Cathars, offering multiple insights which reflected a Magnificent Unknowable Cosmos of untold diversity. They were right at the centre of the true teaching of Christ, and thrived on open debate. Their unwillingness to define and therefore limit themselves into an organized stronghold was perhaps their downfall when faced with "God's Literalist Army". But their consciousness survives; as above so below, we carry this within us. It is our greatest, most precious secret....

As a Hindu story goes..: When the Gods argued on where to hide the secret of the Universe, one said: "Let's put it inside the human being...they'll never find it...." Roberto Assagioli, like many others, took on the search and set out to develop a creative path of guidance suitable for the consciousness of our day. He developed a psychological language and discipline to ground this work, so insight can be translated into remedial action. It is time to re-fortify the Gnostic within ourselves and find our inner Christ – and name this light by whatever feels true, because it is not its definition that counts, but its freedom. This is our birthright; our human essence.

"Peace be with you - may my peace arise
and be fulfilled within you!
Be vigilant, and allow no-one to mislead you
By saying:
"Here it is!" or
"There it is!"
For it is within you
That the Son of Man dwells.
Go to him,
For those who seek him, find him.
Walk forth,
And announce the gospel of the Kingdom."
 (From the Gospel of Mary Magdalene.)

Good news indeed…..

BIBLIOGRAPHY

Armstrong, K.: *'A History of God'* – *The 4000-year Quest of Judaism, Christianity and Islam.* Vintage 1999.

Barnstone,W. & Meyer, M.(eds) : *'The Gnostic Bible'.* Boston & London 2006.

Freke,T. & Gandy, P.: *'Jesus And The Goddess'* – *The secret teachings of the original Christians.* Thorsons 2001.

Guirdham, A.: *'The Great Heresy'* – *History and Beliefs of the Cathars.* The C.W. Daniel Company LTD 1993.

Harvey, A.: *'Son of Man'* – *the mystical path to Christ.* Tarcher / Putman 1999

Bible – *new international version.* Hodder & Stoughton 2000

Hurtak, J.J.: *'Gnosticism: Mystery of Mysteries'.* The Academy for Future Science 1999

Hurtak, J.J. & Hurtak, D.: *'Pistis Sophia '* – *A Coptic Gnostic Text with Commentary.* The Academy for Future Science 1999

Leloup, J.Y.: *'The Gospel of Mary Magdalene'* Inner Traditions 2002

Pagels, E.: *'The Gnostic Gospels'.* Penguin Books 1990

Pagels, E.: *'Beyond Belief'* – *The secret gospel of Thomas.* Pan 2005

Picknett, L & Prince, C.: *'The Templar Revelation'* – *Secret Guardians of the true identity of Christ.* Corgi Books 1998

Picknett, L.: *'The Secret History of Lucifer'* Robinson 2006.

from ANAMNESIS

THE REMEMBERING OF SOUL, 3

Jay Ramsay

What is the gift of your life ?

Beyond naming, an utterance
in your throat's depth, your soul's
intention to live –

Can you recall it ?
You sit in meditation, surrounded by stars.

What are you living for ?
There is an answer so personal
so passionate, beyond all conceiving
in your innermost coding –
that your secret may die with you,
but not before you've had the chance
to witness its luminous traces.

And she, he is your answer
that other one nearest of all within
who shines in you like an icon, a sun.

What else is there ? The spiral climb
hearing your name called through the mist,
ever-stretched towards your blue potential
true self's surrender, that is the only way home.

WARM JUSTICE

CHEAP HOLIDAY IN OTHER PEOPLE'S MISERY?

Keith Hackwood

a communiqué from the belly of the penal machine

Four months ago I began working as a psychosynthesis counsellor in a Category B Local Men's prison. This article is part of my response to the challenges and vicissitudes of my experience so far, in the manner of a communiqué from the belly of the penal machine. Perhaps it is my call to be seen by my peers, and indeed to share with you the strange vapours which spume up from the fumaroles of her majesty's pleasure.

Prisons are in the news again recently, usually in reference to the overcrowding crisis and its effects on any meaningful engagement with the ideological Vaseline of 'rehabilitation'. Despite (and indeed because of) the media coverage and the 'facts' of the situation presented, my confirmed hunch is that few people in society actually have an awareness of what prison means at the start of the twenty-first century, both as experience and as vessel for the processing of difference. Which is interesting since, in a fairly mundane way (and as made plain in Bo Lozoff's book of the same title) 'we're all doing time'. If I allow my hunch to expand further I encounter within myself the question 'how do I, as a counsellor and as a human being, engage directly with the machinery of collective punishment?' After all, this institution represents my will as a member of society, a taxpayer no less, in operation.

Reflections on this theme can be confusingly visceral, requiring new and unexpected shapes within depth-ethics, stretching the plasma of thought between the heart and the head with seemingly impossible contortions of will and synthesis. Yet to ignore the question is to slip back into the comfortable inertia of the primal split. To be recuperated into 'them not me' thinking. In response to paradox perhaps the Grail question becomes necessary, after all whom does this serve?

E WING ECOSYSTEMS

My experience of prison as an environment in which to practice as a counsellor raises more fundamental questions. Is it even possible to form effective therapeutic relationships in an environment of institutionalised authority, denial, punitive action and tangible fear? Assuming that by some fortuitous grace therapeutic work is feasible, can it breathe in this Saturnine place? Can it survive the powerlessness of the individual (any individual, counsellors included) under the weight of the system? Even the most basic needs cannot be taken for granted – our 'professional' sacred cows have no green pastures on the other side of the wall and the architecture of power enthrones Security as master, the power behind the throne of Capital – guarantor of the status quo. This has immediate implications on space and time; for a start there are more locked doors than we ever need 'on the out', (literal barriers requiring the counsellor to wear keys in order to get around, keys that symbolise movement, freedom, power and which glow during sessions unable to contain their own florid symbolism any longer) doors with bars and grilles, barbed wire gates.

Then there's the structure of the day, dictated by lock up times and meals and limiting the maximum theoretical client time to four hours each day. Beyond these factors emerges the grey area of relationships with other staff, in particular uniformed officers and medical staff. Being predicated in the same Victorian gestalt as the buildings themselves the 'system' recognises only uniforms and, naturally, the medical (i.e. 'scientific' or 'value-free') model. Hence scruffy young counsellors can expect a status within the hierarchy varying anywhere between demi-god (perceived as being almost as 'high' as a doctor) and inmate, with behaviours and responses conditioned accordingly. Generally an air of unease and suspicion prevails, since a system in crisis has little time for innovation, yet can equally ill afford accusations of ignoring 'progress'. Within the liminal tectonic slippage of these two positions another space can open up, one in which it is poeisis not dogma that provides the greenish phosphorescent glow. Individually, relationships can and do 'work with what is' enough to allow a range of therapeutic options to be offered, from yoga to one-to-one counselling, even drama and movement therapy. Even in the harshest of environments some plutonic shoots push up. This is achieved at some cost to one's idealism, and often against the backdrop of polarised angst, prisoners accusing officers of brutality and violence, officers struggling to fit human shaped flesh and blood into the square metal boxes provided by the system. To be stood between this Scylla and Charibdys is as daunting as it is exhilarating.

BE REASONABLE, DEMAND THE IMPOSSIBLE

It seems to me that the prison environment neatly summarises the fullness of society's paradoxical relationship with wellbeing and integration, and in doing so constellates the core effects of male wounding. This is not insignificant, especially since the patriarchal paradigm is alive and well and continues to dominate thought, action and belief structures throughout our contemporary world. The inmates represent one side of the split, one colour of wounding, whilst the authority and those who wear it's uniform and take it's pay cheques embody the polarity. It is impossible to avoid the radiation of this split, which manifests in every action and interaction inside the walls. It reinforces the violence of the system itself, and therefore the violence expressed in impotent rage against it. It constellates the operational ceiling of power, requiring obeisance from each participant in its rituals. It becomes the field arising from the ground of being, an unacknowledged ideology invisibly unpicking the threads and stitches of power, desperate to hold the edges of the wound apart even further, to insist upon its own agony, making blood sacrifices to avoid change.

Prison infantilises inmates and staff because it is entirely predicated on the efficient operation of a closed system. It does not recognise individuals. Yet many crimes contain within them a raw desire for individuation and many incarcerated criminals have actively rejected some aspect of externally imposed morality or law. Hence the polarity between woundedness in officers and inmates is most dense around these issues of individuation. The natural tendency for officers is to collectivise, conjoin, seek validation and safety in numbers. The ultimate sanction of prison in the UK is solitary confinement – the very denial of the social, the insistent leading edge of difference, the actualised outsider. In my experience and in general, prisoners exhibit much more readily a tolerance for individual choice and co-operation with change, whereas the officers retain a surly teenage narrow-mindedness in the face of their own wounding. To assert any common humanity between the two sides is more difficult for an officer – it implies that in a very real sense he is the same as the person he is locking up.

En masse the prison service is caught by a paranoia created through its very raison d'etre – it sits within the contexts of capital and hierarchy, believing in its own efficacy and power, expressed negatively through confinement, isolation and punitive regimes. Like Ken Wilber's developmental stage of 'Role-Rep Mind' the individuals who service the system are first required to be consumed by it. It functions like some Terrible Mother, obliterating the horizon, dominating reality with its vast reach. Men in uniform remain boys. Inmates encounter this force through compulsion, not choice – and the dehumanising process is engaged. Where does therapy enter this skewed world, and, vitally, how can it engage with the woundedness of the men within this world, whichever 'uniform' they wear?

In my view this question is almost entirely unconscious. The doctors, nurses, CPN's, psychologists, drug-workers and psychiatrists inside the walls line up opposite the rapists, murderers, armed robbers, car thieves and drug dealers. The energies spiral into the search for 'cures' and 'treatments' but neglect the context of the operation. They neglect the complexities of individual situations, personal (and karmic) histories, they operate within the scientific-positivist paradigm that informs the meta-system of our state itself and is thus 'beyond question'. No-one speaks of healing, no-one speaks of soul, no-one speaks of initiation or archetypal patterns. The transference and counter-transference of power loops endlessly, in many fundamental respects this is no different than any prison in history, existing primarily to isolate and punish, but couching this bare attention in newspeak. Treatment actually means control, cures mean the successful recuperation of an inmate into society. But it is society that is criminalized in such manoeuvres, society that represses and splits off its 'criminal' subpersonalities into the dungeons of the unconscious, in each of us, and acted out in large scale in so many of our institutions and structures.

A cut-off subpersonality will fester and erupt, unable to give its energy to the whole instead it will bleed that life force out of the whole, to empower its own isolated rage. And yet each subpersonality, whether supposedly 'positive' or 'negative' belongs to that whole, relates to it, contains within it the seed of its own redemption or reintegration. Each has formed in response to the fractals of that being through time as they endlessly transform. My belief, and perhaps the point of this article, is that in order for the social whole, the collective of our being, to know itself more completely it must first reintegrate its repressed subpersonalities. In this example, prisons, but the dynamics are as true for economic classes or any institutionalised reifications of power.

Cut-off subpersonalities need to be re-engaged. Their energy is necessary to the balanced health of the whole organism. Living behind protective repression is under-living on a tragic scale, for a population or community as for an individual. As above, so below. Somehow the creative, soulful, wise, just and beautiful dimensions of our being must turn towards the vilified, ugly, monstrous, dangerous and deformed – must welcome their inclusion, acknowledge their co-humanity and uniqueness. The vehicle for this meeting can vary – in my experience it is called compassion. A politics of compassion would acknowledge the vast inequalities, injustices and suffering in every atom of our world – our unification through a common core of transience and suffering, Ichtion's Wheel, Boethius's rise and fall, Samsara. But there is another universal chord, another sacred geometry in the matrix of our connection – that is our imagination, the Christ-like part of humanity that led William Blake to assert that 'every thing that lives is holy', we are each ablaze with 'delicate tenuities', with the 'eruption of the marvellous' which even now sneak under the quickened pace of capital's lust for monopoly of interpretation.

Imagination is painful, much more so than physical injury or wounding. And yet the absence of imagination is a cold entropic death, a state of non-being. Dare we awaken collectively to our own painful imagination, our own origination in the fires of necessity? It is interesting to recall at this point that Roberto Assagioli, founder of Psychosynthesis and an Italian Jew, was himself imprisoned by Mussolini's fascists in 1938 and lost his son as a result of this experience. He was also known for describing himself as a 'thief', making psychosynthesis the hoarding of a lifetime's diverse and imaginal loot, for the benefit of all.

An echo that recognizes the existence of the other
and does not overpower or attempt to silence it.
> (Our Word Is Our Weapon, Subcommandante Insurgente
> Marcos, Zapatista Communique)

In conclusion, and returning to prison, the question remains, can therapy be effective as an agent for integration on a personal and collective level, within the system? I have no answer. I know that the attempts to encounter answers involve the risk of 'being shot by both sides'. I know that lasting answers will not emerge from reactionary authority nor liberal consensus. I know that the status quo is seething with eruptive potential, the caldera shows signs of activity, an eruption is long overdue. In immediate human terms the issues blossom in many colours – sexual and physical abuse, drug dependency and addiction, the limitless anger of the infant and the nihilism of the dispossessed. The puer and the senex continue to stare blankly at one another. Is it crude forms of social engineering or pill-fuelled medical intervention that will break this pattern and relieve the pressure? Is it behavioural programmes predicated on the reprogramming of desire, such as 'anger management' and 'correcting offending behaviour' courses now prescribed as part of an inmate's sentencing plan? Is it the success of corporate America and it's penal architecture, as in the new wave of hi-tech complete isolation 'supermax' prisons? Personally, I defy each of these. No transformation will be possible that depends upon crushing, bending or adapting an individual's will to fit the desired outcome of a system, or that requires the wearing of uniforms, the carrying of security equipment and the isolation of parts from the whole.

The crisis in our prisons is just the red shift of the crisis in our own hearts. As long as we remain ignorant of our human inheritance, as long as we look to externals for validation of our Selves, we remain imprisoned in our learned and dependent beliefs. Perhaps it is time to acknowledge that civilization is no more than a work in progress and that history has not ended. The world we created continues in its immiseration and alienation, underneath the cheap cynicism of mediation. It is against this background that we, if we be healers of any sort at all, must choose to act. We are indeed all doing time, and only the revolution of the heart will suffice.

ALL CRIMES ARE PAID

A Case Study, September 2002

Keith Hackwood

"Modern consciousness now suffers its own uncertainty principle, pressed to recognise that all its reflections do not extend beyond the prism, the prison, of its own unconsciousness, no matter how expanding the universe, how luring the moon."

James Hillman 'Notes on White Supremacy'

GOD SAVE HISTORY: PAST/PRESENT

I work as a counsellor within one of Her Majesty's Prisons, in fact a category B local men's prison, where I am employed for three days each week to deliver one-to-one counselling and group based work. In this case study my intention is to focus on three of my prison clients since these represent well the difficulties and inspirations, possibilities and frustrations of this work.

Clients are self-selecting and by 'application' can join a waiting list, often for months. Some referrals are made via other staff and some prioritisation of need is possible. At the outset I also need to mention supervision, which has been central to my capacity to work in the prison context at all. I shall explore in further detail throughout the integration of supervision insights into practice, as a form of vital 'second attention'. Often my own issues seemed as present & powerful as those of my clients, and focused on a species of ambivalence about whether anything resembling the Psychosynthesis I had trained in and sought after could ever take place in an environment of institutionalised punishment, despair and conflict. The theatre of imprisonment constructs its own relationship with individuals, whether as inmates, officers or counsellors, and the power dynamic is stark – The System comes first, the individual is entirely of secondary concern, when recognised at all. I recall wondering what madness I had stepped into, what symbolic understanding could possibly emerge here, where the brutal fundamentalism of monolithic, materialist and 'value-free' hegemony throw dirty shadows on the Victorian walls?

My longest piece of work in prison to date has been with a client called Rhodri and amounts to fifteen sessions. It is worth noting that Rhodri has made every session – making him unique in my experience of prison work. Rhodri is thirty-five years old, tall, solidly built, with dark hair and black sparkling, deep set eyes. His mouth often curls into a smile, revealing two rows of broken, spiny teeth. His body is visibly scarred, on both arms and on his chest, the result of two serious car accidents and several drug-induced collapses (including a stoned fall into a working cooker resulting in serious burns). Rhodri presents an ambivalence about being alive and has spent the past fifteen years addicted to intravenously administered amphetamine sulphate, heroin, and latterly, crack cocaine, all of which he also dealt. In prison for armed robbery, Rhodri's presenting issue revolved around his pain at being separated from his girlfriend Leanne, and their daughter. Leanne is herself in prison for a copycat offence – they're both serving four years.

As with all my prison clients, except those without security clearance to attend (meaning they are regarded as a risk, of being violent, escaping or hostage taking), Rhodri and I meet in the prison's only counselling room, located above the hospital wing and equipped with a surveillance camera for constant observation of sessions. This is a room with sealed, barred windows, two chairs and a table. Its carpeted, considerably larger than a cell, and offers clients a degree of privacy and 'objective normality' otherwise completely absent from their experience.

Sometimes clients are brought to and from sessions by a prison officer, although staff shortages deriving from the well known crisis in the prison system often prevents this, in which case I escort my own clients. Hence, for better or for worse, I wear a key belt and chain and have access to all areas of the prison (the issue of whether to carry keys was highly charged and unavoidably symbolic for me, constellating relative power and freedom into the body of all sessions in starkly visible form, uncomfortably so at first).

Returning to Rhodri, a strong factor in his presentation for counselling relates to his fear at having his sentence increased (the Crown has been pursuing an appeal with this outcome in mind) – this is his first prison sentence, and it has made a huge impact upon him. The uncertainty around this appeal seemed unjust to Rhodri, his belief was 'they're just fucking with my head'. Most noticeable in his time inside prison has been his withdrawal from and emerging new relationship to drugs. For the first time in fifteen years Rhodri is clean, and his perspective on his own life is radically different, much more visceral and sharp than it could ever have been through a decade and a half of self-administered anaesthesia. After an initial session of history taking, it became apparent that we could work together – Rhodri was in a place where he was prepared to engage with and face himself, he was drug free (and taking weekly voluntary 'piss tests' to prove it) and recognised the weekly hour together as a space to express himself ('I haven't talked this much since coming inside, you can't just lay this shit on people'). This was made clear to me through his range of emotional presence, moving between tears of grief through anger to a clear statement of the 'life or death' nature of his experience, 'I am in prison because something's got to change'. The symbol of this transforming hope very quickly became his three year old daughter, Joely. Rhodri and I agreed to an initial contract of six sessions, to be reviewed at that point with a view to continuing.

The second client I have chosen to include I call Ray. As with Rhodri, we reached an agreement to work 'six sessions at a time', following his introduction at supervision. Ray is forty seven years old, on remand awaiting trial for attempted murder. His presenting issue was very specific, relating to startling memories of his time as a soldier in the British army serving in Northern Ireland during the early 1970s. The fact of being in prison unoccupied for long stretches of time, as well as the physical environment itself, with it's locked doors, barbed wire, uniformed guards and every other trapping of state power, became a terrifying nightmare world, where memories of his military service haunted both waking and sleeping. Ray had lost friends to IRA shootings in Londonderry and bombings in Belfast; he had even participated in putting down a riot at the Maze prison. His descriptions of events past and present and their collision through his own experience suggested the possibility of fairly extensive post traumatic stress disorder. Initially I felt my own potential for being overwhelmed by Ray's visceral imagery, and yet I had made post traumatic stress the subject of my presentation to the training group during the final term of Synthesis. Could this be why, to help me meet Ray? Or was it my first opportunity to be spectacularly exposed as inexperienced, as a fraud?

With the support of my supervision group I found my willingness to find out which, to put myself in the situation as fully as I could. Sessions soon became more expansive, Ray's life history (one of broken relationships, children he hadn't seen in twenty years, dead end jobs and a lingering sense of 'is this all there is?') was dominated by the upright gleam of the military, from a childhood moving around the UK and Germany following his father's RAF career, to his own army service (between 18 and 26 years) and what he referred to as 'the unravelling of my life' at the point of leaving service. I began to see how Ray had experienced the army as abandoning mother, how being in prison now was a source of almost uncontainable irony, shame and outrage. His anger was a new energy, a fuel, a sense of injustice propelling him full tilt towards his own culpability, his own isolation and loneliness. Much as this expression felt authentic and necessary, such anger in this context and from a man on a charge of attempted murder was extremely challenging to work and stay present with for me. I focused on boundaries almost exclusively and felt him respond, remembering Brown's adage "aggression against those simultaneously loved is guilt". Where was Ray's guilt?

Ray is a solidly built, powerful man, with cropped greying hair, big arms and a boxer's face. In fact he closely resembles the actor Ray Winstone, celebrated for portraying hard men and gangsters – hence christening him 'Ray'. My good fortune, and his assistance of me, was discovering his capacity for visual imagery and muscular metaphorical reflection. We worked with relaxation techniques and guided imagery, and very quickly Ray began to meditate and study yoga, with immediate effects upon his volatility. He also joined the drama & movement therapy group, which I co-facilitate. This opening chink of alternative relationship to self, a change of perspective to his own suffering, Ray exploited to the full. I sensed that here was a man absolutely ripe for new experience, a broken child-like innocence looking for connection with something bigger than himself. Very soon my concern in our work moved away from mindfulness of my own safety and became primarily one of pacing, and ensuring adequate time for 'digestion' and linking up of insight, expression, catharsis and collapse. Ray and I have completed twelve sessions to date, and continue to work together.

My third client I call Damian. Unlike Ray and Rhodri, Damian had been denied security clearance to attend for counselling, meaning that I would have to go to him if we were to work together. The reason for this focused upon a history of violence, an assumed hostage-taking risk, and some institutionalised spite, for Damian has committed, and is serving a minimum of fifteen years for, rape. Unsatisfied with the imposed working conditions, even before meeting Damian, I was keen to clarify my options and responsibilities and some of the apparent risks. I was able to negotiate an agreement from the security officer that if after six sessions Damian had presented no risk, he would be allowed to have sessions in the counselling room (a carrot I dangled him readily). I also perused his security file (which was enormous, Damian having had multiple sentences in his short life), and his medical file. I found this material useful in preparing myself to meet Damian, but of limited value thereafter. I was also reliant upon supervision, including additional telephone supervision around the time of my first few contacts with this client, in considering whether to work with him at all.

I first met Damian in his cell. As with all cells it was small, grim, overcrowded, heavy with the thick smell of two men's confined bodies and decorated with varying strengths of pornographic imagery carefully culled from newspapers and magazines (an ironic hell-realm, visually torturing anima in the service of momentary relief from abandonment). He struck me immediately as being highly suspicious of me, intense, as though he were carrying huge amounts of rage and anger. Twenty-five years old, shaven headed, like a powerful caged animal with sharp, clear eyes, Damian was checking me out every bit as much as I was assessing him. He asked me if I knew why he was in prison – I told him I'd read everything the prison had about him, he seemed unmoved. I asked him how he felt, and to my surprise he began to tell me how he couldn't remember the rape, it was 'as if I wasn't there'. He told me he felt remorse, but until he could feel the connection to actually having done it, he was confused, overwhelmed even. The length of his sentence was also of great concern to him.

Damian had a huge record of convictions, over 190, mostly for car thefts, ABH/GBH, the occasional opportunist burglary, but nothing else even remotely sexual in character. I asked him what had happened, why the rape? He said he didn't know, that he'd been alone in a stolen car and had taken cocaine, ecstasy, marijuana over many hours – he was lost, looking for directions to the motorway when he stopped a woman walking home. Then he kidnapped and raped her, before letting her go, saying 'is it any use me apologising?'

This ugly piece of bathos appalled me almost as much as the crime itself – why was this necessary, I asked myself? He told me he was aware of hoping that someone would kill him for what he had done, and that recently he had wondered about his relationship with his mother. I encouraged him to say more and he told me a story of neglect, care homes, youth offending and the almost complete absence of any significant mothering. He said his mother preferred it when he was detained (as he was consistently from aged eleven or so) since 'at least I know where you are and that you're safe'. He added, with venom, 'she'd say that, but she never once fucking visited me in there'. Issues with violence and with the feminine, the abandoning mother, seemed emergent and his degree of self-reflection impressed me more than I had imagined – there seemed enough here to work with. The cat neglected becomes the tiger, I wanted to get underneath that neglect partly to calibrate my own position as a counsellor, and partly because Damian opened up to me, became vulnerable.

In terms of presenting issue, Damian wanted to find a space to explore his own actions, his own pain, without feeling abandoned or punished. I was sure of his genuine motivation, but daunted, very uncertain of my own ability to be the person to go into this territory with him. As our first session ended he insisted I have a copy of his forensic psychiatric report, compiled for his trial, which I accepted. It is important to realise that as a 'sex-offender', Damian was entitled to 'go on the rule' (rule 45, the right of a person convicted of a sexual crime to be held in a segregated unit – usually for their own safety) yet in his own words Damian wants to avoid 'a mug's wing'. His insistence interested me – was it a way of distancing himself from the crime, being on a normal location, rather than separated into a specialist sex-crime wing? It also constellated Damian's thanatos drive, his desire for death, or at least the confrontation of the death threshold – there are plenty of other inmates willing to administer their own form of justice to someone like Damian, except that his well established capacity for violence, and his experience of the system over fourteen years, all conspired against this being easy or likely.

In reading the psychiatric report, and having access to all the statements relating to his case, including the victim and Damian, I noted that in the professional opinion of the assessing doctor, Damian suffers from dissocial personality disorder (ICD 10 F60.2) which is associated with his 'abnormally aggressive and seriously irresponsible conduct' and which is 'sufficient to meet the criteria for psychopathic disorder under the terms of the Mental Health Act 1983'. However, the recommendation was that hospitalisation would be of little benefit to Damian and that 'the interventions he requires can appropriately be provided within the prison system'. The report continued that Damian should be considered for a therapeutic prison environment, that he must complete a 'sex offenders treatment programme' (rather arbitrary and cognitive in structure) and that his prognosis was reasonable due largely to his motivation to change; however, its rather ominous conclusion stated:

'Prison authorities should also be aware that (Damian)'s personality disorder carries with it a significant risk of completed suicide in the medium and long term.'

No Future: context/systems

Before considering aspects of life history emergent through process with Rhodri, Ray and Damian, I will pause to develop the prison context that is always so overwhelmingly present. First there is the context of my employment – I am paid by the prison service, appointed after a drawn out process of security checks. I am now part of the 'us' that defines itself starkly against the 'them' of inmates, except that I don't have a uniform and I don't carry any security equipment. I have been trained in Control & Restraint, though I suspect more for my employer's insurance requirements than my own safety. Detail is evidently of great importance to the system – but this is not a place where therapy is recognised, let alone supported. The priorities are (as explained to me by a senior officer) the safety of staff, the smooth operation of the system, and finally the wellbeing of inmates. Everything that happens in prison is according to that hierarchy of 'needs'. The reason for this prison's apparently groundbreaking experiment in therapeutic interventions is driven by the prison service's concerns about deaths in custody. Suicide, or the fear of suicide, is the prime mover – my brief, if I have one, is to 'stop these people killing themselves, or at least warn us about who's most likely to do it'. I remain mindful of Assagioli's own experience of imprisonment.

However, the prison population presents significant suicidal ideation in around 50% of its membership at any one time. In 2001 there were 79 deaths in custody nationally, 64 in 2000. Overcrowding is rife and the combination of difficult, often unexpressed emotions, fear and isolation all feed into a meta-geometry of self-harm and fantasies of 'easeful death'. Official figures note that suicides are most likely to occur in the first week of custody, often within twenty-four hours, and that 88% of successful suicides are by hanging, typically using bedding as a ligature attached to cell bars or the cell door. My first day in the prison began with seeing the extremely distressed cellmate of a man who had, just the day before, hanged himself. Death is constantly present in this place, which is both Plutonic and Saturnian, an ante-chamber of hell populated by society's unacceptable and un-integrated subpersonalities. A final statistic of note – the general incidence of borderline personalities in the national population is generally reckoned to be around 2%, whereas for male prison populations the figure is around 14% (women's prisons reach 20%) – awareness of the significance of this information for counselling is vital. Could I invite 'death' as a therapeutic ally, an imaginal and symbolic reality rather than a piece of acted-out literalism? And could the system's monopoly of interpretation of death-as-inevitable-end be challenged, synthesised and re-contextualised within my clients' lived realities and within myself? These questions are reflected and held in each line of this case study, in the constant tension I feel between empathic overwhelm and closed-off distancing, they form part of my fundamental experience as a developing therapist, new striations in my own will.

Two of the clients I am focusing on, Rhodri and Damian, have a history of institutionalised care in adolescence. Rhodri was adopted at ten days old and lost his adopted mother at age ten years, on the day of the Silver Jubilee in 1977. Rhodri felt blamed for his mother's death, especially by his 'father' – their relationship deteriorated until his 'father' told him he was adopted, whilst physically kicking him down a flight of stairs. From this point Rhodri's life went underground, into drug taking and eventually drug dealing, making upwards of £10,000 a week selling heroin. He describes himself as having been quite a loner, having two major relationships in his life – a wife (now an ex-wife) with whom he had two children, and his current partner of five years, Leanne, and their three year old child. Rhodri had even tracked down his biological mother and met her some time before being imprisoned – but now feels too ashamed to contact her again, although fascinated and excited to discover seven half-sisters he knew nothing about.

Rhodri is also still in touch with the only man he has known as a father, now aged 82 and unwell, living in Norfolkshire and unable to visit. Their relationship has improved through absence and the passage of time, although as his father approaches his own death (with which he is, apparently, morbidly obsessed) he has seemingly tried to heal and resolve earlier dysfunction and pain. His chief tool in this, at least symbolically, has been the promise of a substantial inheritance for Rhodri, in family property and cash. Rhodri is ambivalent about this, although he clearly has a depth of real feeling for his father, especially in their regular exchange of letters and telephone calls. The likely inheritance affects Rhodri in various ways – it throws into sharp detail his ambivalence about being alive at all and it represents some level of acceptance by the family he was adopted into, yet excluded from. It also raises questions of responsibility, the possibility of an opportunity to break with the drug lifestyle and provide a stable, loving home for his child and partner. Rhodri exhibits an inferior 'feeling function', huge needs for love and recognition, and an omnipotence fantasy, cradling the left-over feelings no-one will take care of.

Much of our work has involved identifying and mapping the topography of Rhodri's will in relation to this possibility. He needs to be a father for his daughter. In order for this to be achievable he needs to experience parenting, and weed the drug addictions rooted deeply within that fertile soil. I have watched Rhodri physically change from an emaciated, deathly junkie to a fit looking and vital man. He has been successful to date in avoiding drugs (which are ubiquitous within the prison), although his fears of relapse are strong. In moments of connection with shadow, and in our consideration of his capacity for self-sabotaging, Rhodri identified the addiction to dealing as being his foremost fear. In his own words,

'I can't do any jobs, I haven't got any qualifications. Why spend eight hours a day being told what to do by some muppet when all I need is a mobile phone and I'm rich?'

Rhodri also had some experience of counselling, linked to a drug project he attended briefly, but as he says, he was just 'going through the motions'. Being locked up has faced Rhodri with the stark reality of his path to this point, and allowed him the opportunity to stare at his life in a way he hasn't done before. My early feeling in our work was that I needed to be supportive of the fragile hope emerging within the situation, as well as present and unshirking in witnessing the pain and the massive ambivalence of this man's life. This is an 'end of the line' situation, as Rhodri put it. However I framed the counselling process and the possible ways we might work, Rhodri had already decided this was his last chance to find any support in making the changes he needed to make. His motivation has been consistently strong, our sessions often very down-to-earth and not without a certain strain of black humour – I feel as though the content Rhodri shared provided me with a context against which I could envisage and hold the ideal model of his identified will, especially at times when he lost his connection with that. He was also able to establish a wider context for his healing process, accessing the prison education department for lessons in English and Maths and in Information Technology, as well as starting a programme of exercise and yoga, connection to his own body. Insofar as this hypothesis is the case, I certainly felt myself attempt the role of 'external unifying centre' or, perhaps the more human role of reparation-making father, even as I was also aware of a certain brotherliness in our connection. This was especially charged for me since Rhodri was born and bred in (and his whole story is located in and around) my own home town. Furthermore, although far beyond my own experiences, Rhodri's story had enough parallels to my own to cause cautionary alarms to sound in my own psyche. Could I maintain my boundaries and not slip into unconscious collusions with this man, or was I developed enough beyond my own issues with drugs and responsibility to be of any therapeutic use? These issues I brought to supervision and I gradually felt reassured that Rhodri seemed an appropriate client for me to work with, with the further guidance that working with his will would provide an integrity to the process which I could come to recognise and trust.

Damian's life story contained some parallel experiences to Rhodri, including being in care for much of his youth, before beginning a long series of custodial sentences and detention in young offenders institutions and then prisons. Damian spoke fondly of his father, who he had recently (within the past year) rediscovered. He especially liked the fact that his father was a drummer and became inspired to write songs and learn to play guitar. Apart form this connection, and several fleeting mentions of siblings and cousins (mostly in connection to other prisons, especially Dartmoor and Bristol, both of which establishments Damian had spent time in) Damian's life seemed empty, dominated as it was by periods of incarceration. I knew at once that Damian's life was unlike any I had encountered this intimately – nothing had really prepared me for it, but here was a man whose usual experience of life was one of being imprisoned – for Damian being 'on the out' was more unusual and, quite possibly, more difficult. The level of institutionalisation present was great, Damian's reality was conditioned by prison regimes right down to the structure of his days, mealtimes, expectations and enjoyments (the arrival of the weekly tobacco ration, for example, known as 'canteen'). I hypothesised about Damian's developmental condition, which appeared to reveal early wounding around attachment to his mother, subsequent abandonment (literally) and an unresolved fury located within an artificially infantilised subsystem of his self-identity. The all-consuming rage of the infant, 'I smash the world'.

In exploring with Damian his sexual history and the significant relationships of his life it was soon clear that, despite fathering at least two children with different, casual girlfriends, Damian had never experienced a committed relationship and never had the experience of a stable home. Rather, he had a catalogue of casual heterosexual encounters without any commitment on either side, and a string of associates and acquaintances with whom he would stay during the brief times between his regular custodial sentences. However, and most strikingly, he had a girlfriend currently and at the time of the rape for which he was imprisoned. This woman, called Jane, he had met on his previous release from prison and they had continued their relationship to date (about one year – the longest relationship of his life). Jane is in her early forties and immediately my responses constellated around mother fantasies. Whatever the accuracy (or not) of these instant hypotheses, Jane was clearly a figure of enormous importance in Damian's life. He wrote to her daily, received letters at the same rate and told me that he spoke with her first thing every morning by telephone (other inmates 'arranged' for him to always get the first use of the wing telephone, out of some impenetrable code of respect, based on the length of someone's sentence – Damian, of course, has the longest sentence of all). He also managed to acquire an acoustic guitar through one of the chaplains, and to begin writing songs and poems, largely for and about Jane. These he shared with me and at moments, performing his songs for me, I began to feel his sensitivity and to sense an enormous feeling of waste in the whole situation. He even began planning a prison wedding.

Through consideration of Damian's life history and my experiences of sessions in his cell (a very imperfect and limiting therapeutic environment) and especially through supervision, it became apparent that my major task was to be a sort of 'life-witness' and to give up my attachments to having something happen in our connection. So dense and impacted were the layers of trauma and wounding, denial and negation within Damian, that the tenuous quality of our sessions (always haunted by the prospect of him being transferred to another prison without warning, a practice known in prison slang as 'being ghosted out') would not allow anything more structured. I tried to meet Damian each session, to be as open and as present as possible, to praise his prolific creativity and expression, and to enquire with earnestness into his suffering and his soul's mystery.

In contrast, Ray's life history contained what he calls 'a very happy childhood'. As mentioned already his early years involved a lot of travel and regular uprooting of the family to follow his father's postings in the RAF. This led to a pattern of disruption in childhood, a sense of interruption and change rather than any long term stability – something I noticed as a pattern in Ray's later life also. Since his harrowing experiences in Northern Ireland and his leaving the army, Ray had had two marriages collapse (the first immediately, after two years, the second after fifteen years), lost contact with two children from the first marriage and the stepchildren of his second. He also has a three year old daughter by a woman he lived with during 1999. In each case Ray had simply left, unable to cope with the pressure he felt himself to be under, unable to face the responsibility he felt imposed upon him. He had even abandoned various houses and flats in which he had lived, leaving everything he owned inside, finding it easier to begin again completely each time.

Since arriving in prison and becoming distressed by flashbacks and problems sleeping manifesting through his PTSD, Ray had gradually taken more control of his experience and begun to open to new paradigms and ways of perceiving life and the world. One growth came from dramatherapy sessions focusing on archetypal stories (especially, Theseus and the Minotaur – the act of confronting inner monsters within their own labyrinthine darknesses, in their own unconscious territory) and on regular experiences with yoga and meditation. I also encouraged Ray to obtain a copy of Bo Lozoff's book 'We're All Doing Time', made available free to prisoners and focusing on spirituality and healing inside the prison system. Ray responded with a series of letters to his ex-wives and his children, in which he attempted to articulate himself and account for his own absence in their lives, whilst identifying the changes he felt himself to be engaged with now. He also began a course of Christian study through the prison chaplaincy and reached the point of being baptised.

This emerging part of Ray has an awareness of the suffering of others, and in particular a powerful sense of justice and service. As his trial approaches Ray has become sickened by the legal process and justice system, witnessing the petty inequalities and paradoxes evident at each level, and connecting this with his own reality and that of his new peers. Ray obtained a job as a cleaner on his wing, a sought after role affording a slightly larger cell and unlock (i.e. out of cell) all day. In this role I have witnessed Ray's support for other inmates, finding time to check on vulnerable prisoners and fulfilling a bridging role between officers and inmates. At the time of writing Ray is about to begin his trial, upon the outcome of which will depend our continuance of work together. His mantra is 'I will not come back here'.

MY BEAUTIFUL SELF: ANALYSIS

In considering an analysis of Rhodri, Ray and Damian, I have focused my energies on psychosynthesis models, although I have also found much use in theoretical maps and practical methodologies from a variety of sources, in particular Gestalt and Existential modes. However, these have been largely deployed 'tactically', whereas the larger integrative framework, the strategic perspective, has been almost wholly (bio)psychosynthesis, seeking to witness both the personality centre and personal self and also the transpersonal dimensions of a client's being. In major part my work to date can be categorised as 'will' work, will being for Assagioli the unfolding six-stage process by which actions toward Self are most swiftly developed. It is important to note this, because in each case, being imprisoned, the clients I work with are experiencing large degrees of disconnection from their own will. Their wills, like their bodies, are in gaol.

Within this overall approach, which marks some of my own growth and development as a counsellor, there must be spaciousness if rigidity and reification are to be avoided. Whereas the prison system makes few allowances for individuality, the counselling experience must, if it is to recognise difference and connect coherently. Vital in this perception has been reflection upon the nature of each individual client, their unique presentation and pathology.

One of the most striking themes spanning the three clients is that of the parental split, informing the deeper reaches of the primal wound beneath. Each man is himself a father, each with more than one child and partner. Each had a damaged, distant or non-existent relationship with his own father, sometimes marked by violence and often by absence. Their early imprinting of masculine archetypes was narrow, with early twists of senex-authority and the puer's need to sublimate this into drug rebellion (Rhodri), military discipline (Ray) and antisocial criminal activity (Damian). At these early stages curtailed educational opportunities, the instability or absence of a primary home, the inconsistency or fragmentation of emotional and psychological development within the family system, as well as complex patterns of poly-drug use (for Rhodri and Damian) all served to destabilise and inflict trauma upon the nascent sense of self.

As well as these 'father' wounds, each client's history is compounded by similar degrees of interrupted or broken mothering. In Damian's case this meant literal absence through the mother's choice (which reminds me of Norman O Brown's words: 'identification with the father involves a transformation of guilt into aggression, denying dependence on the mother'), for Rhodri, being abandoned by his biological mother, then later deserted in favour of death by his adopted mother (with the systemic implications of a potential promise to 'follow' her). Ray's mother, though present, appears to have been meek and timid, a rather distant and mute figure in his memory.

The archetypal resonance of the witch lurks close to these unconscious surfaces, and Hecate, Sycorax and Lilith speak through dreams and actions over time, remaining neglected, unseen, but all the while whispering in the green ear of anima, delineating the bounds of future relationship. This Marie Louise von Franz describes as "a narrowing in" where the archetypes are "in a kind of soup in which everything is contaminated by everything else". This un-mothered infantile recess becomes its own goetic womb, becomes fuel for the more gnostic subpersonalities as it rots down into Psyche's fossil-fuel bedrock. In Rhodri, for example, the faint whiff of natural gas is present in his regular presentation of his appetites and desires. A cluster of ravenous subpersonalities has formed around his un-meetable and unmet love needs, expressing in his past through periods of reckless sexual excesses, risk taking behaviour (including the armed robbery for which he is in prison, the motivation for which was 'I was bored') and of course massive, prolonged drug addiction.

In Buddhist depictions of Samsara, of all human suffering, the god Yama, Lord of Death holds the complete cycle in his arms. There is light and dark and a complex, Heironymous Bosch like mandala, usually depicting a rooster chasing a pig chasing a snake chasing the rooster. These symbols are usually interpreted as representing the cycling of craving, hatred and ignorance, dancing the twelve steps of dependent origination. It refers to the idea that as long as we remain clinging, hateful and ignorant we will continue to create karma and so continue to choose the endlessly spiralling world of suffering and pain. Although not a Buddhist, I have found this a useful centre to occupy in relation to my client's pathologies – attempting to hold a relationship akin to that between Lord Yama and the bestial chase.

In Psychosynthesis terms I imagine holding a relatively unifying centre between antagonistic drives, allowing spaciousness for disintegration into broader self-concepts, tracing relative identifications with personality functions, remembering that the Will best expresses the executive radiance of the Self. I recognise in my clients' binding forces of attachment to suffering, often expressed in extremis, and often in ways reminiscent of infancy. For Rhodri the most lurid binds are those of 'sensuous craving' (kama-raga), for Damian they glitter most in the range of 'doubt that has no desire for satisfaction' (vichikitsa), and Ray's approach towards the threshold of a crisis of duality may be represented here as the bind of 'belief in a separate personality' (drishti). I see these as distorted faces of the personal self.

Each client manifests subpersonalities and archetype-complex relationships to the various parts of their psyche, often conflicting over the scarce commodity of available will. Damian in particular gives many examples of commitment to an action derived from an encounter with his will, only to sabotage his intention with a contrary action – so for instance, after working extensively with his anger and identifying how his pattern is to magnetise conflict, become inexorably, almost dutifully involved, Damian made a series of will statements about self-control, only to attack a fellow inmate with a kettle and take from him a gold chain. In considering this I reflected the splitting

Damian was manifesting, he said that the whole thing occurred because his cellmate (who he barely knew) thought he recognised the other man as someone who owed him money. Damian's identified psychotic condition, dissocial personality disorder, though relevant as a map, felt useless faced with the actuality, the suchness, of his behaviour. Yet at times he demonstrated compassion, protectiveness and sensitivity, both within the therapeutic relationship and among his peers – his ability to create cohesion within his own sense of self, to move between the first and fourth rays/ways, was compromised and at each turn it appeared that the system with which he is so enmeshed sought to prevent this and punish him even for the attempt.

Damian and I did not get the opportunity for an ending of any sort. One week I went to visit him as usual only to find him gone. Ghosted out. The feelings I had were hard to be with, the sense of abandonment now transferred its attentions to me, together with the sense of having failed as a father myself in this situation. We had completed eight sessions, and never once made it into the counselling room. The pattern continued, perhaps some witnessing took place, even a measure of insight, but it remains hard to find much more than the fingerprints of a re-traumatised child on the dividing glass between our realities, even now.

Freud says "denial is always accompanied by affirmation of the denied, and therefore results in a split in the ego". In Ray's case this denial has had many forms – his repressed memories of atrocities on active service (later erupting through his PTSD symptoms), his attachment to the role of carer (at the expense of his own care, and then collapsed into full-blown carelessness for self and others) and the fragile layers of enamel chipped but intact, around his precious belief in 'a normal background, a happy childhood'. As Ray has moved beyond the most painful aspects of PTSD and begun to adjust to the routine of life in prison, a new fraction of his will has become evident. I have seen this as an early but authentic movement towards his personal self, with the rarefied shimmer of the Self beyond the horizon. As his will has moved through painful territories and new namings (such as naming his hatred for his father, then softening into a more self-forgiving space) Ray has developed a connection to the collective dimensions. At first the movement was small, held by his cellmate, whose story Ray was moved deeply by (indeed Ray was instrumental in motivating his cellmate to attend for counselling). Over time this connection has expanded to include his landing, his wing, all the prisoners in this HMP, and now all prisoners in the UK. The vehicle for this expression of will has been his decision to pursue authority and hold it accountable for its actions, as well as to offer it the benefit of his experience and that of others. He has engaged the prison governor in this, and most recently he wrote to the Home Secretary outlining his concerns and offering his informed opinion. He is also in contact with various campaigning groups and ex-offenders organisations and has even begun preliminary enquiries into studying law.

Ray's actions are interesting, but more interesting to me is the way in which he involved himself in the process. He identified his purpose, deliberated upon it, decided to act, affirmed his path, planned how he might have an effect and then implemented the plan. He did this on various levels of collective reality more or less simultaneously, and he maintained a deepening/heightening connection to personal self throughout, culminating in his actual baptism. Ray is known in supervision as Ray of Light.

I IS THE ENEMY: PROCESS

I have already spoken in some detail about process in relation to each client, and their stage of therapy. In broader terms, my way of working has been in constant flux and movement. Often initially I would feel overwhelmed by content, by the impact of unseen others from imploding family systems or by the context of working in a prison itself. Gradually I have learned to loosen my need to digest every morsel of content, in fact to let it be altogether at points. Generally there is a great deal of expression that seems necessary to the client, and my first attention is to witnessing that process, not absorbing it or necessarily doing anything with it. My stock tools are disidentification techniques, symbolic and guided visualisations and gestalt confrontation through empty chairs or imaginal inner spaces. Beyond this I have found little room for technique, although paper based family constellations have been extremely effective in the few attempts I have made. The focus however is strongly on therapeutic presence, the bifocal and non-linear quality of attention and awareness needed to hear between the words. I have been influenced in some measure by the 'fly-by-wire' approach to therapeutic presence, resting in a sense of the inherent instability of the vessel, but able to touch in and out of connection in sequence with the client. This way of working allows space for the unknown whilst enabling a constant stream of feedback, physically, emotionally, mentally and within the matrix of I-Thou connection.

One final aspect, I experience myself as being quite challenging in my working; having allowed support and reflection to develop the focus on will creates a feeling of pushing deeply into something resistant – prison slang would have this called 'being real' – and my experience is that it is both necessary and appreciated. Before starting the job in prison I made and consecrated a wand, symbolising my own will, and dedicated it to Chiron. I use it twice each day. In the Qabalistic tradition the wand connects to the world of Atziluth, or Archetypal reality, and corresponds with the element fire and the quarter of the soul known as Chiah, or life-force. I am conscious of this connection, and it's link to my own fathers (my father helped me shape the wand, my therapist, my supervisor, my peers in Synthesis, and certain other key allies continue to hold me in my will on these many levels, through all weathers) – it balances and protects me, brings Atziluthic awareness through healing soul-essence.

WE KNOW WHAT WE FEEL: SUPERVISION/GROWTH

I have touched on my growth as a therapist, which continues to be extremely powerful. I am acutely aware of my resistances and relative weaknesses as a counsellor and I continually feel tested, but increasingly client contact is the anchor, the part of my experience where I know myself to be 'of electric nature' as Beethoven put it. My feelings regarding brief therapy have changed – I now see the value of this work, and the depth of penetration possible in even a short time. I also know its frustrations, and the peculiarly painful enforced endings which prison insists upon – being 'untimely ripp'd' from a client is an experience I find difficult. Further growth has come through supervision, where the focus of reflection has been directed at me rather than my clients, at my self-nurture and safety.

Today I am better at moving between worlds, at holding the tension between empathy and disidentification, better at remembering to take care of myself as a priority, physically (swimming and regular walking helps), emotionally (more difficult, and transferentially implicated; living alone I feel the weight of clients' enforced loneliness and my own hard to separate sometimes, especially noticeable as a change in my poetry, it culminated in writing a personal article for publication in the journal Ipnosis – writing as emotional disidentification) mentally (in my integrative thirst for synthesis of extremes) and beyond (in the archetypal sense – connection to duende, my chthonic daimon, and in the Platonic ideals of Justice and Beauty).

I WANNA BE ME: SACRIFICIUM INTELLECTUS

In conclusion, I need to honour another dimension in the lapis-alchemy of my journey, the defiance and inflamed angry passion, the Promethean Anarch within, and the painful, beautiful way in which this has come to me, opening me I believe, into a new level of compassion (repointing my own Love pillar, that fallen tower, to balance that of my Will). It has involved a rebalancing of my own functions of consciousness, perhaps my first sustained contact with Jung's 'fifth function' of transcendent fire seeking 'the way to higher development through water.' I feel the 'passionate emotionality' that Jung says 'precedes recognition of unconscious content'. It rests on a series of mirror experiences with these clients, interestingly, since mirrors are not allowed as personal possessions in prison.

I can perhaps best express what I mean through finishing Rhodri's story. He has had his sentence increased at appeal, he is still drug free and working hard – he has also been transferred to a therapeutic community prison, an act of conscious will on his part which I supported with a letter to his trial judge, detailing our work together and his authenticity with it. The last time I saw Rhodri, after a session where we had animatedly discussed the merits of rock music as a vehicle for soul and the unknowable quality of endings, I consciously and deliberately broke prison rules and surreptitiously gave him a tape I had made of music by the Sex Pistols. It was partly instinctive, moist-transference on my part (projecting my own hopes onto Rhodri) and partly a way of subverting external authority. It was a risk I am delighted I took – Rhodri was affirmed, fully met. The risk of full contact, however fleeting, was worth it and of necessity, happened beyond the Saturnian limits of institutional sanction, in the terra incognita of human connection. I felt rewarded, and the defiance inherent in the music itself became epiphanic, newly charged, real. By way of epistrophe I have titled the subsections of this study with the fractured lyrics of Johnny Rotten, a fitting cultural anvil to hammer against and one who holds the polarities of extreme defiance and passionate openness in the name of personal freedom as effectively as I aspire to do.

"wherever you go, Tibet, India, USA, Brazil, compassion is always compassion. It exists beyond personal history. That concept is a real concept in the sense that we find it, we don't create it. But true nature goes beyond even that."   A.H Almaas

BIBLIOGRAPHY

Almaas, A. H. *The Pearl Beyond Price*, Diamond Books, USA 1988

Assagioli, Roberto *The Act of Will*, Platts, London, 1999

Assagioli, Roberto *Psychosynthesis*, HarperCollins, London, 1993

Benson, Jarlath *Working More Creatively With Groups*, Taylor & Francis, London, 2000

Bey, Hakim *Temporary Autonomous Zones*, AK Press, 1996

Bey, Hakim *Immediatism*, AK Press, Edinburgh, 1994

Brown, Norman O *Life Against Death – The psychoanalytical meaning of history*, Wesleyan University Press, USA, 1985

Binswanger, Ludwig *Being In The World*, Souvenir, USA 1975

Cobb, Noel *Archetypal Imagination – Glimpses of the gods in life and art*, Lindisfarne Books, London, 1992

Cobb, Noel *Prospero's Island – The Secret Alchemy at the Heart of The Tempest*, Coventure, London, 1984

Franz, M.L. Von *Shadow & Evil in Fairy Tales*, Shambhala Publications, Boston, 1995

Freud, Sigmund *The Complete Psychological Works of Sigmund Freud Vol 18 'Beyond the Pleasure Principle', 'Group Psychology' and Other Works*, Vintage, London, 2001 (Edited by James Strachey)

Hillman, James *Re-Visioning Psychology*, HarperCollins US, 1992

Hillman, James *The Myth of Analysis*, HarperCollins USA, 1992

Hillman, James *Notes on White Supremacy – Essaying an archetypal account of historical events*, unpublished essay

Suicide Prevention Annual Report – Deaths In Custody Unit, HM Stationery Office, London, 2001

Jung, C. G. *The Archetypes & The Collective Unconscious*, Routledge, London, 1991 (Translated by R.F.C. Hull)

Jung, C. G. *The Gnostic Jung & Seven Sermons To The Dead*, Theosophical Publishing House, London, 1982 (Translated by Stephen Hoeller)

Loy, David Lack *Transcendence – The problem of death and life in psychotherapy, existenialism & Buddhism*, Humanities Press International, New Jersey, 1996

Lozoff, Bo *We're All Doing Time*, The Human Kindness Foundation, Los Angeles, 1990

May, Rollo *Man's Search For Himself*, Souvenir Press, USA, 1982

Nietzsche, F *Beyond Good & Evil*, Penguin Classic Edition, London, 1990

Nietzsche, F *Thus Spake Zarathustra*, Penguin Classic Edition, London, 1961

Preece, Rob *The Alchemical Buddha – Introducing the psychology of Buddhist Tantra*, Mudra Publications, Exeter, 2000

Parfitt, Will *Psychosynthesis: The Elements and Beyond*, PS Avalon, Glastonbury, 2006

Parfitt, Will *The Core of a Psychosynthesis Training, and Loving What We do : Doing What we Love*, (www.willparfitt.com), 2002

Platts, David E. *A Basic Psychosynthesis Model of Counselling & Psychotherapy*, (www.chebucto.ns.ca), 1999

Romanyshyn, R *The Soul In Grief – Love, Death & Transformation*, North Atlantic Books, Boston, 1999

Russell, Douglas *Seven Basic Constructs of Psychosynthesis*, Psychosynthesis Digest, Volume 1, Number 2 – 1982

The Sex Pistols *SexBox1*, Virgin, London, 2002 (3 CD edition)

Tift, L & Sullivan, D *The Struggle to be Human – Crime, Criminology & Anarchism*, Cienfuegos, Michigan, 1980

Dear Me

Marilyn Mehlmann

I know that I'm not good enough for you.
You see, I know you too.
Don't think you have me fooled
with all your talk of weaknesses and sins.
Objections overruled.
For all your fears I give you not two pins.
I know you're perfect.

Sometimes in your eyes
I see a glimpse of something huge and wise,
serene. A fragment of the universe.
I know, you see.

But what I need to tell you is that this
is not enough. The universe is
in your eyes. And this is not enough.
No way that I could love you as I do
without the pain, the weaknesses and fears.
What does perfection know of tears?
What does perfection know?

I know that you're not good enough for me
till you can find forgiveness in your heart
for your own self, in fragments it may be.
And every blessed fragment will be part
of our humanity.

That's good enough for me.

Four Fundamental Questions
– Four Fundamental Answers

Anonymous

It is often that the truth is right before our eyes and we deliberately choose to ignore it. Our conscious minds are always trying to make heads or tails of the phenomena around us by indulging in the science of knowledge. The finiteness of our intellect and our senses guarantee the incompleteness of our endeavor. At the same time the art of wisdom is left forgotten and things that are simple and beautiful are discarded as naïve and unscientific. Yet generations of people have tread through the ages with these answers. Some may call them superstitions and a condemnation of the emancipation of human intellect. Others may cling to them as holy writ and even kill and be killed in their names. Despite their use by individuals and their effect on our society these truths remain what they are and these answers are there for anyone with enough guts to disidentify from the false security of his intellectual birdcage.

The alchemists dealt with this art of wisdom. This occult movement that people regard as the beginning of science is also holding fundamental answers to fundamental questions that have always been asked by human beings since the beginning of time. In this essay we will try to provide correspondences between the four fundamental existential questions and the four alchemical artifacts that are provided as answers to the student of their secrets.

Existentialism poses four fundamental issues-questions around which all psychotherapy revolves. These are:

Freedom
Death
Loneliness
Meaning of life

Alchemy provides four corresponding artifacts:

The Philosopher's Stone
The Elixir of Life
The Universal Solvent
The Caduceus of Hermes

FREEDOM - THE PHILOSOPHER'S STONE

Can man really be free in a world where he is torn between black and white, pain and pleasure, necessity and inevitability? Can we make any choice without having to mourn for the loss of the alternative we didn't choose? Can we live with the guilt of our choices? Is there a measure to our responsibility to the people around us? How much can we give and how much can we take? What do we do when our measures differ from those around us? Are we satisfied with the ethical minimum of the law or do we strive for the ethical maximum of our principles?

Existential psychotherapy quotes responsibility as the answer, yet this certainly leaves many of the above questions unanswered. Beyond this responsibility lies a deeper sense of who we really are and what actually motivates us to take responsibility and enables us to make these choices with a light heart. Yes, these choices can be made with a light heart. We just have to know who we really are and realize that at any given time there is only one choice we can make according to our true self. The different aspects within us can serve different purposes and different introjected commands. Yet there is a place where all these quiet down and are used as counsel and not as commands.

Where our center can choose according to its intrinsic wisdom, according to its true needs and qualities. We have all known this state when whenever we made a difficult choice that affected a lot in our lives and yet we made it equanimously and at peace with ourselves because we knew that this was the way to go from deep within. When we miraculously didn't care anymore about the objections of our environment because we understood deep within us that in the end we could not allow ourselves to make any other choice. This place deep within us is our true self – The Self in Psychosynthesis – that holds all the wisdom we need to make these choices. The difficult thing is to go against our true self. It is then that we feel guilt and regret about our choices because we have followed a false messiah to our salvation. Even when we make the same choice – externally – that our true self would have, but we make it with our intellect and because a part of us commands us to do it, we may still feel guilt and regret because we didn't do it from deep within as free men but from an external command as slaves.

This ability to go within ourselves and find our true self and follow its wisdom is the philosopher's stone. The stone which constitutes the cornerstone of our existence. Which is stable and fundamental to our core existence. Which teaches us to be ourselves not because we cannot disobey our introjected commands but because there is a supreme happiness and equanimity in accepting our true natures. This is the inner inevitability that can utterly destroy the outer determinism. Even death is gladly received when our true self is harmonious to this choice. Every choice and every problem can be turned into gold with a small chip from the philosopher's stone. The universal wisdom that is reflected in our true self is enough to illuminate everything into becoming a perfect golden choice.

To obtain the philosopher's stone one has to delve deep within oneself and change his false self into the image of his true self. We have to destroy our false usurping king-our survival personality-into the true legitimate king and truly be our Father's son. The old usurping false self is to be drowned or given to the wolves. That is the unconscious repressed feelings or the repressed instincts are to be listened to and incorporated into our personality. Through these outlets we are no longer wasting energy in keeping our character armor to repress these feelings and instincts. We also are more in touch with our inner world and eventually we discover what it is to just be ourselves. It is neither destructive nor dangerous as we were once taught. It might be inconvenient to some people but it is extremely convenient to us. This kind of selfishness is fundamental to a meaningful relationship with ourselves and with others as well. By letting the old false self be devoured we search within us and we find the hidden philosopher's stone. We establish a connection with our true self. This dissolving process was portrayed by the alchemists with the following Arcanum:

VITRIOL

Visita (Visit)
Interiora (the interiors)
Terra (of the earth)
Rectificando (and by rectifying yourself)
Invenies (you will find)
Occultem (the hidden)
Lapidem (stone)

DEATH - THE ELIXIR OF LIFE

How can we live our lives knowing that we are going to die? Knowing that we are going to die anytime now and we might not know it and not control it? How can we create anything knowing that it will also die and we are not going to enjoy it after we are dead? Knowing that nothing lasts and all we hold dear is going to be lost? Knowing that we are subject to pain and loss and decay? How can we bear the pain? How can we bear the hopelessness? How can we bear the darkness around us and within us? How will we ever get enough?

Existential psychotherapy proposes that we stay in the here and now and live our lives as they come and fully engage in them as much as we can moment by moment. Not to live for the future or the past anymore than we have to and see ourselves in our present situation. Yet there is something more than this intellectual command that we may behaviouristically hypnotize ourselves to follow. There is a fundamental truth behind this edict: there is a profound joy in just existing and this existence is intertwined with the whole universe. We are all one. We are not disconnected but absolutely one and the same with everything in the universe. All our dualistic wants and needs and qualities are essentially a collateral effect of our individual manifestation in this identity we hold as a live member of the homo sapiens community in this planet. Yet all these things that make us who we are and we so proudly cling to for the definition and fortification of our individuality are not essential to our existence. Take these all away and we still exist. Strip us of our stories and our preconceptions and we still exist. OK, you say, we still exist, so what? We are left with nothing we are empty husks, devoid of content and meaning. And here enters the beauty of it: we are neither empty nor devoid of meaning in this state. We are open to the sheer joy of existence. A joy that teaches us that the supreme pleasure is to exist. That there is no need to prove anything and to anyone. That we are perfectly and absolutely OK as we are. That evolution and degeneration are both OK because there are parts of the same wonderful game of existence. This cosmic game provides us with such joy and happiness and harmony that we get addicted instantly to playing it. That is reason enough to stay alive and continue to play this game. We can disidentify from our individual qualities and histories by realizing we are fundamentally OK because we are integral parts of the universe and this whole cosmic game.

That the universe is fundamentally OK just because it exists. This fundamental joy of existence is only realized when we empty ourselves of the lesser joys of life and we are open enough and empty enough to feel this higher pleasure of sheer existence. The Hindus call this pleasure of existence Ananda, the king cobra that is the king of all snake-pleasures: the only snake-pleasure that is not poisonous however hard you squeeze it. The only pleasure you can freely partake of as much as you wish and it will never enslave you. Its addiction is deliverance and its pursuit is already accomplished. Only when you lose yourself you can truly find this joy within you.

The alchemists connected this elixir of life, this aqua permanens, with intense death and intense life situations. At the threshold, one can lose oneself and see the bigger picture. At the moment of orgasm, even the basest rapist can feel what it is to be part of everything. At the moment of death, even the most unrepentant criminal can see the glory of the universe enfolding him. These memories of these instances are what can fortify us to realize that life is eternal as long as we hold this remembrance in ourselves. Living in the here and now takes on a new essence. It becomes living in everywhere and forever. We know we are part of the universe and we need not worry neither about our own end nor about the end of the universe because the joy and the harmony is so fulfilling that the circle is already complete. This relationship has everything already and there will be nothing to miss as unaccomplished. It is like losing a relative you have loved and have been loved by very much and you feel that the relationship was complete between you. There is nothing to grieve for because there was nothing left to get from this relationship. The memory is sweet and the essence of your parting is fulfillment and equanimity.

LONELINESS – THE UNIVERSAL SOLVENT

How can we bear loneliness? Can we get on with our lives alone and forgotten? Is it possible to leave a part of yourself unwanted and repressed? Why do I have to bother with other people? Why don't they want me? How can I make them want me? Why do I feel so alone? Why are we all alone in the end, even when others are around us? Is it our destiny to be utterly alone in this world?

Existential psychotherapy glorifies self searching as the answer to loneliness. By knowing and accepting our parts we end intrapersonal loneliness. By knowing the way we interact with other people we can establish more meaningful relationships and by accepting that we are alone in the world in an existential level we can more firmly accept it and bear it.

The alchemists knew that we are not alone in this world and they had the universal solvent to portray this secret. The universal solvent is universal love. Love connects people to each other and to the world around them. This love provides understanding and connection to all things. It forgives, it nourishes, it consoles, it heals, it mirrors, it accepts, it respects, it honors, it mellows, it satiates, it gives, it receives, it dissolves and it rectifies. All things can be made whole with this love as long as the will is there to surrender oneself to this love unconditionally. It solves all complexes and all character armor is dissolved under its power. We don't have to know how our character works and how we interact with others to rectify that with our intellect. We just need to love and let ourselves be loved in return. It magically changes the environment around us and ourselves towards the environment. We are connected through this love to the whole universe and we know that we are never alone because we are integral parts of the universe. This love makes us realize that unquestionably.

MEANING OF LIFE – THE CADUCEUS OF HERMES

Where do I come from? Where am I going? Why am I going there? Who am I?

Some Existential psychotherapists deny the existence of the meaning of life and focus on realizing and accepting this lack of meaning as a means to staying in the here and now and being happy without a meaning. Others acknowledge the relativity of individual meanings to life and perhaps even categorize them. The latter are more keen to accept the quintessential need for a meaning for us to live a fulfilling life.

The answer is there and we still choose to keep our eyes closed as small children who continuously deny their teacher's lessons because they want to go out and discover them on their own. The choice is to be respected but it is a huge waste nonetheless.

The caduceus is composed of four elements: the black snake the white snake, the staff and the winged solar disk.

The two snakes are the two opposites in our lives: love and will, right and left hemisphere, wisdom and understanding, assertiveness and passivity, action and reaction, entropy and syntropy, destruction and creation, evolution and degeneration, happiness and misery, love and hatred, severity and mercy, security and validation, insecurity and devaluation, protection and persecution, benevolence and retentiveness, giving and taking, wild and tame, male and female, good and evil, yin and yang, raja and tama, ida and pingala, sun and moon, harmony and disharmony. We are always under the choice between the two opposites, we are in effect under the laws of dualism.

The staff is the central core of our existence around which the two snakes of dualism revolve and entwine. It is the central stabilizing force that keeps the two opposites in equilibrium. It is both the medium solution, the choice of a place between the two opposites and the sum of the different parts at the same time. The caduceus is nonetheless incomplete if we suffice to use this equilibrium as a mere middle solution between the two opposites. It means that we are merely trying to assuage both our opposites desires by treading the middle path of lukewarm mediocrity. The winged solar disk is the path of sublimation, the higher ideal that guides us to be our true selves in connection with universal harmony. It is the path of wisdom.

We can be passionate and dedicated when we follow this path just as we can be indulging in the joy of existence and still not be poisoned by its sublime pleasure. There is an overcoming, a sublimation, a higher ideal, a distinction between the dual and the whole, the gross and the light, the baser and the higher. The choice is not within the boundaries of the line drawn between the two opposites but in a point above this line where any choice can indeed correspond to a point in the line below but at the same time is beyond this boundary of dualism. It is the path of individuation, where every act is consonant with our higher self. The universal higher self that is reflected in our own individual true self, no longer impeded by our own individual false self. We are given wings to overcome and fly in the skies of personal choice guided by universal harmony. Anything we choose is right because it is our own choice in the universal game. As long as we perceive this universal game we know we are part of it and that this consciousness provides our actions with responsibility and meaning just because we do them under this universal consciousness. We are no longer bound by the laws of duality as long as we are disidentified from our personal false selves. The meaning of life is simply that it exists and that it is extremely joyful to participate in this game of existence. The game includes duality and choice, pleasure and pain. These are to be honoured as parts of the game and fully engaged with. They are not the game itself but parts of the game, a means to an end. The end is the game of existence. If we confuse the means with the end we will be stuck in a prison of our own making. If we see the glory of the meaning of life we will engage in dualism disidentified and unattached so as to get the higher joy of existence out of dualism and not the lesser joy of dualism out of existence. If we crucify our higher selves to the glory of the lesser we will keep searching futilely for a meaning where there is none to be found. If we crucify our lesser selves to the glory of the higher we will be able to see the meaning of life where it really exists.

VOICE OF HEART

Roderick Field

And my heart, I knew it was singing
so I strained to hear its song

And what did it sing . . .
It sang, it sang:

. . . and when at last his lips did part
A new voice spoke through open mouth
I am the shape, the voice of heart
I can but only speak the truth

. . . and when at last his chest was rent
A new eye looked with tender stance
I am the sight, the eye of heart
I see with love in every sense

. . . and when at last his head was held
A new thought sprang from heart to mind
I am in love to think the world
I know the bridge out to inside

. . . and when at last his loins were fed
A new child shone, was shadow's light
I am the son, the child of heart
I am the end of harrowed flight

And its song, once sung, then was.

WHY FORGIVING OURSELVES
AND EACH OTHER IS
THE PATH TO GLOBAL JUSTICE

John Bunzl

When we protest against transnational corporations, politicians and unaccountable global institutions such as the WTO, the IMF and the World Bank; when we protest against those we regard as causing or exacerbating global warming, ecological destruction, pollution or the widening gap between rich and poor, we inevitably blame them. Often, we go further to blame individuals who may shop at supermarkets, or who fail to buy Fair Trade or organic foods and so on. In protesting against them, or in decrying their behaviour, we inevitably point our fingers at them: "YOU are the ones who are destroying our world!" In fact, it's not too much of an exaggeration to say that the Global Justice Movement's principal mode of action is protest; a mode which inescapably implies the blaming of one section of society or another, or one institution or another, for our global ills. And to be fair, there's a lot to protest about and without protest these important issues would never come to wider public attention.

But dire as our global problems undoubtedly are, should not the question be asked as to whether, in some sense, we are not all to blame for our present predicament, NGOs and global justice activists included? After all, who amongst us is so utterly de-linked from the global economy as to be able to honestly claim not to be contributing in some way to present problems, be it by driving when we might walk, by buying the products of transnational corporations when something more eco- or socially friendly might be better, or by failing to buy organic food when cheaper non-organic alternatives better suit our budgets - or by flying to holiday or conference destinations and thus contributing disproportionately to global warming emissions? Because for any of us to pretend that we are beyond reproach is not only likely to be untrue, it leads inexorably to a kind of "eco-fascism" whereby self-styled "eco-warriors" vilify and victimise the rest of us who, for one reason or another, apparently fail to live up to their criteria for what is required to "save the planet". Indeed, the reality is that through our individual and collective choices, lifestyles and socio-economic system, all of us play a part, to a greater or lesser extent, in exacerbating our increasingly dire global predicament. So to pretend otherwise is not only divisive and untrue, it ultimately serves only to divert us from what should be a common effort to find solutions and instead leads us into an endless loop of factional, 'us and them' blame and counter-blame.

And if we are all to blame, perhaps we should take the further step of asking ourselves whether the corporate executives or market traders we commonly regard as being in positions of power are really in any position to significantly alter their polluting or socially irresponsible behaviour? It should after all be clear that in a competitive global market any corporation single-handedly taking on a greater measure of social or environmental responsibility - and thus increasing its costs in the process - would only lose out to its competitors causing a loss of its profits, a reduction in its share value, a consequent loss of jobs and, ultimately, the prospect of it becoming the target of a hostile takeover. You don't need to be a rocket scientist to conclude that, in a global market, corporations can generally only afford to behave as responsibly as the aggregate behaviour of their major competitors permits and, since they cannot reliably count on them to simultaneously take on higher standards, it is virtually impossible for one or a restricted number of market players to make the first move. So while it's clear that corporations could take some small steps towards more responsible behaviour and should be encouraged to do so, we shouldn't fool ourselves into thinking that they have the power to make the really substantive and fundamental changes needed to solve our global problems. Indeed, they manifestly don't.

As George Soros points out, the same goes for global investors and fund managers. With respect to his own role he explains that: "As an anonymous participant in financial markets, I never had to weigh the social consequences of my actions. I was aware that in some circumstances the consequences might be harmful but I felt justified in ignoring them on the grounds that I was playing by the rules. The game was very competitive and if I imposed additional constraints on myself I would end up a loser. Moreover, I realised that my moral scruples would make no difference to the real world, given the conditions of effective or near-perfect competition that prevail in financial markets; if I abstained somebody else would take my place."[1] So it's not corporate execs or fund managers who are destroying our world, it's the system in which they – and we— are all implicated. WE – all of us – are destroying our world.

After all, do global justice activists really think business leaders are any less aware of our environmental crisis than anyone else? Of course they're not! But they're caught in a vicious circle of destructive global competition which systematically prevents them from behaving in the way activists – and they themselves – would like. In his book, "When Corporations Rule the World", David Korten astutely observed that "With financial markets demanding maximum short-term gains and corporate raiders standing by to trash any company that isn't externalizing every possible cost, efforts to fix the problem by raising the social consciousness of managers misdefine the problem. There are plenty of socially conscious managers. The problem is a predatory system that makes it difficult for them to survive. This creates a terrible dilemma for managers with a true social vision of the corporation's role in society. They must either compromise their vision or run a great risk of being expelled by the system."[2]

That's not to say, of course, that some corporations

or CEOs aren't greedy or careless, or that we should become apologists for poor corporate behaviour. But more often than not, it is destructive competition and the fear of losing out, rather than pure greed for profit, which daily drives the socially and environmentally detrimental decisions of business executives. For as they rightly point out: "If we don't do it, our competitors will" – and in a globally de-regulated market, they're right! So what is the point in blaming them when they're caught in a system which effectively prevents them from behaving otherwise? And are global justice activists and NGOs in any position to point fingers when, were we in the shoes of corporate executives and subject to the same competitive demands, we'd likely be behaving in much the same way? So it is not corporations or their CEOs at whom we should be directing our primary fire, but at the destructively competitive global market system of which they are merely its most high-profile prisoners.

And what about governments; the institutions who are responsible for "the system"; our leaders who are supposed to regulate markets to balance social and environmental interests with those of business? In a world where capital and employment quickly move to any country where costs are lower and profits therefore higher, what chance do governments have to impose increased regulations or taxes on business to protect society or the environment when doing so will only invite employment and investment to move elsewhere? Environmentalists commonly decry government laxness in properly regulating corporations but what choice do governments have when they cannot count on other governments doing likewise? Any government making any significant move to tighten environmental or social protection regulations would face the prospect of uncompetitiveness, capital flight, a loss of jobs and a resulting loss of votes. Again, that's not to say that governments are powerless to do anything at all to improve matters or that we should stop pressuring them. But it does mean that their room for manoeuvre is extremely curtailed to the point where they, too, are largely caught in the same vicious circle like everyone else. So, governments of whatever party are now constrained to pursuing only those narrow policies they know will not displease world markets; a pathetically narrow range of policies which reduce democracy to a hollow kind of pseudo-democracy; an electoral charade in which whatever party we elect, and whatever the party's manifesto may have stated, the policies actually delivered inevitably conform to market demands and to each country's need to maintain its "international competitiveness".

So activists should ask themselves whether they would act greatly differently were they to be sitting in government instead of our politicians? When significant strides to protecting society or the environment mean losing jobs and votes, would we really behave much different to the politicians we so commonly decry?

As I have hinted, at the root of the present world predicament lies a vicious circle of destructive competition which no-one can be said to be in control of and no-one can therefore be held wholly responsible for. Furthermore, the global institutions of the WTO, IMF and World Bank whom we might expect to be in control of the global economy are, in fact, operating under the delusion that competition is always a beneficial phenomenon; a delusion forced upon them by their understandable inability to control the free movement of capital and corporations. For in having no control over their free movement, and thus in accepting that state as a "natural given", they are necessarily lead to prescribe yet more competition (i.e. more structural adjustment, more privatisation, more tax cuts, more fiscal austerity, etc) as the cure to our global ills and not less. In failing to realise that economic competition becomes destructive when it fails, as at present, to occur within the framework of adequate global regulations that protect society and the environment, the WTO, WB and IMF serve only to exacerbate the very problems they think they're solving. Those in charge of the institutions we expect to exert beneficial control over the global economy and whom we commonly believe to be "in power" are, therefore, relatively powerless to influence its out-of-control competitive forces.

So, by blaming governments or corporations or international institutions, we actually accord them far more credit than they really deserve. For in blaming them and in holding them responsible, we imply that they have the power to substantially change the system when we should instead be recognising that the lunatic herd mentality of global markets has already taken over the asylum. Disconcerting though that realisation may be, all those we think of as "in power" are in fact as much prisoners of the system as the rest of us. And were the leaders of the Global Justice Movement to take their place, would they be in any better position, given the radical and global free movement of capital, to take greatly different decisions? I think not. Of course this should not mean that our protests should stop – far from it! But what it does mean is that we should not fool ourselves into thinking that protest or other conventional forms of NGO action can ever be adequate to bringing about lasting, substantive and beneficial solutions; it means that each of us who truly cares about this world must earnestly seek for another way.

Surely, therefore, the greatest mistake we can make in our fight for global justice is to blame others for our sorry global predicament as if we ourselves were blameless or as if we could do any better? All the while we fail to recognise that we are all to blame, or that we would ourselves likely behave in much the same way as those we presently vilify, we perpetuate division, discord and resentment; we build adversarial barriers instead of removing them and we thus make impossible the atmosphere of cooperation, understanding and forgiveness needed to foster an atmosphere of global community; an atmosphere in which the productive negotiation necessary to finding appropriate solutions could evolve. When – finally – we take all this on board, far from being overcome by a feeling of desperation and despair, paradoxically we reach a crucial and fundamentally important intellectual and spiritual turning point. A point at which we can move to a new and liberating level in our thinking and being. We move from what the prominent American philosopher, Ken Wilber, calls 'first tier' thinking to 'second tier' thinking; from nation-centric thinking to world-centric thinking; from what he calls 'flatland reductionism' to integral holism. So once we stop blaming others, we start to see that, in reality, no single person, group, organisation, country, religion or culture can be singled out. We start to see that even those who benefit hugely from the status quo are in no position to actually change the system and we start to see that we are all caught – to a greater or lesser extent – in the vicious circle of globally destructive competition: a "prisoner's dilemma" from which there is, ordinarily, no way out. In short, we start to see – finally – that we are all in the same boat. From a collective realisation such as this, we would have gone a long way to creating the pre-conditions for building a genuine global community: the conditions of forgiveness and non-judgmental acceptance of ourselves and each other; the inclusiveness necessary to beginning our collaborative search for global solutions. After all, it is upon such a state of genuine Global Community that any properly functioning global democracy must surely depend. In short, we would have created the conditions in which we could recognise the reality that we are ALL ONE; all one in the recognition of our common human fallibility and 'brokenness'; all one in the celebration of each others' differentness, all one in the brother/sisterhood of humanity and all one in the eye of our respective God.

Fortunately, this latest and most essential of humanity's evolutionary journeys has already begun through the work of a number of organisations around the world whose perspective has moved beyond the 'first-tier' mode of protest, blame and 'either/or' thinking to the 'second-tier', non-judgmental, world-centric, 'both/and' thinking needed to solve global problems. For as Einstein rightly suggested, "no problem can be solved with the same thinking that created it".

One organisation that seeks to embody this new thinking is the International Simultaneous Policy Organisation (ISPO) which offers us all – activists and business executives alike – a means by which we can firstly take back control of our present, hollowed-out pseudo-democratic processes and, secondly, how we can co-create the policies necessary to achieving environmental sustainability and global justice. Finally it offers the crucial means for citizens the world over to bring our politicians and governments to implement them without any nation, corporation or citizen losing out. It thus turns the destructive, competition-led politics of globalisation on its head by offering global citizens a practical and peaceful way out of the 'prisoner's dilemma'; a veritable way for all of us to take back the world with a new politics of citizen-led, international co-operation for our emergent – but yet-to-be-born – sustainable global society.

Notes:

1 *The Crisis of Global Capitalism – Open Society Endangered*, George Soros, Little, Brown and Co. 1998.
2 *When Corporations Rule the World*, David Korten, Kumarian Press & Berrett- Koehler Publishers, 1995.

for further information:

International Simultaneous Policy Organisation

www.simpol.org

CONSIDERING
THE PHILOSOPHER'S STONE

Mike Stillwell

D. *"Voldemort singled you out as the person who would be most dangerous to him, and in doing so he made you the person who would be the most dangerous to him, and gave you the tools for the job!"*
(Dumbledore talks to Harry, in The 'Half Blood Prince')

All in a dream I wandered, seeking truth,
Through strange symbolic landscapes of the soul
Finding great wonders; – a basilisk's tooth,
A dragon's egg, and books of spells, and all
Manner of marvels in that magic place.
But as I walked (the hound of doggerel
Close by my side), I chanced on, by some grace,
A Tree, or Fountain (I could not tell,
For 'twas invisible) The waters fell,
Then rose to fall again – or was it fruit
That thudded down and seeded in that dell,
To grow? A Child King climbed to crown from root.

I fancied his story might assist us;
Yours sincerely, Hermes Trismegistus.

1)
We look for meaning in a fairy tale;
Know Freud named complexes for old Greek myth,
We've guessed the meaning of the Holy Grail;
And know who Arthur was, and Wayland Smith.
We've studied Dante in his native tongue,
And know our way around the Tree of Life;
We know what stories 'mean', from balls of dung
That scarabs roll, to what befell Lot's wife.
But have we really understood that all –
Not some but all tales tell us of the soul?
That novels, movies, tales both great and small,
Each shows one person taken as a whole?
How stories – people, places and event –
Show aspects of one soul's development?

2)
Even a silly joke shows different parts
That meet and seem at first to promise well.
People connect and talk perhaps, it starts
To look as if the force for good will tell.
Then with a word it's all turned upside down
Our laughter is a measure of surprise
At being taken in, we smile not frown
As a defence, at hope's sudden demise.
So with all stories, when we hear one told
(or read it in a book, or see the play)
We take the characters that we behold
And match them with our own inner ballet.
As with all stories; there's two warring sides –
One force for synthesis, one that divides.

3)
We make as we are made, and spin our tale,
Sometimes in words, or how we make our world;
Ask others in to listen, or to play,
Listen or play in turn as theirs unfold.
Why do we tell? To speak of where we fell?
Is that why we bow others on our stage?

Or sometimes, rarely, can one weave a spell
That shows the way on every precious page?
Shows the Whole Thing, the pieces and the board,
The moves, the players and the game they play,
And every detail seems to strike a chord
Of what we'll gain or what will slip away;
And do we, listening, say 'If this were me –
Then this and this and this must come to be.'?

4)
I'm here to tell of one such epic tale,
That speaks of all the parts we have inside
One part of us is fighting to prevail,
With other parts opposing or allied.
I'm speaking of the Harry Potter books
By J.K. Rowling, This is a review
Not of their literary worth as works of art
But as a guide to what we all go through.
We must imagine every different place
To match a similar place inside our soul,
And every character, each different face,
To match a part of us; part of our all,
And take all happenings that then unfold
As similar to our personal inner world.

5)
The story opens in a quiet street.
In Little Whinging, at the evening's fall,
And there a senior witch and wizard meet;
Professors' Dumbledore, McGonagall.
They speak of the Dark Lord's recent attack
Upon the Potter house. Lily and James
Were killed, but by some miracle their son
Survived the death spell and, so rumour claims,
He Who Must Not Be Named was overthrown
By a mere infant, no one knows quite how.
Harry, 'The Boy Who Lived' is being flown
Through the night sky by motorbike, and now
Is bought to earth, safe from all further harms

And cradled in a giant's gentle arms.

6)
Rubeus Hagrid, Keeper of Keys and Grounds
At Hogwarts School, brings him to Dumbledore
Who lays the infant Harry safe and sound
Into the sheltering porch of Number Four.
And there in Privet Drive young Harry sleeps
Quite unaware that all across the land
Magic folks meet in many a muggle street,
Glasses are raised in many a wizard's hand
To toast 'The Boy Who Lived', and the defeat.
Of Voldemort and the Death-Eaters reign.
Harry sleeps on, a letter in his hand
Penned to His Aunt and Uncle, to explain
How orphaned year-old Harry needs a place
To grow up in a family's embrace.

7)
Let's pause to look at what we've found so far.
First is baby Harry, named for a king.
Destined to do great things, he bears a scar
Upon his forehead, and the very thing
That should have killed him marked him out for fame.
Harry's an orphan with his parents dead
(Like every superhero you can name);
He's bought up by his relatives instead.
An older witch and wizard leave him there –
The closest thing to grandparents he'll find –
He also has a wild man's gentle care
But these three turn and leave the child behind;
The Dark Lord gone for now, Harry's best chance
For safety is to grow up at his Aunt's.

8)
How can we match these parts with who WE are?
How can this story help us understand
What makes US tick? What are these 'parts of self'.
And what exactly is our inner land?

Well, first if all, you may have noticed that
A child will sometimes scold itself and say
– As if a parent's voice were stored inside –
"Bad boy! (or girl) Mustn't do that!" when they
Are doing something wrong. And if they're sad
Or hurt, you'll see them rock or soothe themselves
With words like, "Shhh, don't worry, never mind".
Perhaps you've even done these things yourselves.
It's like we form these 'foster parents' for
Those times when real ones aren't there anymore.

9)
One, the 'Critical Parent', holds the rules,
And tells us when we get it right or wrong
The 'Nurturing Parent' offers care; they're tools;
Advisors if you like, recorded from
The adults round us, but they're caricatures;
A baby's nursery view of dad and mum,
Not our real parents. But, from time to time
They're also who we sometimes can become,
Not just an inner voice. Another part,
Though taped with the recorder on ourselves,
Contains our early needs, or IS those needs.
 Against all moderation it rebels.
This, with the superego pair, makes three;
Three ego states that form a family

10)
Just like the Dursleys; – father, mother, son.
Critical Uncle Vernon's always mad
At things that don't seem 'normal' or 'correct',
Sees his foster child as wrong and bad,
But shows his best side to his only son.
Aunt Petunia dotes on Dudley too,
A 'smother mother', she spoils her child
To bits, while Harry barely gets his due.
Like coins, the Dursleys have two different sides, .
And Dudley too; – bully, or fearful kid
If others hold the power. He meets his needs

Using others. He's what a baby did
To get its way, or how that baby feels
When hurt, alone, unloved, or missing meals.

11)
Into that setting Harry's now arrived,
A cuckoo in the nest, they seem to feel.
In many ways ill-treated and deprived
Cut off from future, past, and what is real
Inside an alembic – we hardly hear
Of anything outside the Dursley's sphere.
Like an homunculus inside a jar
Harry grows up 'til his eleventh year.
Psychology suggests an ego forms,
A buffer 'tween parental introjects
And id imperatives, but Harry here
Just manages himself. Magic protects
Him, (though he doesn't understand the source)
He is a centre of syntropic force.

12)
Those parts of us that are the Dursleys are
Supposed to guide and love and show our needs
But can attack, neglect or even be
A cruel or needy child. Harry succeeds
By being different; everything they're not,
Not trying to run the Punch and Judy show
For his own ends (that role has been reserved
For Voldemort) but he, it seems, must grow
In Privet Drive, and later must return
So he can call it home until the times
Are right for him to take on the Dark Lord
To punish him, for all his many crimes.
Now knowing what the Dursleys may portray,
Who, then, is Harry Potter, would you say?

13)
So now we've looked at Harry's foster home,
Lets turn to look at Albus Dumbledore,

Headmaster at Hogwarts School for Witchcraft
And Wizardry, and see what he stands for.
An older man, foremost among his peers,
Embodiment of wisdom, he's in charge
Of Harry's care throughout his childhood years,
Protecting him while Voldemort's at large,
First placing him to grow at number four,
Then guiding his education from the time
When Harry goes to Hogwarts. Dumbledore
Is obviously a wizard in his prime
Who's realised his potential and so now
Devotes his life to showing others how.

14)
A Wise Old Man, an Adult and a Child
Are integrated in his laughter-lines
And twinkling eyes, and Dumbledore, though mild,
Personifies authority at times.
Like all the other parts, sometimes a voice
Inside, and sometimes who we seem to be;
He educates us, but gives us a choice;
that quiet certain voice within that we
Know knows, outside the box of space and time,
Whether it comes through others, or we find
We speak; the same wisdom; however heard,
That sows a seed that unfolds in our mind
And heart. He holds our purpose, our true wealth
An archetype close to the Higher Self.

15)
Professor Minerva McGonagall,
Transfigurations teacher, Deputy Head,
We first see as a cat upon a wall
Who turns into a human witch instead.
Where Dumbledores initiating force
She's more concerned with form, she seems quite stern;
Although her heart is good she will enforce
The rules – the kids are there to learn
And woe betide them if they play the fool!

Dumbledore's female counterpart, she's named
For the Roman wisdom Goddess. Her rule
Is strict, but still her fairness is acclaimed.
A sprightly seventy, but full of fight; –
Our deepest understanding of what's right.

16)
At his eleventh birthday week's approach
Letters come for Harry; first one, then two,
They multiply each day, an avalanche,
No matter where the Dursleys move him to
So he can't read them. They find an island.
 Far from anyone; Uncle Vernon's sure
No one can reach them through a howling storm.
But midnight brings a pounding on the door!
A giant knocks it in, then makes a fire
By magic in the fireplace, brews some tea
Cooks sausages, and pulls a birthday cake
From a coat the size of a marquee.
It's slightly squashed, but Hagrid's clumsy care
Replaces Aunt Petunia's, then and there.

17)
When Uncle Vernon points a gun at him
The giant pulls the rifle from his hands;
Bending it in a circle at a whim
And then makes sure that Harry understands
Harry's a wizard, and that Voldemort,
Not a car crash, killed Harry's mum and dad,
That Harry must leave home now to be taught
At Hogwart's School. When Rubeus gets mad
With both the Dursleys for keeping the truth
From Harry, he takes their place as guide
And carer, and curses their spoilt youth
With a pig's tail, showing on the outside
What Dudley is within; and he makes sure
Harry receives the call from Dumbledore.

18)
Who then is Hagrid? Half man, half giant,
A wild man, very strong. Harry says when
Indoors he looks 'too big to be allowed'
Twice tall, five times as wide as normal men
He has no side, no ounce of meanness there,
And though he's none too bright he has a heart
To match his size. His home is on the edge
Of the wild forest; Hagrid's set apart
From other teachers, and he teaches Care
Of Magical Creatures. This hairy man,
This hunter dressed in furs, this protector
Of wild and monstrous things, does what he can
To serve the school, but he feels most at ease
In his crude hut, or striding through the trees

19)
Of his dark forests. Have you a Hagrid?
It's big, that part, but sometimes it takes years
To understand how big, and very strong
And difficult to kill. Strong too in tears,
In loyalties, in courage and in fears,
And prone to drink. This deep instinctive side
Not who we want to be, but who we are
That wears it's inside out on the outside
And that we try to hide most from ourselves.
Out basic creature nature can't ignore
What makes us thrive or ail; our Hagrid part,
Instinctive, feeling, knocking down the door
The wild half-beast in us (and this is strange)
Passes Wisdom's message, 'You must change'.

20)
Now Harry has to buy what he will need
For wizard school; he goes in Hagrid's care
To Diagon Alley, and. he finds there
A magic world that he was unaware
Existed. The 'muggle' and the magic
Side by side, as sun and moon shine down on

The same land at different times, or waking
Consciousness and dreams are acted out upon
The stage of who we are; – the theatre's
The same, and sometimes the sets and players.
Are of both realms. In Dragon Alley
Harry visits wizarding purveyors;
Walks through the Leaky Cauldron and beyond
Buys robes and spell books, gets his owl and wand

21)
And meets Draco Malfoy, an arrogant
First year at Hogwarts like himself, yet not
Like Harry. Draco shows he's different
By his contempt for others. He has got
A sneering attitude and he looks down
At those not from a wizard family.
Malfoy is being fitted for a gown
At Madam Malkins shop; we seem to see
Them contrasted side by side. Harry's sure
Draco's like Dudley, and when Draco calls
Hagrid 'a sort of servant' it is clear
They can't be friends. When Draco drawls,
Asking If Harry's parents were 'our kind'?
It's Harry's opposite we seem to find

22)
And now Harry's rival. Remembering
Our premise of all stories mapping out
The aspects of one person relating
Over time, then their rivalry's about
Which self will 'win', which strategy is best.
Which part will be successful; – Harry's way
Or Draco's? They take sides in a contest
And both choose different masters. Who's to say
If Draco's snide remarks and bullying
Or Harry's quiet courage win the day?
And what is it that either stand to win?
Will Dumbledore or Voldemort hold sway

And what is it they want? Harry decides
Not to join Slytherin, and chooses sides.

23)
Before we carry on, imagine that
A friend asks you to listen while they talk
A problem through. You start to notice that
A triangle emerges, though they balk
At seeing it in themselves; – a harsh judge,
A looking-after bit, a victim part
That's sometimes nasty. This pattern won't budge,
In them or relationships; but you start
To see a part of them you glimpse between
The others. Different somehow, not one
Of 'the family'; three dimensional,
Unlike the rest. Or let's say you've begun
To feel you know them well, then find immense
Resources of uncommon common sense –

24)
Or a deep sense of what is right and wrong –
That seem to come from somewhere 'higher up';
A sense of what they may be. Or a strong
Sense of what they need causes you to stop
And realise that our body-being needs
Just what it always did. Or maybe you hear
With some surprise a part in them that feeds
On other's failures and conceals it's fear –
And so succeeds – at the expense of those
It belittles. Or even catch a glimpse
Of that dark aspect hardest to expose
Who would be Lord at everyone's expense.
These, then, are the people from our story;
Are they, too, in YOUR inner repertory?

25)
When Harry's bought all he needs – he's rich
In wizard gold, and has a vault piled high

With golden galleons, left by his witch
And wizard parents – Hagrid says goodbye
And puts him on a train to Little Winging
With a ticket to take the Hogwart's train
In a month's time. Harry's life is changing
And can't still be the same; he can't remain
In Privet Drive much longer. If a map
Portrayed this challenge, then the lowest sphere
is the Dursley's house; above that, perhaps,
Muggle London, where magic doors appear,
First at the Leaky Cauldron Pub's location
Then between the signs at Kings Cross Station

26)
Where next he finds himself. He's off to school
But can't find platform nine and three quarter
(between spheres 10 and 9) He feels a fool
Until a witch, there with her sons and daughter,
 Shows him the way. A scarlet steam train waits
And Harry boards the red Hogwarts Express.
It's on the train that Harry Potter meets
Ron and Hermione, who we soon guess
Become his greatest friends. Back to our map
Let's put another sphere for Hogwarts School
Above the other two, but in the gap
Between this and the last, we'll take a rule
And draw a line across, and either side
The homes of Harry's friends, just as a guide.

27)
Do YOU know what it's like to step outside
The pressures of 'The Dursleys'? From the rules
And criticism, the oversupplied
Or absent care, the greed and fear – the roles
And nagging voices? Joining the real world,
And seeing so much more, like coming out
From a bad film? You and the world feel filled
With possibilities. And all about

You start to glimpse the hand of something far
Beyond coincidence behind events; –
A sense of magic. You realise there are
Doors. You have two guides; first, your inner sense
Of Wisdom shows you who you want to be,
The Wild Man who you are. Both hold a key

28)
To your true nature. Wisdom can come down
Because he is a vision of the Whole,
While the Wild Man is at home on the ground
And wherever we find instinct. We're told
Dumbledore trusts Hagrid absolutely.
Hogwarts lies at the centre of our map
And is our Individuality.
Where the above and the below meet, slap
In the middle of the egg, with Harry
The centre of awareness of our tale,
And focus of its structures. If we carry
On up to the line that is the veil
James and Lily are Will and Love each side.
Above, a phoenix and two Heads reside.

29)
Ron and Hermione are Harry's friends,
And, though I dislike using one word each
To summarise them, 'thought' and feeling' tends
To describe what we seem to see in each;
Though which is which is quite another thing.
Hermione, a know-it-all, likes rules
And books and being top in class; working
To pass exams, while Ron usually feels
He's second best. His family is poor,
Even his rat and wand are handed down.
Later the three become friends when they floor
A mountain troll; Ron brings it to the ground
With a spell, while Hermione tells lies
To cover up, so they become allies

30)
By using what they seem to struggle with
Ron with his head, Hermione her heart.
Harry gets through things with the help of both
And rarely are the three of them apart
But on the train, Harry and Ron are first
To be special friends. Malfoy insults them.
Instead of harm the result is reversed.
And Harry and Ron's friendship seems to stem
From that moment; – an oft repeated theme,
How opposition activates the force
For synthesis. The afore-mentioned scene
fighting the trolls another case, of course.
So, mind and feelings strengthen and progress;
He with his chess, she with a party dress.

31)
And so to Hogwarts. A rambling castle
With a jumble of towers and battlements
Far from muggle eyes. As the train's whistle
And the daylight fades, the First Years commence
A magic ride by candlelight across
The lake in little boats, to their new home
For years to come. A vast and sprawling place
Looming before them. How, in this poem,
Can I explain it? Have you ever dreamed
Of being in a place, then finding one
Much larger, with many rooms, that seemed
Strange but familiar? People you know on
some floors, but many you don't elsewhere?
A dreaming place that you were unaware

32)
Existed, but all the same you've been there
Many times before on other nights. If
Your sense of recognition served, you'd swear
This was a place that once you lived in. With
The dream a new and bigger place is found
Inside ourselves, through a forgotten door,

A broken wall, a tunnel underground,
So too here, the boats find a caverned shore,
Through a frond-hung cave, under the castle
Where they climb stone steps and wait nervously
To be sorted into 'houses'. Until
They've tried the sorting hat – which will decree
Their place – they cannot join the feast and be
Part of this larger personality.

33)
The four school houses echo the elements
Of astrology. Gryffindor is fire
And values valour, courage, and a sense
Of chivalry. Hufflepuff's earth, and more
Concerned with patience, hard work and fair play;
A badger to Gryffindor's red lion.
Ravenclaw's air, and values the display
Of intelligence and wit; it's blazon
Is an eagle, while Slytherins portray
Their house as a silver snake, relying on
Cunning and ambition to get their way
By any means. The houses hinge upon.
Instinctual energy, the physical,
The rational, and the emotional.

34)
As they are 'sorted' Harry's nearly last
And sits beneath the hat while it decides
Which house to put him in. It seems to cast
About, unsure which to pick. Harry guides
It by thinking , 'Not Slytherin'. It calls
Out "Gryffindor!" and Harry joins his friends.
Each house has a table on the Great Hall's
Floor, a Staff Table at one of the ends,
Making a pentagram. The ceiling is
Enchanted to show the constellations
Of the night sky. Candle-lit chandeliers
Hang in the air, different decorations

Grace the walls according to the season;
A place of feasting and celebration.

35)
The Teachers sitting at the High Table
Remind us of the seven liberal arts
Of medieval times; together able
To give Wisdom; each discipline imparts
Part of a whole. Dante linked these seven
With the seven known planets of that time.
Perhaps the hall's ceiling showing heaven
Is mirrored here. Dumbledore at his prime
The eighth, in a golden chair, with seven
Teachers at his side teaching the old arts;
Seven functions of the psyche, given
The forms of functionaries. Harry departs,
After the feast, for bed, by winding stair;
Troubled by evil dreams his first night there.

36)
As Harry's learning starts, my poem ends.
The challenge; – to see stories as aspects
Of someone in development; a lens
To view tales through. That which we write reflects
That which we are, and this applies to
Our stories, games, books, jokes, films, dreams and lives
Far more than conscious metaphors like
'Pilgrim's Progress'. The internet contrives
A better map of the collective, just
By what it is, than any mythmaker
Could achieve. The characters we've discussed
Weren't, I imagine, meant to 'mean' whatever
I've said here. They're all God's signature
In us. We're the Stone and the adventure.

37)
First we see Privet Drive, a place so small
There's only room to pass bad feeling round
But not to grow and change. Then comes a call

From somewhere else, to find a larger ground
Of being; – a bigger pot. It seems we
Need (and have) a system of containers
Inbuilt and waiting, like a family tree;
Aspects of who we may be, as trainers
Of parts of who we are. We can unfold
Into this filing system and so grow
Through these relationships; a 'school' where old
And new and might be meet. It's complex, though
We sense it's structure in all that we are
And make and tell, like a passion flower

38)
With different patterns round a centre. Here
We have a vision of the magic world
Creating something that has lasted for
A thousand years. For centuries, we're told,
The structure holds, though faces come and go
As pupils come and learn, and then move on,
Some to have children, while others, we know,
Are teachers in their turn. Musing upon
The theory that we make as we are made,
What does this mean in us? The vision of
A Fountain, or Tree returns, a cascade
That rises, falls, then rises over… years?
Or lifetimes? Through four houses for students
And a High Table for each higher sense.

39)
This school for souls becomes a training place
For mini-personalities based on
Aspects of our nature; each childish face
A face we wear at times, some we put on
To tell a joke, some we'll try out for 'best'
If it appears to help us meet a need.
There's no assurance Harry beats the rest
As who we really are. Each one – a seed
For self. But hey, that's where I go when I

Reflect on this one book. And there's the joy
Of seeing stories in this way; to try
Out ideas, then see if one can employ
Them with oneself. A framework for insight
As well as a delight in its own right.

40)
If works of fiction can be said to show
Some aspects of the person writing it,
Whatever the setting used, and help us know
Parts of their inner tale, then we can fit
Ourselves into their framework, seeing how
Our stories match, like trying on a glove; –
We all have hands. Like a dream may show
our state of play inside, consisting of
Things borrowed from the prop cupboard of our
memory, used to represent our world
Within, and charged with meaning. Yet an hour
Later another dream might be revealed,
Similar in meaning, using a whole
New symbol-set for the same parts of soul.

41)
Perhaps you know mythopoetic lands
Through visualisations, have walked in
Sun-warmed meadows of the mind, have held hands
With angels, met a wise old bean, or been
A diamond? We may take guided tours
Of the soul's country, or let a daydream
Lead us deep within ourselves to the shores
Of meaning, and beyond, and it may seem
The story only happens when we're there;
But it continues, in that unconscious place
(we are unconscious of it – unaware –
Not it of us) perhaps without a face
We'd recognise, or any face at all;
Energies in the Dance Perpetual.

42)
But once we let imagination clothe
Them, metaphor can take us for a walk
To see where it may lead. Let's say we loathe
Draco in us – our aspect that will talk
Sneeringly of others; bully and snob
And bigot – and we fight with him in us
At each turn. We might do a better job
To see his fearful side (as Harry does,
Later on), and maybe feel compassion.
Or let's take Dumbledore. What does it mean
When the time comes that our wise old teacher
Leans on his pupil for help? Harry's seen
To be growing up, while Wisdom's nature
Turns frail; – When 'he we may turn into'
Says, "I'm not worried, Harry, I'm with you."

43)
We tend to see the Wise Old part of us
As always there, always the same, but if
It's like a grandfather… Perhaps we must
See ourselves as a family tree, and give
Some thought to what transpires in families,
What changes over time, and so not just
See the self's development. And what is
Dumbledore's link with a phoenix? We must
Play lightly with these musings. Perhaps they'll
Open doors, give insight, make things expand;
Perhaps not. But try it. Take any tale
From any source. Try it on your hand
Like a glove. Wiggle your fingers to see
How it fits; - then we'll talk of alchemy.

END WORD

44)
Let's take another story, like Star Wars;
The orphan Luke Skywalker come of age

On a desert planet on the far shores
Of space. Two droids appear now at this stage –
Protocol and repair robots. A Wise Old
Jedi Knight starts to teach Luke to fight, then
Takes him to Mos Eisley. Here, we are told,
They can get a spaceship (like Harry's train)
To the larger universe. Their pilots
Are a loner and a Wild Man; two sides
Of one man/beast aspect. It seems the plot's
The same, a hero caught up in the tides
Of a conflict that spans generations;
Same type of thing, different locations.

45)
If we had simply found a formula
For writing books, or making lots of cash
From movies, then so what? But who we are
Shines through, whether the story's good or trash.
We might read Campbell and base our tales
On 'The Hero With A Thousand Faces'
But WE show through despite this; what prevails
Is us, our structure, our inner places
And who we sometimes are. Lord of the Rings,
The same. Four races, Dark Lord, Wise Old Man,
Yada yada yada. All wars and kings
And heroes. But match it to your own plan
And see if you agree (or think I'm odd)
The worst kept secret is the name of God.

46)
Recall that 60's program, 'Lost in Space'?
Absolute tosh, but still it has it all.
Three generations of the human race,
Two each of each sex, and, if you recall,
An alien chimp, a robot and a spy
Called Doctor Smith, lost in a spaceship.
Or 'Through the Looking Glass. Try to apply
Our lens. A chess game; Alice takes a trip
Through a magic mirror to Story-Land

Where nursery rhymes are real. A pawn crossing
The board to be a queen. We understand
These are Lewis Carroll's aspects passing
Before us. The same set, a different glove.
How did he show awareness, will and love?

47)
What part of him is Alice? What part of
Rowling is Harry? Why different sexes
To the writer? Must this go hand in glove
With a true 'soul's story'? What perplexes us
Is finding a guide. Well, how about Jung?
He has a lot to say on Anima
And Animus. There's Wise Old Philemon,
Archetypes like The Hero, and there are
Even personality tests based on
His understanding of the elements
(bit of a shame he put in 'intuition'
Where 'instinct' used to go; It makes more sense
With intuition where the quintessence
Is formed. But still, his insight is immense!

48)
Being so intuitive himself, no
Wonder he did that) What a perspective
He had! The Self, The Trickster, The Shadow;
Individuation, The Collective!
Only… (I'll whisper this), comprehensive
As it is, It's still… another story.
Being accurate and not offensive,
Is Analytical psychology
The truth, or a Tradition? You might have
Noticed I find Qabalah and The Tree
Of Life a useful guide. I also give
Psychosynthesis credit as the key
To its understanding, but…they're ONE door
To truth, and yet another metaphor

49)
However brilliant. Anciently, stories
Have been used for transformation. We
Identify with a hero's glories
And defeats, and match the aspects we see
In the tale, whether friend or enemy
Of the hero, with other parts of us, also
Developing. A force of syntropy
Takes charge, weaving events. Future calls to
Present to transform the past (I wonder
Sometimes if that's why dreams seem syntropic; –
Because the self is buried there under
The conscious, bending each theme and topic
Along an axis of meaning towards
Wholeness. Just by it's presence, it accords)

50)
So with a myth or sacred play we hear,
Or act a part, and link parts of ourselves
We those that are portrayed, and we appear
To transform as the characters themselves
Transform – which bit is 'up' and how things go.
In A.A. people listen to 'the chair'
Tell of their struggle with alcohol through
Painful years, until they found through their despair
The gift of desperation, met by grace,
That changes lives; or can do, if we face
Things as they really are. We can embrace
The similarities we share, or chase
The differences all the way to hell.
So stories can save lives, and souls as well.

51)
Take Robin Hood, the stories or the films
– I like the one with Herne in, but that's me –
And list the characters; – who helps, who harms
The hero? What are the places? Let's see
Who's mentioned but off-stage; what the world's like;
What's the beliefs that govern it? Let's try

Not to dismiss with a word, or mistake
Labels for explanations, like 'Bad Guy'
For the Sheriff. How's he bad, and why would
He need to kill Robin? Or take Hamlet,
Another family drama. Yes, we could
See it as tragedy, but I bet
Strong-armed Fortinbras wasn't complaining;
It's syntropy we find entertaining

52)
However brutal. I could carry on
(American Beauty is good, and the
Hudsucker Proxy, and... and... and so on.
The story doesn't matter. We can see
Every story as a glimpse of the same
Pattern. Even the story of the year
Acted out through all our lives. Every game
We invent has it. It shows through most clear
In all our classification systems;
A library index, a chart of fish in a fish shop,
A list of cars, or birds or gods or gems.
A Liliput Lane village, a Big Top
Of circus folk, a body's organs, all
The rooms in a house, all of these recall

53)
The parts of self. And if these parts can move
And relate to each other, then we see
God. If it can't move He can't get in (you've
Got a problem, then). Movement is the key,
For that is story. As a therapist
I might see, as it were, a game of chess
Inside my client. If I can resist
Sitting to take one side, or make a mess
Giving advice, she can talk of her game,
The state of play, how each piece in it feels;
Exploring, expressing. The candle flame
Of self flickers and burns strong; something heals.

That could never be if I'd sat at her board
And moved her pieces. Does that strike a chord?

54)
How much more with groups. Just to keep it safe
And personal is all it takes. Story
Takes charge, if no-one tries to run things with
An agenda. But hey guys, I'm sorry,
This poem's long enough and you've been good
To read this far! With such a lot unsaid
We'll wind it up. Stories; you've understood,
Can be taken personally instead
Of as just – stories; and this applies to all,
Not some of them. Google 'Egg Diagram'
For a basic map. But try to recall
'A story is one view of who I am,
Not who I am', Metaphor's good but not
(like views) if it's the only one we've got.

55)
And stories – stories are not just in books
But are our lives, and characters not just
Our parts inside but parts we play. It looks
The same story. I sometimes feel there must
Be a place somewhere deep - within? – that is
The original. Oh! I almost see
Their faces! And oh, the adventure! This
Is where I'm needed but I'm here. Round me
I see people on the street like them but...
Shorter, taller, older… like coming out
From a play; there's people like the cast but...
Different; pieces of splintered mirror.
There's things that I must do. I ache to go.
So.. if you find the door, please let me know.

56)
An egg. At the bottom, the past. In here
We live in a world of projections. Here
We start, awareness, cradled in a sphere

Of protection, of love. Then pressure; we're
Pushed to be born by some other will. We're
The done-to bit; – awareness, we're born. There
Outside is love too, and will too to steer
Us, in one person, then as two, then we're
The sphere, for them and our done-to bit where
We record them. Each have 'good' and 'bad'. Here
Trust is born, and so too self-centred fear
And the battle of self and ego. Clear?
Two sides. Two ways. The ego leaves this sphere
To try to rule the rest of us with fear.

57)
Self follows, passing the three advisors –
Sometimes a daily challenge – leaving the
Punch and Judy show of nursery dramas
For a larger place. Using the story
Of Harry, we may suppose there's many
Houses, many triangles, each with a
Part of self, a sub-personality; –
That's where evolution comes in, but hey,.
Just thinking out loud. From that gateway place
We step within the archetypal realm
Which is the Vale of Soul-Making, embrace
Our instincts, feelings, mind, and start to learn
From higher functions met in the centre;
Each Inner sense as teacher and mentor.

58)
There we develop, in the middle zone;
Awareness. We can redeem that below
By reaching up for help – the dotted line –
To that above; here is the way to grow.
An image for you – the magician with
One hand stretched down to help, and one upraised.
Below, a child ruled by cruel parents. If
We can help him pass them (care helps, and praise),
And he side-steps ego waiting above,

He's here at the centre. Thus we redeem
Ourselves, with help from Who We May Be; as
Water bubbling from the Wellspring's stream.
All the fiends and fighters, saints and devils; –
Love, will and awareness on three levels.

59)
Before that Wondrous Tree or Holy Spring
Invisible I saw the waters fall,
Then rise to fall again – or heard them sing -
Or felt them rise within – I can't recall
Exactly. Perhaps... was... was I that Tree?
Or did I fall, so far! so far to climb!
Did I aid him that did? Or... was it me
That tried to hold him back? Or maybe I'm
The one he did it for. I do not know,
I have no explanation. I bow to
The source of continuous creation
And thank God, for I reap where others sow.

So. Rain, wind, earth and sunshine make a tree –
Out of what? That, my friends, is Alchemy.

FINIS

Dancing

The Twelve Steps Of Soul

Exploring how astrology can impact
upon and inform therapeutic work

Keith Hackwood and Mark Jones

Part 1: evolutionary astrology and personal psychosynthesis

Meaning & the Multidisciplinary Mandala

In this article it is our intention to eavesdrop on the interesting and engaging dialogue that is ongoing even now, between the therapeutic modality of Psychosynthesis and the visionary totality of Evolutionary Astrology (EA) as expressed in the books 'Pluto: The Evolutionary Journey of the Soul' and 'Pluto II: The Soul's Evolution Through Relationships'. In so doing we will be paying our dues to the founders of each tradition, the little known Roberto Assagioli and the largely unknown Jeffrey Wolf Green, two men very much of their time whose scintillating ideas and systems have yet to have their full impact upon our world, and whose obvious differences draw a quality of harmonic resonance, one from the other. It is this complementarity that we wish to explore in the following article, rather than any specialist technical or overly fastidious accounts of the operations of astrology or therapy as modes of knowing the world.

Firstly, let us say something about astrology in general and Jeff Green's system of Evolutionary Astrology in particular. The zodiac, upon which all western astrology depends, carries twelve signs or constellations made up of archetypes grouped in six pairs of opposites (such as Leo-Aquarius or Aries-Libra) which hold the creative tension and spectrum of possibilities engendered therein. In the fullest sense, the zodiac is therefore a symbolic representation of the totality of consciousness in potential. All possibilities and manifestations of consciousness are representable (and, so, knowable) by means of the zodiacal wheel. In much the same way as Assagioli's Egg diagram is a model of the operation of consciousness and the movements of the psyche, so the zodiac describes similar movements within a cosmic field, knowable via an individual birthchart, but always placed in the trans-human context of apparently vast movements of time (for example, no human being will experience the full cycle of certain planets used within astrology, since the period of their orbits around the sun is greater than that of a human life; for example Pluto takes 244 years to complete one orbit and hence is said to operate in generational, as well as purely personal octaves. Contrast this with, say, Mars, which takes 2 years to orbit the sun, and therefore has a much more 'personal' cyclic influence). Also like the Egg diagram, the zodiac is a map, and as we all know useful as any map certainly is, it is not the territory. Astrology, and especially Evolutionary astrology then, operates by means of wheels within wheels – creatively angelic, like the descriptions of Ezekiel and like the observed motions of the heavens above our benighted heads.

All civilizations and cultures have made use of astrology and often developed its precision and effectiveness to levels of refinement to rival anything our projective technological worldview has manifested. It is in this tradition that we wish to place Jeffrey Wolf Green and EA, and for this reason that we will argue for EA as offering much to the psychotherapeutic endeavour. So what makes EA special? Firstly, we would do well to note its focus, which is primarily placed upon the distant planet Pluto. Pluto, god of the underworld in Roman mythology (Hades in the Greek pantheon), twinned with its moon Charon (the ferryman),

speak deeply of intensity. Pluto rules the eighth zodiacal sign
Scorpio, which is often characterised in newspaper or 'cookbook'
astrology as being about sex, death and inheritance. For EA the
Pluto/Scorpio archetype is the soul. The soul is viewed through
the lens of Pluto, in all its incarnational history, with all its stored
potential and wounding, without taboo, without judgment, but
with absolute honesty, necessity and intensity. Simply put, this is
why EA is of interest, not only to astrologers or even transpersonal
therapists, but to clients – to us all. It provides a methodology
by means of which we can engage with the language of soul –
the logos of soul, psychology. Hence, for EA Pluto is the natural
psychologist, who brings penetration and depth to the experience
of being a soul. From a psychosynthesis point of view we might
call this experience whereby soul integrates into personality,
the I. Similarly, the dialogue between an individual soul and
the archetype of Pluto as Soul mirrors our understanding of the
I-Self axis, an inseparable double-mirroring of the timeless Self
within the lived body, the wave and the particle simultaneously
participating in an indivisible revelation, the generative mystery
of which we could call, with Keats, conscious soul making.

The question now arises, to what extent does EA impact
upon or inform therapeutic work?

THE SKY (RIGHT NOW) AT NIGHT

Let us begin to address the question we have set by means of
a tour of the major thematic emphases to be found in the night
sky at the time of writing (Easter 2005). The most striking notes,
from an EA perspective, are sounded by Pluto (currently in
Sagittarius), Uranus in Pisces, Neptune in Aquarius and Saturn's
movement from Cancer into Leo.

That Evolutionary Astrology   provides a clear
methodology to identify potential prior life traumas is an
enormous gift. That so many have developed such therapeutic
precision and insight over the last century of the evolution of
modern psychotherapy is another tremendous gift. The proposal,
at least in part, of this analysis of the planetary positions in the

sky and their meaning for us as human beings is that there are the beginnings of a cross fertilisation between these two disciplines. The work of Robert Sardello in such texts as 'Love and the World' and 'The Soul of the World' have shown what kind of interchange can occur between thinkers as profound and diverse as Jung and Steiner. In this essay, encouraged by some of the initial meditations on the nature of the transpersonal planets we propose that extending this dialogue toward Evolutionary Astrology and allowing its intense reply could open up whole new areas that as Synthesists we wish to nurture.

Just as in an individual's chart Pluto is our bottom line so within the collective picture does it contain an underlying theme of the evolutionary dynamics of any given time within the collective. Pluto in Sagittarius speaks powerfully about the nature of truth, the experience of faith and the fundamental or natural laws underpinning creation. Jeffrey Wolf Green's work in bringing EA into the world has emphasized the seminal notion of natural laws working within the totality of creation (as symbolised by the 12 archetypes within Astrology). A natural law may be contrasted with a man-made law. It is a man-made law for example in Britain that one must pay 40% tax if one earns over a certain figure, it is a natural law, for example, intrinsic to Psyche that we do not encourage children in our care to go and play on a motorway! At points man-made law and natural law co-incide, for instance in the realization that there is always a cost or price to pay for taking another's life; at points they depart, in for example the notion that this cost is reversed as a prize in examples of genocide throughout the world. Without wishing to pin these fundamental natural laws to anything as clumsy as a list Jeffrey Wolf Green traces the origin of these laws and our dialogue about their use or our judgments about them through an analysis of Pluto's Nodes.

Very few astrologers much less the general reader are aware that all planet's have nodes, not just the famed example of the Moon's nodes. The Nodes themselves represent an abstract point in space where the orbit of the planet intersects the ecliptic on which the circle of wheel of the zodiac resides. The upward or ascending motion of the planet creates the North Node the descending motion the South Node. Just as in EA we are able to trace the history of any given person through the south node of the moon so we can trace the history of any planetary function through its own nodes. In the case of Pluto the South Node is in Capricorn, which leads us to meditation on the underlying history of Pluto, the issue of the unconscious and depth security within the Soul stem at this time, from within the Capricorn archetype. Within this archetype, through the phenomena of the precession of the equinoxes, the shift from astrological age to age, most famously in the much heard cry in our own time of the transition from the Piscean Age to the Aquarian Age, Green notes the phenomena of sub-ages: that half-way through the approximately 2,000 years of each age its sub-age, or polarized archetype comes into influence. On this calculation the age of Capricorn as a sub-age of Cancer would be seen to predominate around 6,500 B.C. a time which Green links (via for example the anthropological work of Riane Eisler in texts such as 'The Chalice and The Blade' and 'Sacred Pleasure') to the rise of a patriarchal society from the vestiges of the prior matriarchy.

With the South Node of Pluto in our time in Capricorn we could posit on a larger collective level that we are all born with deep security issues stemming from this transition and the resulting imbalances that this transition has brought through culture and religion. Is this born out through our experience today? By this reckoning some of the fundamental struggle for truth, for a living definition of religious experience or faith, that comes through Pluto moving through Sagittarius would include a massive struggle within patriarchal systems of political and religious thought, the difference if you like between natural and man-made laws. I think most of us would agree that this broad backdrop contains many of the issues that dominate our time with the rise of the Christian right and the neo-conservatives in the U.S, with the rise of fundamentalism in that form and through the Islamic world. On a more personal level it can be sensed within the ongoing struggle for equality within the world, for at the heart of the Sagittarius archetype is a nomadic experience, a tribal origin in the so-called 'primitive' cultures, itself a patriarchal branding. As books such as Marlo Morgan's 'Mutant Message

Down Under' clearly echo the work of many anthropologists that the 'primitive' cultures held a wisdom within their relationship to the environment and to each other that is simply breathtaking in its complex harmony with the consciousness of the earth. Indeed the phenomena of this consciousness, that James Lovelock called 'Gaia', is another correspondence with the Sagittarius archetype in EA. The movement of Pluto, harbinger of death and transformation through Sagittarius denotes a clear shift in our recognition of our involvement with Gaia as we struggle to surpass the history of our involvement as simply takers from the earth (Pluto South Node in Capricorn) through the illusion of our supremacy through the Industrial revolution and our cataclysmic attitude to the earth's resources.

It is within this collective picture that we see our clients who are appalled at such injustice, who vent their anger on protests against war and the rape of the third world. Here we place our own dialogue with what is true, against the memories of so many distortions of that truth. Within Sagittarius at its most realized spirituality is a natural phenomena of existing within the earth's love on a conscious level, through Capricorn and the resulting distortion of patriarchy the earth is like woman, a secondary force that must be held subservient to the priest/man and his needs. The earth and woman must be covered or else bowed before the phallic light. Indeed from this perspective all consciousness emerges from this solar light energy, even as evolutionary biologists begin to discover that creation needs only heat in the depths of the ocean to create from her womb.

In the archetype of Neptune we find the collective unconscious in EA, we find the divinity, the final surrender to the totality within the final archetype. The South Node of Neptune is in Aquarius, at a point where Neptune has just been transiting the last few years, returning to its own origins. These are origins, to follow Green's meditation on the ages that stem from the last Aquarian Age 25,000 years ago! A time that in his far meditation (not dissimilar to the level on which Rudolf Steiner based the parameters of his teaching) Green associates with the culmination of the matriarchy, its high cultural phase. Green's vision of the matriarchy is held within certain native cultures still alive today, even partly their glories lie in the imagination such as the native American Indians or the indigenous peoples of the Amazon basin etc – a life characterized by living within the boundaries of what the earth can provide, characterized by giving, sharing and inclusion. In such societies being ostracised from the tribe represents the ultimate punishment and often-literal death. Within such cultures equality was key – from the shaman to the humble fruit picker all were respected, as all were essential to the good of all. It is this loss within patriarchy of the sense of connection on an essential level to the others working with and for you that is so causal in the alienation so much a part of the Aquarian archetype in today's world. Whilst Green is inviting no simple return to primitivism a la Rousseau he certainly challenges through his meditations on the origins of Planetary functions (through their Nodes) the complacency of the modern consciousness in its tenuous grasp on the more existential concerns.

Much of the alienation coming through the Aquarian archetype today stems also from the relation of Aquarius and Uranus to trauma. This is one of the key insights within Green's Evolutionary Astrology relevant to all today, and maybe especially therapists, with Neptune in Aquarius at the same time as Uranus is in Pisces. This is what Astrologer's call a mutual reception – because the ruler of Pisces (Neptune) is in Aquarius at the same time as the ruler of Aquarius (Uranus) is in Pisces. At its highest Neptune corresponds to healing through reconnection to spirit. Aquarius/Uranus corresponds to far memory, a memory of the earliest events of this life, memory of inter-uterine experiences so carefully recorded through Stan Grof's extensive research and his identification of Basic Peri-natal Matrices, and also, through EA, a memory of other lives, the prior lives of the Soul or mind-stream as it manifests extensions of itself throughout the space-time continuum. Within this far memory Evolutionary Astrology delineates the impacts of history, both personal and collective, in the development of each self as held within the natal chart and influenced by the planetary conditions in the sky at each time.

With this mutual reception of the Piscean and Aquarian archetypes we are pointed to the highest goal or potential of healing and reconnection to spirit (Pisces/Neptune) which takes place through the individuation journey or reintegrating the self within all its experiences contained within far memory (Aquarius/ Uranus). Green's genius in Evolutionary Astrology has been to identify a form of Post Traumatic Stress Disorder effecting people from prior lives. A Vietnam war veteran himself whose encounter with a Vietnamese Buddhist monk whilst serving with the U.S. Marines led him after the war to several temples in the U.S. and a reconnection with his teacher Paramahansa Yogananda, Green is no stranger to the issues of trauma. Whilst serving within the war he was exposed to vicious Agent Orange poisoning which leaves him even now too weak to travel and teach as he used and led to one of his children being born with a genetic disorder congruent with the kind of damage he himself suffered. Yet in his analysis through his own profound relationship to the astrological signatures Green has been able to identify the causes of many issues and traumas in the present life within prior life events. For example in this life he was born with a strange birth mark on his chest and a residual anger that led him into the Vietnam war in the first place (in a kind of 'prison or fight' deal offered by the American authorities). He would later understand through prior life recall a life as a native American Indian rushing home from a successful hunt to see his family butchered and find himself shot in the chest as vainly he tried to save them.

Outside of his personal story, which we recount partly here simply as context, Green has been able to explore the Plutonic question 'why?' within astrology to take western astrology to a depth that previous only eastern modes held – i.e. a direct understanding of how prior life causes shape the current life and destiny. If we take the meditations on the planetary placements in the sky now in Easter 2005 and their history of origin through the planetary nodes we can see a general healing and therapeutic concern for all of us working in the healing professions whether we work directly with it or not. This is a crucial point for by working intensively with the issues in the present, by allowing the archetypes of that work through dreams and visualisations or just through the intensity of the encounter, we build the temenos in which such healing can occur. Not that direct work is unnecessary, as Psychosynthesis therapists we may open to, say, hypnotherapy to explore these very avenues for the benefit of the experiential integration of those we work with. Yet even with the less direct approach we are concerned here to make the case for how serious this enterprise of integration within the far memory can be – so many of our clients today have issues and are profoundly stuck upon themes and problems that originated and were often compounded through trauma in previous lives. The condition of the planets in the sky at this present point make clear that acknowledgment and the initiation of healing modalities to work with and through this realisation are part of the shift required as we move from the Piscean to Aquarian Age.

In analysing the South Node of Uranus we return to the theme we began with as it resides in Sagittarius – i.e. the nature of our individuation (Aquarius/Uranus) lies in our capacity to experience our own truth, our inner wholeness. Just as Ken Wilber in his multi-dimensional model of the human psyche identifies the centauric stage as the integration of the body-mind (only possible through retraction or awareness of the persona and relative integration of the shadow) so through Sagittarius, the centaur, the teacher of the hero's, the being who integrates animal (horse), man (upper body) and spirit (through the flight of the arrow of truth) are our may aspects unified into the field of our personal truth if we can find a way to be with that truth within the world. As Sardello so simply and so radically pointed out it is no good simply to enter therapy as a fantasy, a recollection with our innerness, such innerness is inert or as so much candy floss where compared to a lived experience within the field whereby such innerness is simply openness to the sophianic stream of the Soul of the World rushing back to meet us as innerness steps outside. All our individuated power stems from our relationship in truth with the natural laws of this living Cosmos, all trauma originates in the breaking of this tryst between our individual being as it exists with the being-of-all. All trauma is simply and ultimately a lie, all lies whether from oneself to another or simply within oneself will generate trauma…

In Evolutionary Astrology in distinction from most other Western forms of astrology, Saturn/Capricorn is perceived as the structure of consciousness, both from the level of how we structure our own individual consciousness to the nature of the space-time reality in which we inhabit the 3D world. In its polarity, Cancer/Moon, we have the nature of the individual ego, the formative experiences of the early home-life, the nature of emotional imprinting and via the polarity, Saturn, the structure of the emotional body, the nature of the ego type. As Saturn makes the shift from Cancer to Leo we see symbolically a collective shift in the structure of consciousness from one of individual security, true security coming essentially from within, from an acceptance of the self and the particular formative experiences that shaped it into a need to engage with the endeavour of building or actualising that self through its own creative engagement with the world. In this way, for the next two and a half years, the structural principle of consciousness as it manifests through the collective (and by definition we can thereby only talk of generalised influences in this context) invites us to an increased engagement with our creativity and the feedback such creativity engenders between ourselves, the community and world in which we live. In a way this essay, a collaboration between two friends in their mutual encouragement of each other's creativity, is a statement within that general shift. A desire to put one's creativity on the line, to risk a response from the world in whatever way it may choose, to risk to think and create from multiple platforms in a way that sustains the multiple ways in which the self has perceived its own creative evolution within the world and the myriad of different teachings that have aided such a project. Whilst this is always an issue in life, just as there is always a Saturn and always a Leo archetype, whilst Saturn lives inside Leo such issues are focused and highlighted within the collective psyche.

SO WHAT?

So what, indeed. What opinions might we be able to form in relation to this information gleaned from a quick tour of the night sky at this time? How might it be helpful to us as busy, professional therapeutic practitioners with heavy client-loads and little enough time as it is? Well, in lieu of personal answers to these relevant questions, the first evident point to make is that the sky provides us with information out of which we can decode archetypal context for any individual life (our own included) on earth at this time. We can begin to place ourselves and our clients within a specific matrix of energies being triggered and shaped through cosmic motion and soulful intervention within the collective. This may in turn give us an unique perspective from which to view the issues being brought to us, the themes developing in our own professional and private lives, and the 'thing most needful' (where such exists and can be known). It is also a wonderfully elevated platform from which to study cultural psychopathology, but more of that in Part 2.

In the interests of grounding this starry gnosis, gleaned as it is from way above our heads, it is important to speak of the body. Not just the physical, cellular body, the locus of activity for soul interfacing with world (for bioPsychosynthesis), but also the emotional body, and for what some healers have termed the 'knowing field' generated between therapist and client in a successful enough I-Thou state. We have all had the experience, be it alone or with an Other, but what is the content we access at such times? What is it we see-feel, that is bigger than our I-personality, more vivid than our subpersonalities and yet doggedly elusive and mysterious, even as it affects us in the moment? For EA the answer is simple – we are encountering the stored residues of our own prior lives as information in the here and now. The soul (Pluto) remembers, and since soul is no other than body in a state of natural law (only distorted patriarchal monotheisms insist upon a splitting off of soul from body, and a subsequent dualistic masochism of body hatred and transcendent yearning) the body, in its cell-structures, also retains the information of all life, morphogenetically resonant and available right now. For the same reason (patriarchal distortion) we can also posit the notion that many of our prior lives within the gestalt of 'history' have included deep woundings – deep trauma – through the misshaping of the natural by the transcender hierarchy (for example, a life lived as a native forcefully taken from a culture of matriarchy and suddenly subject to the impositions of empire manifested in religious terms (one god not many) as well as social/economic terms (slavery), producing pain, trauma, perhaps brutality and death, certainly confusion, despair, maybe guilt, anger, fear – all of which the soul remembers and seeks to work through, not only alone but also in relation to those other soul's whose paths intertwine with ours). This is where we discover the 'evolutionary' part of Evolutionary Astrology, in the notion of the soul evolving in relation to the personality through time, not only within the span of a single life, but across many, many lives. Jeff Green proposes that because of this we are all born, to some degree, already traumatised – trailing not only Wordsworthian 'clouds of glory' but also personal and collective traumas of the deepest, most impenetrable kind.

At this point we should also note the ways in which EA connects very well with certain other therapeutic modes, most notably that of prior-life regression work as that carried out under the ægis of post-Erickson hypnotherapy. Also worthy of note is the work of the Dutch regression therapist Hans Ten Dam, whose incredible book 'Deep Healing' ties in very precisely with the operation of EA, as well as offering much to the Psychosynthesis approach.

The emotional body, the physical body and the knowing-field create a matrix through which the therapist can assist the client in orientating him or herself in relation to their prior-life trauma. The prior-life trauma in and of itself, is no different than the issues which they present (or obfuscate) in their current life, this is not about some highly wrought mysticism or baroque psychism, but rather the concrete operation of healing through time via the only time that exists, the Now. One tell-tale sign of the proximity of prior-life material, which again we have, no doubt all experienced, is that of the response-that-is-out-of-all-proportion-to-the-apparent-stimulus. In other words the client whose thoughts and feelings seem excessive in relation to the trigger – the woman who knows her husband is cheating on her no matter what the assurances of 'reality', or the man who feels inadequate in his inner-life and cannot form relationships, no matter how supportive his environment or how perfect (or ordinary) his childhood. There are countless variants of course, but the emotional tone and the frequency of repetition within the clients' awareness are clear significators of prior-life trauma. As is current life trauma, since in evolutionary terms we often get stuck where we always got stuck, or become enmeshed in the archetypal patterns we have not yet ensouled. In EA these issues are often referred to as 'skipped steps' and they show up regularly in the birth charts of clients – pointing clearly at 'the elephant in the living room' from the soul's point of view, and requiring the conscious resolution of current and prior-life traumas in relation to the specifics of the original wounding (be it learned guilt, sadomasochism, an overpowering sense of lack, a need to dominate and oppress or whatever other form it might manifest within). The soul mediates time through the language of psyche – in other words, when we are in the place of our I we have access, through the Self, to all of our karmic experiences in all apparent times – when we are fully 'in the now' we are, mysteriously, in every 'now' we have experienced – not as Keith Hackwood or Mark Jones, but as a soul. From the soul's own side (which ego and even I can never know) time is a sort of play-dough, colourful, useful for making shapes, expressive – but prone to dry out and become dead and useless, and utterly foul to the taste!

ME, MYSELF & I-THOU

As we have seen, from the larger sweep of the transhistorical perspective we can trace a human movement from prehistoric hunter-gatherer nomad to agricultural matriarchy, in which certain principles of natural law appear. From this point the story becomes increasingly one of patriarchal dominance, reflected in the increasing usage of metals, the technology of weaponry and the organisation of priest-king and state structures. The necessary balance sought by the individual soul occurs within a context of global, generational and cosmic soul patterns and cycles, and within the individual soul level another useful calibration can be posited. For EA this calibration is grouped around nine divisions in three broad stages – the so-called evolutionary stages. It is important at this point to note that these stages are described primarily in terms of state, not station – so in their application to a client, or to ourselves, or for that matter, to the varying dynamics of our subpersonality populations, it is the basic state where our consciousness resides on a day to day level that we are aligning with and naming. Hence, when we learn that there are three major categorisations of soul, Consensus, Individuated and Spiritual, and that each has three stages (first, second and third) we take the lid of a host of self-judging and fantasising dynamics ('I must be first stage spiritual', 'I can't possibly be in the consensus' or whatever), hence it is important that we use our critical distance, our deepest and highest sense of where our soul is, in its manifestation through our relationships and activities in the world. All souls are equal in potential, the spiritually realised state is always possible and available – and yet the workings through of karma, the resolution of 'skipped steps', the healing necessities of our unresolved trauma in relation to self, world and other all affect our state and colour the nature of our 'ground of being'.

It is said, very broadly and imprecisely, but by way of clarification, that at any given time 75% of souls manifesting on Earth will be in the broadly consensus state – meaning that their concerns will primarily be with the here and now of material existence, of this life and this life alone, of power dynamics that are most at home in dominating others or projecting needs outwards. This state resembles the herds of the animal kingdoms, with its higher ends representing leaders of the state, much as modern politicians do. In the consensus there is nothing to be gained from seriously questioning anything – reality stops at the end of the nose. A good example of the consensus state is the way in which people believe what they are meant to believe, without question or personal enquiry – astrology is hokum, say the astronomers – and so it is for most people.

A further 20% of souls will be in the individuating state – which in turn is said to be the state in which the soul spends the longest amount of time and undergoes the most desperate afflictions, tests and sense of alienation. Here we find everyone from the cultural revolutionary to the psychotherapist, engaging with the forms of a social and global structure, which will largely be experienced, as marginalizing and threatening to the emergent sense of 'I'. The key threshold of the individuation state is to realise the necessity of the spiritual (not the religious, since organised religion largely exists in the consensus state, as a means of mass control more than a means towards enlightened soul-realisation). The final 2% or so of souls incarnating at a given time will be those in the three spiritual states, moving through karma of teaching, of releasing guru projections, of developing the purity of their teachings and agency in the world.

From a therapeutic point of view it is highly unlikely that the bulk of people who are primarily identified with consensus reality would ever present for counselling or therapy (or an astrological consultation, for that matter), except where such activities are culturally sanctioned (witness, say, the mainstream 'acceptability' of yoga in the last decade or so – and the way in which it ceases to be about the royal road to conscious evolution through dedicated yogic practice and becomes more a lifestyle choice, a marketing opportunity, a diet/exercise fad for ex-Spice Girls, and ultimately, a pale imitation of what 'yoga' truly means. This is how the consensus operates, to retain control in a small hierarchy and maintain the status quo at all costs). Similarly, it is equally unlikely that anyone in the higher spiritual states would ever present for therapy, both because of their relative rarity, and due to the fact that their basic evolutionary state would, by definition, be developed beyond the psychological. This is not to say that any individual great teacher or guru does not still have issues, emotionally or psychologically, regarding control or value, or desire energy – however, such issues are encountered through the vaster parts of the being that are already connected with realised spiritual states (interestingly, it is within spiritual organisations that this dynamic most surfaces as something potentially workable by means of psychotherapy, an opportunity for group Psychosynthesis as a counter to the anti-shadow, pathology of the sublime that can arise in and around highly spiritualised teachers and communities).

The vast majority of any practitioner's clients will emerge from those 18% or so of souls currently identified with the individuated state, so it is these we shall concentrate on a little deeper. Whilst all souls are equal in an absolute sense, some are more equal than others from the relative perspective of any given moment in time. Those in the first stage of the individuated state will largely be characterised by the dynamics of the 'inner lie'. In other words, their outer lives may relate very strongly to the consensus, they will generally have jobs (often good jobs) and be outwardly attached to the culturally acceptable goals of success, the accumulation of wealth, security and so on. However, their secret lives will mirror the growing split between the outer appearance and the inner reality – the swelling gnosis that what was once enough no longer suffices. The right job, house, car, partner, holiday, hairstyle, diet, friends or clothes increasingly fail to paper over the cracks apparent in the psyche. It is as though the soul knows that these objects are not where life's focus needs to be. Often there ensues a series of life events or crises to 'force the issue' and bring the soul in question into confronting itself in the light of these issues.

This leads us to the second stage of the individuated state, perhaps the point of maximum isolation and alienation from the soul's perspective, and often the most confusing and painful point on the journey of the personality self. Here it is as though everything is broken. Consensus reality no longer works for the individual, it seems little more than a hollow sham. However, the crisis ensuing from leaving the herd has not yet resolved itself – the state mirrors that of the caterpillar inside the pupæ, melting its form and yet not yet unfolding the blueprint of the form to come. Hence, it is a time of maximum vulnerability, and a place wherein many souls have received much wounding, as they work to shed prior-life conditionings, and yet, typically, meet with no validation from the world around them or the people they share their lives with. This is the archetypal leaders of the protest movement, for example, acting out their alienation and, often, inherently more evolved than the political leaders they seek to overthrow. What matters most here is freedom, absolute radical freedom. And yet what manifests is often a distortion, an enactment of the woundedness rather than the healing potential of the situation, and hence often re-traumatising occurs (for self and others).

Therapeutically, building trust and the good-enough therapeutic relationship with person's whose primary identification is with the second stage of individuated consciousness is a substantial challenge. These are souls in extremis, some will take a suicidal trajectory, some will act out in self-harming, eating disorders, addictions of all kinds and a host of other gnarly psychopathologies, railing against the existential meaninglessness of human suffering and angry to the depths of their being. However, it is precisely this client group that a modality such as Psychosynthesis (which allows individual freedoms, holds its own models lightly enough and with a fly-by-wire subtlety and precision, and yet also offers the maps through which a soul may encounter its broadest dimensions in a safely non-dogmatic way) can serve most effectively. It serves us as therapists to realise that, at least from an EA perspective, this is what we are often engaged with in the counselling room – the business of soulmaking, soul-reparation, prior and present life healing and the envisioning of uncensored potential pathways towards the stabilised 'I', and beyond. The deepest need of the second stage individuated person is to find their own freely chosen and inwardly validated spiritual path. Few (if any) will use this language or frame their issues this way, and yet the application of even basic EA techniques, as shown here, demonstrates the truth of the assertion. We are, as someone said, midwives of soul; and as someone else said, no community is complete until it can hold its own births and deaths consciously – so, as a community of transpersonal therapists, we are not only in the midwife business, but if we are authentic, we also often perform the functions of the executioner, the headsman, removing false hopes of a return to regressive consensus states, or flights of superego fancy. It is, perhaps, for this reason that the client pays us – as in the past one paid the hangman or axeman, to ensure a noble, swift and clean death. The stakes in our work are often that high, whether we are always conscious of them or not.

Let us conclude this section by talking of the third stage of the individuated state. Natives of this state will be seeking to understand their unique individuality as distinct from society and to act accordingly in authentic and integrative ways, whilst also attending to their 'baggage' – their relationships to others (who may or may not share their evolutionary state), their need to become congruent in all the major areas of their lives (issues such as creating 'right work' or resolving longstanding difficulties with parents for example). Again, a therapy such as Psychosynthesis has a great deal to offer to people in this state, especially as they move to explore the leading edge of their innate spirituality and to generate forms for expressing this in authentic, worldly ways. It is also a highly creative state, and often responds well to the kind of visualisation work found in, for instance, Piero Ferucci's work.

WOULD YOU BELIEVE?

Evolution, broadly speaking, happens in one of two major ways – either through a cataclysmic event or crisis, or via a continual growth. This is as true for the soul's evolutionary journey as it is for the origin of species from a materialist point of view. The shaping and growth of the soul through time, as described through the techne of EA, coupled to the mapping of consciousness and the therapeutic applications made possible through modes such as Psychosynthesis, together constitute a threshold moment for psychology itself. The potential exists for the founding of principled, open and synthetic means of arriving at human understanding of the totality of consciousness through the lived experience of an individual life in relation to the cosmic context, the marriage of the vertical and horizontal axes. This (and other) form(s) of spiritual technology equips us to work multidimensionally with our own experiences, as well as those of our clients. As the soul is divided for the sake of consciousness, so it returns to a unified state in the name of that same consciousness, now fully expressed and cyclically ripe to dissolve. This is the story of separating desires moving through the desire for reunification with oneness – the soul's story, the story whispered by Pluto, who sometimes speaks of Love and Will. Let's conclude this first part of our exploration of EA/Psychosynthesis, with its emphasis on the personal journey, with a quote from the guru and inner-teacher of Jeffrey Green, Paramahansa Yogananda. "Mankind is engaged in an eternal quest for that 'something else' he hopes will bring him happiness, complete and unending. For those individual Souls who have sought and found God, the search is over, He is that something else." *Man's Eternal Quest*

Works Cited

Eisler, Riane; *The Chalice & The Blade*, Thorsons, London 1990

Eisler, Riane; *Sacred Pleasure: Sex, Myth & the Politics of the Body, New Paths to Power & Love*, Element Books, Dorset, 1996

Green, Jeff; *Pluto Volume 1: The Evolutionary Journey of the Soul*, Llewellyn Publications, St Paul, Minnesota, 1998

Green, Jeffrey Wolf; *Pluto Volume II: The Soul's Evolution Through Relationships*, Llewellyn Publications, St Paul, Minnesota, 2000

Morgan, Marlo; *Mutant Message Down Under*, Harper Collins, London, 1994

Sardello, Robert; *Love & the World: A Guide to Conscious Soul Practice*, Lindisfarne Books, Massachusetts, 2001

Ten Dam, Hans; *Deep Healing: A Practical Outline of Past-Life Therapy*, Tasso Publishing, Amsterdam, Netherlands, 1996

If you would like to read Part 2 of this work, please visit:
http://schoolofevolutionaryastrology.com/school/blog

BIOGRAPHIES OF CONTRIBUTORS

Alan Robinson

Alan works in private practice in Somerset, as an accredited psychotherapist. Formerly he had a successful career in commerce and took advantage of a redundancy opportunity to train in Psychosynthesis in Bristol, gaining his diploma in 2000 and BACP Accreditation in 2004. He is also married and has three 'grown-up children' and two grandchildren.

For more information, including contact details, see www.counselling.in-somerset.net

Ellis Linders

Ellis has a background in the performing arts and holistic medicine. In 2001 she experienced a spiritual emergency which triggered an onset of severe M.E. Since that time her inquiry into meaning and transformation in consciousness transition continues to be at the root of her healing journey. She completed Will Parfitt's distance course in Psychosynthesis in 2006 and is currently studying Transpersonal Psychology and Consciousness Studies at Liverpool John Moores University (Distance Learning).

Ellis lives her life as a "hermit in the world" in beautiful Somerset.

John Bunzl

John has lectured widely, including to The Schumacher Society, The World Trade Organisation, The Lucis Trust and at various universities. He is a company director living in London. He has three children.

Having had only a passing interest in international affairs and in the thinking of E.F. Schumacher, in 1998 the idea for Simultaneous Policy suddenly occurred to him as a potential means for removing the barriers which prevent many of today's global problems from being solved. In 2000 he founded the *International Simultaneous Policy Organisation* (ISPO) and launched the Simultaneous Policy (Simpol) campaign. In 2001, he set out the campaign in his first book of the same name. The Simpol campaign has since steadily been gathering increasing attention, recognition and support amongst citizens, activists, non-governmental organisations, politicians, business people and many others.

In 2003 he co-authored his second book, *Monetary Reform – Making it Happen!*, written with the prominent monetary reformer, James Robertson. In 2009 he authored a third book, *People-centred Global Governance – Making it Happen!*

Email: info@simpol.org

Jay Ramsay

Jay is the author of over 30 books of poetry and non fiction including his anthology, collated with Will Parfitt, *Into the Further Reaches – an anthology of Contemporary British Poetry celebrating the spiritual journey* (64 poets: PS Avalon, 2007); Out of Time - Poems 1998-2008 (PS Avalon); *Places of Truth - journeys into sacred wilderness* (Awen, 2009), and *The Poet in You* (O Books, 2009), which reproduces part of his unique poetry and personal development course *Chrysalis – the poet in you* (since 1990).

Jay is also a UKCP accredited psychosynthesis psychotherapist who has lived with psychosynthesis since his mid 20's, and is in private practice in Stroud and London NW3.

More about his work – and workshops at Hawkwood near Stroud – can be found on www.lotusfoundation.org.uk, and www.hawkwoodcollege.co.uk,

Keith Hackwood

Keith Hackwood is based near Newport, South Wales and works as a Psychosynthesist therapist and superviser in the local university, as well as in private practice. He enjoys writing in its many forms, as well as spending as much time as possible outdoors.

Keith can be reached via hackwoodk@aol.com

Mark Jones

Mark is a Psychosynthesis Therapist, Evolutionary Astrologer and Hypnotherapist working in private practice in Bristol. Mark is the main teacher of Evolutionary Astrology in the U.K. and frequently lectures and teaches at the EA and Norwac conferences in the United States. A Llewellyn spring 2010 publication *Insights Into Evolutionary Astrology* features a chapter by Mark on the planetary nodes and their collective significance. Mark is currently in the process of co-writing a book with Keith Hackwood on the planetary nodes and the history of civilization, the origin of depth psychology and the atomic age.

Mark has a website www.plutoschool.com and can be contacted for individual therapy foussing on personal potential and life-meaning, astrology readings that can map the deep patterns that motivate our lives, and astrological tuition.

Marilyn Mehlmann

Marilyn, a UK citizen resident in Sweden since 1967, is married with children and grandchildren and has a Diploma in Applied Psychosynthesis from Gothenburg, 1993. Since 1995 Marilyn has been General Secretary and Head Trainer of *Global Action Plan* (GAP) International, including training and consultancy work worldwide and involvement in action research including applications of empowerment, and development of new methods for accelerated collective learning.

Marilyn's current (2009) focus is on sustainability, leadership, and social change processes, including a new development program Leadership for Sustainable Development, and an ongoing series of workshops QED Coaching in Sweden, Belarus and other countries.

http://www.globalactionplan.com

Mike Stillwell

Mike Stillwelll began training in Pyschosynthesis in 1992, and works full time as an alcohol counsellor. He lives in Hertfordshire, and his interests include historical European martial arts – particularly duelling with sword and buckler - and the Sikh martial art of Gatka.

After a long day's work he likes nothing more than listening to the Harry Potter books read by Stephen Fry.

Previn Karian

Previn is a psychosynthesis practitioner who has extended his work into multi-modality therapy. As Resonance Practitioners, he runs a very full private practice in Bournemouth and Southampton. He is known in some circles for his extensive and provocative book review articles in left of field magazines such as Ipnosis and Transformations.

He is a member of The Counselling Society who have also accredited his training modules in ten different schools of psychotherapy for the training arm of Resonance. He is also a member of The Squiggle Foundation, PCSR (Psychotherapists and Counsellors for Social Responsibility), a participant member of IPN (Independent Practitioners Network) and a devotee of Frank Zappa ("Music is the best!").

Rachael Clyne

Rachael Clyne lives in Glastonbury where she practices as a psychotherapist and counsellor. She graduated from the Psychosynthesis Trust in 1986, since then she has co-ordinated spiritual counselling training courses and worked in a wide range of settings. Her self help book *Breaking the Spell – The Key to Recovering Self-esteem* (PS Avalon 2005) has proven a great success. She is also a published poet (*She Who Walks With Stones* (PS Avalon 2006) and *Acclimatising* (2008) and performs in a trio of poets called Strange Sisters.

She is inspired by nature, and all aspects of the human journey, which she expresses with depth and a good deal of humour. She believes that cultivating local community and learning to share is the essential way forward in the 21st century. "We are entering the greatest transition humanity has faced: it's transpersonal or bust!"

Ricky N. Lock

Ricky is a Psychosynthesis Counsellor and EMDR Therapist and is also a registered healer with the BRCP. His work also includes working as a trainer at the Psychosynthesis & Education Trust in London. His motivation for this work is to help people to find their own inner wisdom, strengths, qualities and creativity, so they can live a happier and more fulfilled life.

Ricky have been interested in reading and writing poetry for many years and his favourite poets are William Blake, Lord Byron and the world war one war poets, Wilfred Owen, Siegfried Sassoon and Rupert Brooke. He started writing poetry around 10 years ago as a way of discovering and expressing his own hidden feelings and to broaden his understanding of how he viewed the world. His poetry has given him many hidden jewels and a deepening awareness of himself as well as a new way to relate to others. He has had poems published in America as well as here in England.

Ricky enjoys running and playing squash and walking along coastal footpaths, and is also an avid reader.

Email: rickylock@btinternet.com
Website: http://www.selfsight.com

Roderick Field

Roderick was born in South London in 1965. After a brief but entertaining education, he moved north of the river and began his career as a photographer. Now a qualified psychotherapy practioner, travelling photographer and writer, he is on a mission to capture the essence of what it is to be human.

"With an emphasis on spontaneity, I prefer the quality of natural light and the immediacy of digital capture. The emerging theme is the journey, inner and outer, moving ever towards the light. I look for the wonder in the unlikely, surprising moments of life being lived. I am drawn to it and catch it with my camera so that I have it still, to share."

Roderickfield.com

Will Parfitt

Will is the director and editor of PS Avalon and the author of several books including *Kabbalah For Life* (Rider, 2006), *The Complete Guide to Kabbalah* (Rider, 2001), *Psychosynthesis: The Elements and Beyond* (PSA, 2006), and *The Something & Nothing of Death* (PSA, 2008).

Will trained in Psychosynthesis and has more than thirty years experience of working with personal and spiritual development. He is a UKCP registered psychotherapist, leads training courses in England and Europe, and has a private practice in Glastonbury, where he lives, offering psychotherapy, mentoring, coaching and supervision.

will@willparfitt.com

DEDICATION

To all the contributors to The Synthesist journal
this book is a selection of the best of the best,
but *you are all the best.*

Alan Robinson, Alan Rycroft, Alison Lyons, Ana Marko, Ash Charlton, Barbara Barnett, Barbara Saunders, Caeia March, Cathie Gibson, Derby Stewart-Amsden, Edvaldo Pereira Lima, Fathieh Saudi, Frank N. Millard, Georgina Yael Johnson, Helen Yates, Henry Shukman, James Adam Whiston, Jay Ramsay, John Harrington, John Parks, Joyce Hopewell, Kathy Cybele, Keith Hackwood, Kenneth Sorensen, Kristian Cole, Lydia Corby, Margaret Jacobson, Marilyn Barry, Marilyn Mehlmann, Melanie Reinhart, Mika Devi Genaine, Mike Stillwell, Norman Jope, Owen Ahrmanian, Paul Murphy, Paul Valentine, Previn Karian, Rachael Clyne, Ricky N. Lock, Roderick Field, Shakti Genaine, Shamai Currim, Shanasa Anne Fifield, Signe Ohlsson, Vivian King, Vivienne Fogel.

FURTHER PSYCHOSYNTHESIS READING

ASSAGIOLI, Roberto
Psychosynthesis Turnstone 1975;
The Act of Will Platts Publishing 1999;
Transpersonal Development Smiling Wisdom 2008

BROWN, Molly Young
The Unfolding Self Helios 2004

FERRUCCI, Piero
What We May Be Turnstone 1982;
The Power of Kindness Tarcher 2007

FIRMAN John ad GILA, Ann
The Primal Wound SUNY 1997

HARDY, Jean
A Psychology With A Soul Arkana 1987

HUBER, Bruno
Astrological Psychosynthesis HopeWell 2006

PARFITT, Will
Psychosynthesis: The Elements and Beyond PS Avalon 2006;
The Something & Nothing of Death PS Avalon 2008;
Kabbalah for Life Rider, 2006

RAMSAY, Jay
Alchemy Thorsons 1997;
The Crucible of Love O Books, 2005

SCHAUB, Richard & Bonney
Dante's Path Gotham Books 2003;
The End of Fear Hay House 2009

WHITMORE Diana
Psychosynthesis Counselling in Action Sage 1995;
The Joy of Learning: Psychosynthesis in Education Aquarian 1990

There are various editions of all these books available through major internet retailers or to order at your local bookstore.

There are numerous resources available on the internet relating to Psychosynthesis; very comprehensive info can be found at:

http://two.not2.org/psychosynthesis

where you can download for free many articles by Assagioli and other Psychosynthesis writers.

INDEX

Psychosynthesis related books available from PS Avalon

Self-Development

Psychosynthesis: The Elements and Beyond Will Parfitt
"a splendid book and well-written" Psychosynthesis International

The Something and Nothing of Death Will Parfitt
"this simple but profound book" Scientific and Medical Network

Breaking The Spell: The Key to Recovering Self-Esteem Rachael Clyne
"sensible and insightful...and possibly life-changing" PET Newsletter

Finding Your Self Through Madness Nicki Holland
"an extremely accessible account, avoiding complicated jargon" Revisioning

Poetry

Into The Further Reaches An anthology of contemporary British poetry celebrating the spiritual journey. edited by Jay Ramsay
"ambitious and wide-ranging" Peter Abbs, Resurgence

She Who Walks with Stones and Sings Rachael Clyne
"An inspiring and liberating collection" Caeia March

Out of Time: Poems 1998-2008 Jay Ramsay
"an unlocker of imprisoned souls and a true healer" Kathleen Raine

The Heart's Ragged Evangelist Jay Ramsay
"Jay speaks of the sacred and enduring ... and the power of love" Roselle Angwin

100 Sonnets of Galactic Love Keith Hackwood
"words embodied with meaning, carriers of endless possibility"

Charon's Hammer Keith Hackwood
"a man so in love with the world as to permit moonlight to sleep in his ears"

Dead Leaves Owen Ahrmanian
"entices the reader towards a soulful resolution"

Through The Gates of Matter Will Parfitt
"a fascinating selection from a life time of writing poetry"

PS AVALON PUBLISHING

PS AVALON PUBLISHING
Box 1865, Glastonbury,
Somerset BA6 8YR, U.K.

As well as publishing, we offer a comprehensive education programme
including courses, seminars, group retreats, and other opportunities
for personal and spiritual growth. Whilst the nature of our work means
we engage with people from all around the world, we are based in
Glastonbury which is in the West Country of England.

Our books are available through amazon, all good internet stores
and orderable at your local bookshop. For full details please visit:

www.willparfitt.com

Lightning Source UK Ltd.
Milton Keynes UK
UKOW04f1805070214

226111UK00001B/20/P